Miracle
IN EAST
HARLEM

A Manhattan Institute Book

TIMES **T** BOOKS

RANDOM HOUSE

Miracle
IN EAST
HARLEM

The Fight for Choice
in Public Education

SEYMOUR FLIEGEL
WITH JAMES MacGUIRE

Grateful acknowledgments is made to the following for permission to reprint previously published material:

National School Boards Association: Excerpt from "Friedman Does the Right Thing" by JoAnna Natale from the August 1990 issue of *The Executive Educator.* Copyright © 1990 by The National School Board Association. All rights reserved. Reprinted by permission.

The New York Times: Excerpt from "Schools That Dare to Compete," March 25, 1982 editorial. Copyright © 1982 by The New York Times Company. Reprinted by permission.

Albert Shanker: Excerpt from an article that appeared in the August 9, 1992 issue of *The New York Times.* Reprinted by permission of Albert Shanker, President of The American Federation of Teachers, 555 New Jersey Avenue, N.W., Washington, D.C. 20001.

Library of Congress Cataloging-in-Publication Data

Fliegel, Seymour.
    Miracle in East Harlem : the fight for choice in
public education / Seymour Fliegel with James
MacGuire. — 1st ed.
      p.   cm.
    ISBN 0-8129-2039-2
    "A Manhattan Institute book."
    Includes bibliographical references (p.   ) and
index.
    1. School, Choice of—New York (N.Y.) 2. East
Harlem (New York, N.Y.) I. MacGuire, James
II. Title.
LB1027.9.F57 1993
371'.01—dc20   92-56810

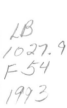

Map illustration by John A. Field

Book design by Susan Hood

Perhaps the greatest accolade of all was when word got back to us that the tour guides on the Circle Line cruise around Manhattan were pointing out the Manhattan Center to tourists and telling them it was "the miracle school in the miracle district." To a bunch of hard-core New Yorkers, the White House and national TV were great, but the Circle Line! That was *really* something.

Contents

ALTERNATIVE CONCEPT SCHOOLS
COMMUNITY SCHOOL DISTRICT 4

NAME OF SCHOOL	LOCATION
1 Academy of Environmental Sciences	JHS 99 - 410 East 100th Street
2 Block School	PS 108 - 1615 Madison Avenue
3 Bridge School	PS 101 - 141 East 111th Street
4 Career Academy	Alt. School Center - 240 East 109th Street
5 Central Park East I	Jackie Robinson Complex - 1573 Madison Ave.
6 Central Park East II	PS 171 - 19 East 103rd Street
7 Central Park East Secondary School	Jackie Robinson Complex - 1573 Madison Ave.
8 Children's Workshop	PS 96 - 216 East 120th Street
9 College of Human Services JHS	PS 121 - 232 East 103rd Street
10 Creative Learning Community	Jackie Robinson Complex - 1573 Madison Ave.
11 Da Vinci	PS 206 - 508 East 120th Street
12 E.H. Maritime	JHS 45 - 2351 First Avenue
13 E.H. Performing Arts School	PS 50 - 433 East 100th Street
14 E.H. School for Health & Bio-Med	JHS 45 - 2351 First Avenue
15 E.H. Tech	PS 72 - 131 East 104th Street
16 Harbor Performing Arts School	Alt. School Center - 240 East 109th Street
17 Hurston Academy	JHS 45 - 2351 First Avenue
18 Isaac Newton School for Math & Science	Manhattan Center - 116th St. & FDR Drive
19 JHS 50	PS 50 - 433 East 100th Street
20 Julio De Burgos	JHS 99 - 410 East 100th Street
21 Key School	Alt. School Center - 240 East 109th Street
22 Manhattan Center for Science & Math	116th Street & FDR Drive
23 Manhattan East	JHS 99 - 410 East 100th Street
24 Manhattan West	PS 171 - 19 East 103th Street
25 New York Prep	PS 102 - 315 East 113th Street
26 Northview Tech	PS 155 - 319 East 117th Street
27 Rafael Cordero Bilingual School	JHS 45 - 2351 First Avenue
28 River East	Manhattan Center - 116th St. & FDR Drive
29 Science & Humanities	PS 96 - 216 East 120th Street
30 SEARCH	PS 109 - 215 East 99th Street
31 Talented & Gifted	Alt. School Center - 240 East 109th Street

MAP OF COMMUNITY SCHOOL DISTRICT 4
BOROUGH OF MANHATTAN

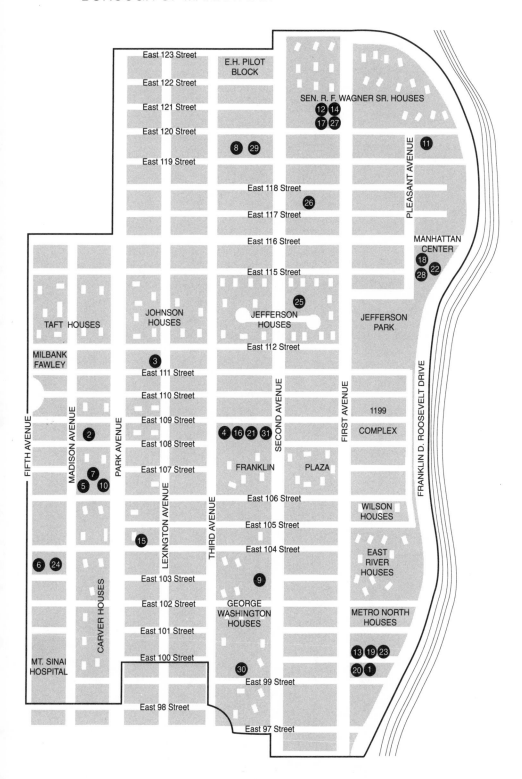

Acknowledgments

We would like to thank the Manhattan Institute and the Center for Educational Innovation for their support on this project. Their confidence in its ultimate success and steadfast encouragement have been invaluable. In particular we would like to single out Richard Gilder, Chairman of the Manhattan Institute and most generous of school benefactors; Peter Flanigan, Chairman of the Center for Educational Innovation; and William Hammett, Lawrence Mone, and Raymond Domanico for their interest in and insight into the story we set out to tell.

The people of District Four were all most generous in sharing with us their experiences. To name them all would require a book as long as this one. They were principals, teachers, students, board members, politicians, parents, and local observers. We thank them all.

Claire Wyckoff and Faye Levine of the Center for Educational Innovation were invaluable allies in revising the final draft. Elizabeth Skok, Allison Hertog, and Jill Lances, also of CEI, were of great assistance as well. Our thanks to Richard Vigilante, who edited early chapters of the manuscript, and especially to Paul Golob of Times Books, who so expertly edited the entire manuscript and was a constant source of constructive criticism and support.

Our families have been most supportive, especially our wives, Sonia Fliegel and Alane MacGuire. Richard Fliegel should be especially commended for taking time off from his busy teaching and writing schedule to help jump start his father's book.

In addition to being listed in the bibliography, several sources deserve special mention. Ray Domanico was most helpful in interpreting data provided by the New York City central board of education. David Bensman's studies of the Central Park East Schools were a valuable resource in reconstructing CPE's early years. Michael Feller's unpublished thesis of the Harbor School for the Performing Arts and the East Harlem Performing Arts School provided us with first person perspectives we could not have otherwise recovered. Mary Anne Raywid provided good suggestions on the early chapters and vital ideas for chapter 12.

Much of what may be judged good in the book owes some debt to those mentioned above or to others. We alone are responsible for any flaws.

S.F.
J.M.

New York
October 1992

Miracle
IN EAST
HARLEM

1

A Miracle but
Not a Mystery

T his is the story of how the public schools of one of New
York City's poorest neighborhoods broke a decades-long
pattern of defeat, failure, and frustration to become centers of
learning and hope.

In 1973 Community School District Four in East Harlem was
the worst of the thirty-two New York City school districts. Only
16 percent of the children enrolled there were reading at grade
level. Dropout rates were high, and many of those who did
graduate could barely read or do simple arithmetic. Truancy
rates were astronomical. Absenteeism was rampant among
teachers, many of whom were deeply demoralized. Indisci-
pline, violence, deteriorating physical plants, and monstrous
bureaucratic indifference had all combined to create a failing
school system.

By 1987, however, 63 percent of students in District Four
were reading at grade level. And though East Harlem contin-

ued to be one of the poorest and most culturally deprived neighborhoods in the city, District Four had risen from 32nd to 15th place among the city's school districts, surpassing the achievement level of more affluent districts. Twenty-six new schools, with new philosophies, have opened in the intervening years. The dropout and truancy rates have declined dramatically, and teachers and parents feel a renewed interest in and concern for the schools with which they are involved. A love of learning is in the air, and East Harlem's students now go on to higher education in unprecedented numbers, many of them on prestigious scholarships.

What accounts for this overwhelming transformation? Simply put, District Four freed students, teachers, parents, and educational administrators to work together to build what they all truly wanted: schools and a school system that put children first. What happened in East Harlem occurred across a school district larger than the entire school systems of many American cities, a district that includes fifteen thousand students, eight hundred teachers, and fifty schools. What was done there can be done elsewhere. The revolution of District Four can become the path of the future for our nation's schools.

There is an apocryphal story about an old man who was asked how to change our schools. He replied that there are two choices: the natural way and the miraculous way. The natural way, he asserted, is if a band of angels comes down from heaven and transforms them. The miraculous way is if a group of teachers, working together, do it. This is the "miracle" of District Four.

It started simply enough. At first, one unusually dedicated teacher had an idea for a school that would cater to the special needs of chronically undereducated and troublesome kids. Starting a new school that did not fit in with established procedures would normally have been almost impossible in the largest and most bureaucratic school system in America. But nobody really wanted these kids, and because nobody at the central Board of Education cared enough about the worst school district in the city to keep them from trying something new, and because the local district authorities were desperate to try anything that might work, the teacher was allowed, even encouraged, to start a small, experimental school.

Then another gifted educator wanted to start a school using

some of the theories about progressive education which she and other colleagues had been debating and refining throughout their teaching careers. After that a third school began, offering a specialized curriculum utilizing the performing arts as a center of interest, which won a wide following in the East Harlem community.

Though very different from one another, all three of the schools were successful, especially when compared to most of the other schools serving East Harlem. As these schools flourished, other educators began to see the possibility of starting additional schools, each of which would address a particular need within the neighborhood. Heartened by the initial success of the first three schools, the district school officials encouraged these new efforts and supported them both at the local level and in the inevitable battles which followed with the New York City Board of Education.

These early schools, the beginning of our network of alternative schools, were all small. In a small school no one gets lost. A sense of community, even family, can be forged. In small schools, with their familiar atmosphere, young people who might slip through the cracks in a large and impersonal institution can bloom. In East Harlem we believed that a school is not just a building, and so we often grouped several small, alternative schools within the walls of a single traditional public-school building.

Then came the most crucial development—the decision that would transform a few scattered innovations into a system for innovative education, a rebellion into a permanent revolution.

With the new alternative and mini-schools flourishing and student performance on a heartening rise, the district decided to permit parents and their children to choose whichever school they wanted to attend, instead of automatically assigning students to the school nearest their homes. It was further decided that no one would be forced into a failing school; those that could not attract or keep students would be shut down. Because the new schools were small, taking up only a portion of a public school building, shutting one down only meant abandoning a failed idea, not demolishing bricks and mortar. A new school could be tried in its place and face the same critical tests of achievement and attractiveness.

As the first director of District Four's Office of Alternative

Schools, I was a major participant in getting the new schools off the ground. I had grown up in the New York City public school system and knew that the level of stagnation of its bureaucracy was matched only by the enthusiasm and ability of the bright-eyed children who populated its classrooms. In instituting this system of school choice in East Harlem, my colleagues and I decided to give our students the same option that their more affluent counterparts have when they choose among public and private schools. What is good for the children of the rich, we reasoned, is also good for the children of the poor.

The idea of choice is simple. In this country we are free ideally to choose everything about our lives: where we live, where we work, what doctor we go to, where we bank, where we shop, what we do with our spare time. I live in Queens today, but when I want to get a haircut I still get in the car and drive back to the Bronx where I grew up. I pay six dollars in tolls to exercise this choice—but getting a haircut is serious business to me. How much more serious business is the freedom to choose a child's school! All around the world people have been shedding authoritarian structures which had inflicted immense human suffering along with physical, intellectual, and moral degradation. They see in our free institutions a hopeful and promising way forward, which is why, for all its faults, people from around the world are still struggling to find a place for themselves in the United States. Our freedom is not merely an ideal; it is something that we put into practice, however imperfectly, every day.

Except in one crucial area: public education. If we are free to choose our supermarkets, our barbers, our sources of news, and our places of worship, why are we not free to choose how and where our children will be educated? Some, of course, will say that we are already free to choose: If you don't like your local public school, you can always send your kids to a private school. That works well for those who are affluent, but what about those who are not? What about the poor, who may be working as hard as any of us but who have not yet escaped poverty? And what about their children? It's all very well to say that you have a choice to send your child to a private school, or to advocate a voucher system that may make it easier for some to do so, but in fact 88 percent of the schoolchildren in this country attend public schools. Even if we were to double the capacity of all private and parochial schools, we would *still* have 76 percent of our children in the public school system. Public education has always been and will always be the linchpin of American society. If this country is to live up to its ideals, the children of the poor should be able to enjoy the same benefits of choice as are available to the children of the well-to-do.

It would be one thing if public education today were really doing its job, but the depressing truth is that it is not. We are assailed by the failures of our educational system day after day, year after year. Despite two major waves of educational reform in the 1980s, student performance has not significantly improved. In fact, American students are falling further behind their counterparts around the world. Despite the protestations of the teachers' unions and educational technocrats, the inescapable fact is that our schools are not doing their job, and part of the reason is that the people involved—teachers, parents, and students—do not get to choose where they will be.

The simplest argument in favor of public school choice is a rather crude analogy to a free-market system: The laws of supply and demand will ensure that good schools are rewarded while bad schools suffer and ultimately fail when no one selects them. The corollary of this argument is that, given a choice system, schools will compete with each other for students and will therefore improve academically in order to attract their maximum market share.

Though this is a powerful argument, it tells only part of the story. Market forces alone will not solve our educational problems. We also need an intensified commitment from individual teachers to the vision, mission, and goals of the schools; patience and support from administrators; and a commitment to learning on the part of students and parents. It is not the free-market system that provides these, but another kind of energy unleashed by implementing choice—the sense of ownership.

If you own something you treat it better than if you didn't own it. That goes for a screwdriver, a CD player, a tennis racquet, or an automobile. It goes for a pet or a piano. It also goes for a school.

Many parents, particularly poor parents, are a bit intimidated by a school. In Hispanic communities, for example, the tradition is not to question a teacher, even if new ideas are needed. Students, too, can feel intimidated by educational institutions. And even teachers sometimes get frustrated in their work, adopting a "let's just get through the day" mentality if they feel that their participation is not valued.

Those attitudes disappear, however, once you have freely chosen to become a part of a given school. You feel a sense of pride and excitement in that school. You feel that you belong to that school, and that the school belongs to you. In short, you feel that you are an owner of that school. And when you feel that you are an owner you are willing to go to great lengths to make sure that the school is as good as it possibly can be.

Ownership enhances participation and performance, and people who feel like owners of their schools are more likely to band together into communities capable of setting goals and solving problems. In these situations teachers are willing to work overtime and on weekends, parents are eager to participate in extracurricular activities, and students feel motivated to devote extra time to their studies. The supervisory staff is similarly motivated. Principals are free to offer positions to teachers, who are in turn free to accept or decline those offers. Together they choose the kind of school they want to create: Fast track or slow? Highly disciplined or laid back? Around what theme, be it science or social studies, do they want to organize? And the parents and children decide which of several competing schools they want for themselves.

Compare this for a moment to a typical city high school. A principal is assigned to a school and, once the probationary period is completed, is tenured in that building. The principal does not choose his teachers, nor do the teachers choose him or his school. They, too, are assigned. Neither the principals nor the teachers choose the organizing theme of the school or the curriculum or even the very textbooks—all these are decreed from the central bureaucracy. And, finally, neither the parents nor their children choose their schools; they too are assigned, depending on where they happen to live. And no matter how unsuccessful such a school may be, new students continue to be assigned to it each fall.

Is it any wonder that fewer than 40 percent of inner-city

public high school students graduate on time, and that less than half of those go on to further education?

Choice offers options, alternatives, the opportunity for inspiration, and a way for young people to find out who they are and what they might like to become. The absence of choice in many cases—especially in failing schools—offers suffocation, hopelessness, the learning of how not to learn, and a general feeling of futility, of not having any role to play in society. It is such feelings that make young people susceptible to deadening life-styles and desperate, violent remedies. Choice offers a way out of that trap.

It is, therefore, not surprising that public schools get better when people are free to choose among them. That's what happened in District Four, a school district in a community with the largest percentage of "underclass" population in the country.

If it could happen in East Harlem it could happen, as the song says, anywhere. Indeed, decades of formal educational research could almost have predicted what happened in East Harlem. So could common sense, at least with the help of hindsight. But the prevailing educational system in New York, and throughout America, has been organized in such a way that ignores both the best research and our own common sense.

Choice has led to a renaissance of the East Harlem public schools, creating more congenial environments for students and teachers alike. First of all, the schools are smaller, so teachers and students are able to form personal relationships, and a sense of community is established. James Coleman, professor of sociology and education at the University of Chicago, feels that the biggest difference between public and private schools is the sense of community that many private schools are able to maintain. Moreover, the dropout rate in East Harlem declined noticeably once we began operating schools that catered to the individual needs of our students. National studies show that as early as third grade children of the "underclass" begin to ascertain that the system does not include them, and they begin to opt out mentally; the students in District Four, however, know that the system does include them, because their choices, hopes, and aspirations have helped define the schools they attend.

Choice has also rejuvenated the teachers in East Harlem, many of whom were frustrated by the bureaucracy's rules and regulations, which had stifled innovation and ambition. These teachers were invigorated when they found that they were free to design their own curricula and run their own schools.

In District Four we told teachers with ideas for their dream schools, "Go ahead and try them. We'll support you." The most common initial reaction was disbelief. Their second reaction was to go out and start a lot of wonderful new schools that did not look like one another or like regular public schools. Not all the schools worked, but most did and were an enormous improvement over the old schools. Even though these schools were so different from one another, they worked because the teachers who ran them were no longer cogs on a bureaucracy wheel but creators, owners, visionaries, and idealists. These are the qualities that lead people to become teachers in the first place; it is how most of the burned-out and demoralized teachers who populate our school system started out. The opportunity to develop their ideas and pursue their dreams reinvigorated their drive to teach and unleashed an enormous amount of energy and idealism which was of incalculable benefit to their students.

Of course, not every teacher became an educational leader. There were those who felt stuck in failing schools but did not know how to get out of their ruts. When their schools were reorganized, some of them fit right in to the new regimes and were revived too. Others did not fit in, but we transferred them to places that made sense for them, and many then blossomed in their new surroundings.

Finally, choice worked for parents as well, by involving them in the process and substance of their children's education in a way that they had never been before. District Four parents do not run the schools—they would hardly have time, and they expect teachers and administrators to do that. But the choices parents make help shape the system. Parents decide on topics for parent workshops, and participate in full-family conferences to resolve problems. Thus they, too, feel like owners, and they are happy to be more deeply involved with their children's education than they used to be. Previously the children noticed their parents' resentment and alienation from the schools and felt discouraged. Now there is less alienation and more enthusiasm and commitment among the parents, and that carries over to the children.

Our discovery of choice was almost inadvertent. We were not trying to prove a theory—we didn't even have a theory. We just had the worst school district in the city. But we also had the willingness to say yes to people who had the vision and the drive to make things work, the willingness to let people do their best instead of forcing them to cope with the system at its worst.

East Harlem is not a laboratory, but a very real (sometimes all too real) part of American life. And District Four is not a pilot program. It has been providing the benefits of choice to its students since 1974, and it will keep doing so for many years to come. If choice can revive learning and hope in one of the country's poorest neighborhoods, it can have similar success across the country.

I want to make clear once again that when I talk about choice it is in regard to public schools only. Students attending private schools already have choice. The 88 percent of America's students who attend public schools deserve choice too, and we owe it to them to provide a superior education. In the past few years, public figures across the political spectrum have endorsed public school choice, including Bill Clinton, George Bush, Governors Rudy Perpich of Minnesota and Booth Gardner of Washington (both Democrats), and former Governor Thomas Kean of New Jersey (a Republican). A recent survey reported by the Hubert Humphrey Institute at the University of Minnesota showed that 76 percent of the parents in that state favored choice in public education.

Yet choice also has its opponents and critics. Most of the opposition comes from entrenched educational groups who fear they will lose power if parents and students, rather than bureaucrats, become the crucial judges of school performance. The truth, however, is that teachers and administrators are actually among those who benefit most from choice. As a system, choice is hospitable to many different educational philosophies, thus fostering greater satisfaction and fulfillment in a teacher's and administrator's work. Other critics raise serious concerns about the potential for inequity in a choice system, and I will address these concerns directly later in this book, for there are also sound, reliable ways to overcome them. Members of the educational establishment never tire of saying that choice is not a panacea—and I would be the first to agree. In education, there is no such thing as a panacea; human variables present too much complexity. Choice is not an end in itself but a means toward achieving quality education for all our children.

Sure, we made mistakes in District Four and hit a lot of roadblocks, but the real beauty of choice is that mistakes are not forever. Nobody forces parents to keep their children in schools that are not working. A choice system is flexible enough to shut down failed schools, open up new schools, and fix mediocre schools without catastrophic confrontations.

Effective education requires hard work, commitment, focus, and a productive learning environment. These qualities are necessary for teachers and for students. Choice alone cannot supply them. But what choice can do, particularly where a school system is failing, is to unleash the latent positive energy in students and teachers and bring it to bear on the educational process, thereby eliminating the institutional and social barriers to constructive change, getting bureaucracy out of the way, permitting people to concentrate on what is of vital importance to them, and letting people teach and learn.

That is the power of choice. Choice alone will not solve the myriad problems facing education today, but it can help create an educational setting in which such problems can be addressed and resolved. In this way, choice acts as a catalyst for widespread and beneficial change.

There is nothing mysterious about how choice helps us accomplish this goal. At the heart of the East Harlem experience is a fundamental but often underestimated attribute of human nature: People want to do good. Teachers want to teach well. Given a reasonable environment, most students want to learn. School administrators, too, have good intentions; after all, most of them started out as teachers themselves. But bureaucracies have a way of stifling constructive change. The beauty of choice is that it gets bureaucracy out of the way. It frees people to do what they want to do and assumes that their goals are worth pursuing.

Bureaucracies presume that people will be indifferent and will fail if left to themselves. In District Four we presumed that if we give people the opportunity to excel, they will do their best and succeed.

Naturally, we cannot run public schools on a system of complete laissez-faire. The schools must be accountable, not only because public monies are being spent but, more important, because they have been entrusted with the future of America. The primary difference between a choice system and a bureaucratic system, however, is in the method of accountability.

Under the bureaucratic system, a central network of administrators and officials keeps watch on school performance. Because the bureaucracy must watch the schools from afar, it tries to make the system as uniform and easy to regulate as possible. The goal thus becomes the limitation of failure rather than the liberation of success—by issuing rules and demanding reports, by crushing difference and discovery, by stifling invention and independence. Such a strategy is particularly ill-suited for a job as subtle and demanding as educating young human beings. The inability of large bureaucratic agencies to run effective schools has been exhaustively documented by the educational research of the past several decades, and by the experience of anyone who has ever attended or taught in an urban public school.

Under a choice system, the schools are accountable to parents and students directly. Bad schools will find it impossible to justify their budgets or support their staffs. They must either improve or be shut down, thus supplying the crucial element of accountability and enabling students and parents to escape bad schools.

Some defenders of the status quo claim that choice exists within the public school system already, through the establishment of magnet schools. But such choice is limited to an elite few, those who understand how to manipulate the system, while the overwhelming majority of students are at the mercy of failing schools. On the other hand, there are ardent proponents of choice who grab onto the simple but crucial idea of shifting accountability from bureaucracies to parents and miss the rest of the story. They think that this simple mechanism is such a good idea that all you have to do is introduce it, then walk away, and magical things will happen.

Such expectations are balloons waiting to be burst. Real choice, which means the ability to choose among genuinely different *schools of quality,* takes time, patience, dedication, professionalism, and commitment. Just changing the rules so that parents can choose schools does not guarantee that there will be schools worth choosing. Only the slow and often arduous work of freeing all the players in the system—and the system itself—to create good schools will do the job.

In recent years, choice has become the most important issue in public education, and it is well publicized whenever schools are discussed. Nonetheless, its mechanisms and processes—as well as its long-term promises—are not widely understood. As the issue is debated more frequently at the national and local level, it is important for everyone concerned to have a clearer understanding of what choice really is.

The story of District Four is both a concrete history and an ongoing reality. It is the largest and longest experience with public school choice on record, and it is a rich and vivid tale. Even our mistakes and failures have provided valuable opportunities to reflect upon and refine the practice of choice, a process that continues to this day.

Wherever they are undertaken, choice systems will face challenges and obstacles. But the East Harlem experience demonstrates that meaningful change can take place under the most difficult conditions, against amazing odds, and despite the most entrenched opposition.

This book explains what choice is and what it isn't in a very simple way—by telling the story of how one failing inner-city school district became a world-famous success. Along the way the lives of countless students and teachers were transformed for the better. The story of District Four is not merely the history of an abstract educational concept but a story about real people, many of whom you will meet in these pages. And the greatest part of the story is that what they did can be done by others—by anyone, in fact, concerned with providing the next generation of Americans with a superior education.

This is the story of how choice transformed the schools of East Harlem, and how its fruits exceeded our fondest dreams.

2

History, the 'Hood, and the Schools

At first blush, East Harlem seems an unlikely place to launch an educational revolution. One of the toughest and poorest neighborhoods in America, the district stretches from 96th Street to 125th Street, from Fifth Avenue to the East River. It is a low and, for the most part, fairly flat area of Manhattan Island, and at one time in geological history East Harlem lay beneath a deep prehistoric sea. Later it became a dense inland forest, settled by Weckquaesgek Indians from the Midwest after they had discovered the Hudson River estuary, the fabled "river that ran in two directions" of which their ancestral legends told. They were hunters, trappers, and fishermen.

By 1664, the Dutch had displaced the Indians, and the English had taken over from the Dutch, and the lush forests of upper Manhattan had become prized farmland. Manhattan's fields yielded wheat of such high quality that New York flour became famous, the foundation of a booming trading economy. As city streets supplanted the fields, new waves of immigration overwhelmed the island. Newly prosperous Germans fled the Lower East Side to avoid the newly arrived Italians and poured into the more desirable environs of East Harlem. The members of British and Dutch descent of the Harlem Club responded by moving their headquarters right out of the neighborhood.

Racial and ethnic intolerance has thus long been a part of the East Harlem story, and has remained part of it through successive waves of Irish, Jewish, black, Italian, and Hispanic immigrations. My father's family, Jewish immigrants from Russia, lived on 120th Street between Second and Third Avenues before moving north with the tide to the relative prosperity of the Bronx.

And I remember very well the days when East Harlem was the center of Italian voting power in New York City. First Avenue and 116th Street was called "Lucky Corners," because politicians like Vito Marcantonio and Fiorello LaGuardia traditionally ended their campaigns there. On one occasion a group of my "Cellar Club" companions and I set out for one of these rallies from the Bronx in a horse-drawn wagon. A policeman stopped us on the Boston Post Road and castigated us for not treating the horse "like a human animal." Yet Marcantonio managed to win, even without our support that day. A member of the American Labor Party, Marcantonio was considered a Communist by some, but he was a tremendously effective spokesman for the poor through his seven terms in Congress, and the people of East Harlem loved him. Today P.S. 50 on East 100th Street is called The Vito Marcantonio School.

By the thirties, the great black flight from the Jim Crow South was bringing large numbers of blacks into East Harlem and other northern parts of the country, but even larger numbers of Spanish-speaking people, mostly Puerto Ricans, were coming as well. After World War II, the Hispanic population of New York City grew to well over half a million, many of whom settled in East Harlem. Black residents accepted the Spanish-speaking newcomer, but as far as the white community was concerned, he was black. The Hispanic insisted that he was Spanish, not Negro, and often refused to learn English to

16

prove his point, thereby further insulating himself from mainstream society and its opportunities. The new immigrants adapted quickly to East Harlem's tradition of ethnic mistrust: For years, the Spanish street name for policeman was "la hara," after the proverbial hard-bitten Officer O'Hara.

The ethnic conflicts of the neighborhood have long been exacerbated by its poverty. The East Harlem of past generations resembles the East Harlem of today in that the majority of people live in substandard housing. In 1935, East Harlem tenements that had been built to house fifty people often held up to four hundred. Today, many of these tenements remain, and the public housing projects that have been replacing them since the fifties are too often ready-made ghettoes themselves.

East Harlem today is no longer the lush land prized by the Indians, the Dutch, and the English, but "Spanish Harlem," a name that raises a host of associations, none of them agricultural. So it comes as a pleasant surprise, in walking through the neighborhood, to see dozens of gardens flourishing, reclaimed by residents from the garbage-strewn vacant lots that symbolize the area's decay. Surrounded by condemned buildings, extreme poverty, and mean streets, the gardens stand as affirmations of life, of mankind's hunger not merely for food but for a better life, and for hope itself.

Outside of these pockets, alas, East Harlem is not a garden, but it does have its pride. And its position as the home of the American mainland's oldest and most vibrant Puerto Rican community is intact. Even so, the last forty years have not been kind to this part of New York City.

In 1950, 7.9 million people lived in New York City. By 1980, nearly a million of them, 11 percent of the city's population, had fled. Once a great manufacturing center and a fount of relatively well-paying blue-collar jobs, the city in those years lost much of its manufacturing base and a huge number of jobs. A combination of economic and cultural factors, which economists and sociologists will be debating for decades, spawned a large and persistent "underclass" without jobs, functioning families, or ties to the larger society. Between 1972 and 1982, three hundred thousand apartments in New York, nearly 2 percent of the housing stock, were abandoned. In East Harlem the loss of housing began much earlier. As early as the sixties landlords were finding that they could no longer run their buildings profitably. Some torched their buildings for the insurance, while others merely walked away. Other buildings were destroyed by residents, in riots, or by the drug trade.

Today the East Harlem landscape is marked by whole blocks of razed tenements—urban craters—except for those few spots where enterprising citizens have made gardens. Some subsidized public housing has replaced the old housing stock, but always impersonally and often grotesquely. Harder to replace has been the neighborhood's collective memory and the fragile web of community that makes the difference between people short of cash and people short of hope. Local institutions have declined. Even Harlem's leading bank, Freedom National, which boasted Jackie Robinson as one of its founders, was declared insolvent by Federal regulators in 1990. As in other inner-city neighborhoods across America, family structure has deteriorated disastrously in East Harlem, while AIDS and crack have exacted an ever increasing heavier toll.

In the 180 square blocks of East Harlem, where 120,000 people eke out what livings they can, per capita income hovers around $4,000 per year. One in seven East Harlem adults is out of work. More than one in three gets some form of public assistance, among the highest welfare rates in the nation. As in the city at large, violent crime is out of control. According to the New York City Bureau of Police Statistics, the number of violent crimes reported in East Harlem is about twice that of the city-wide average.

Along Third Avenue from 100th Street north, grocery stands sell tropical food—yucca, yams, plantains, and mangoes. There are furniture and clothing stores as well, and the street life is buoyant and seemingly normal. But the store owners are often from other ethnic groups—Asians, Dominicans, or Yemenite Arabs. It is hard for local young people to identify with this kind of entrepreneurship. Aside from the occasional *farmacia*, bodega, or barbershop, blacks and Puerto Ricans own few business enterprises. This lack of role models is significant when one considers that the schools are 59.8 percent Hispanic (this group made up almost entirely by Puerto Ricans), 35.4 percent black, and 4.8 percent other groups.

Walk across to Lexington Avenue to some of the older, seedier, public-housing projects and the scene is very different. Groups of young males with hooded eyes hang out together on street corners, the shock troops of a major commercial enterprise: drugs. Many are hawking their wares openly—heroin, methadone, cocaine, crack, angel dust, and pot. Even marijuana today is a potent, hazardous drug, twenty times stronger on average than it was in 1968, thanks to the agronomical ingenuity of its growers. Crack vials and hypodermic needles litter the gutters and doorways of "shooting galleries," usually vacant lots or condemned buildings. Drugs are a major force in the local underground economy, with kids selling on the street in order to support their parents, and dealers often working out of understocked grocery stores.

In neighborhoods like East Harlem, however, the greatest killer of young males today is not AIDS or crack—it is homicide. Nearly 70 percent of violent crime in the city is committed with guns, up from 20 percent in 1960. Although our experience in the schools does not support the figure, New York City police estimate that half of all fourteen-year-olds now possess illegal handguns. The homicide rate among black men aged fifteen to twenty-four rose 66 percent from 1983 through 1988, and in 1990 many of the country's largest cities set new records for murders in a single year. More than 90 percent of the increase grew out of the rise in the rate at which young men were being killed with guns. According to the National Centers for Disease Control, it is now more likely for a fifteen-year-old black male in an inner-city neighborhood to die from homicide before reaching his twenty-fifth birthday than it was for a United States soldier to be killed on a tour of duty in Vietnam.

Violence has become a ritual of inner-city culture. Teachers in the school system a generation ago certainly saw their share of violence, but it was radically different. People had fistfights after school. Occasionally gangs got involved in turf wars. Today young people get killed for their coats, or their sneakers, or for looking at someone the wrong way, or for not looking at someone at all. In 1991, over 120 innocent, uninvolved bystanders were killed in New York by stray bullets. In the 1991–1992 school year alone, three students were shot and killed in Thomas Jefferson High School in Brooklyn, horrifying the city.

19

By every meaningful measurement, life has gotten more difficult and more dangerous over the past thirty years for young people growing up in our nation's poorest neighborhoods. Material poverty has increased as jobs have been moved to other areas and real wages have fallen. But poverty of the spirit has grown even more quickly, showing up as despair, anger, frustration, and alienation from the normal bulwarks of life, especially work, family, and community.

Public schools did not at first respond to the challenge presented by this radically altered landscape. Public education, after all, was yet another part of our country's deeply troubled social fabric through the sixties, seventies, and eighties. In its 1983 report, *A Nation at Risk*, the National Commission on Education found that 40 percent of students could not draw inferences from written materials, while two thirds could not solve a math problem involving a sequence of steps. Moreover, traditional performance standards had become meaningless: Though homework had decreased and real student achievement had declined, students' grades had nonetheless risen. Saul Cooperman, a former Commissioner of Education in New Jersey, summarized the state of decay: "Each generation of Americans has outstripped its parents in education, in literacy, in economic attainment. For the first time in the history of our country, the educational skills of one generation will not surpass, will not equal, will not even approach those of their parents." The authors of *A Nation at Risk* called America's neglect of its schools "an act of unthinking educational disarmament."

If this were true of the country's public schools as a group, it was especially true of the schools in New York City, afflicted for years (like most urban school districts) with academic performance even less satisfactory than the sagging national average and with social problems that threatened to overwhelm an already feeble academic effort. The once vaunted public school system, a product of nineteenth-century morality and political muscle, had been gradually overwhelmed by new social realities.

The 1960s and '70s were a time of exhausting and debilitating social conflict in America and throughout America's schools. In New York the conflicts were especially severe. New

Yorkers still speak of the "school wars" of that era, with little exaggeration. The partial decentralization of the city's huge and monolithic school system was an attempt to ease the racial conflict that grew out of the demonstrations and riots of that era, while at the same time the prolonged 1968 teachers' strike pitted the prerogatives of a largely white teachers' union against the aspirations of minority parents and community activists.

Social conflict and political infighting not only disrupted school schedules but also had a demoralizing impact on teachers. Amid all the politics and contention, good teaching became secondary. While community and racial conflicts provoked fistfights at school-board meetings, demoralized teachers settled for damage control rather than education. The system accepted low test scores, and a general malaise pervaded the schools. The big thing was not to teach but to control the kids. "A good school," the saying went in those days, "is a quiet school." The final result was reduced emphasis on teaching and learning, and for the most part, administrators and teachers in the schools accepted what became the status quo. Too many rules, regulations, resource shortages, and frustrations of every kind had broken down the innate desire of teachers in the system to do their jobs well.

In such an atmosphere, expectations were lowered, and student performance quickly followed. Placing blame became more important than providing meaningful education to the children of the poor. I always found it moving to see the way children came to school on the first day of the year, dressed up, eyes shining with curiosity and excitement, enthusiastic, and eager to learn. But it broke my heart to see how quickly such attitudes changed within a failing school; by December those same kids could become bored, sullen, and withdrawn.

It doesn't have to be that way.

Good teachers are artists, not automatons. Like most artists, their jobs, at times, may require more perspiration than inspiration. But the inspiration—and aspiration—must come first. In a system in which the first rule is "Keep your head down," few, including teachers, who do not get paid much and whose work is hard, can look up and see their dreams. They work largely for love of their students and for the satisfaction of helping them. They work hard because they want to do good. Crush those higher motives and there is little left to keep them going.

My opinions about how schools and teachers function best have grown out of my own experiences in the New York City public school system. I started my teaching career in 1957, as a sixth grade teacher at P.S. 129, an innovative "demonstration" school that had just been established by the City College of New York in West Harlem. It was there that I began to learn how good an inner-city public school could be. The principal, Margaret Douglas, was a tall, dignified woman, highly regarded for her work as principal of another Harlem elementary school, and one of the first black principals in the city. As I was one of the top ten student teachers from City College selected to staff the school, she took me under her wing, and with her help I learned that you can accomplish a lot within the system if you are creative and willing to share the credit.

I started teaching at P.S. 129 before the building was finished; my first sixth grade class was housed in a nearby junior high school. This experience unintentionally taught me an important lesson: a school is not a building. My colleagues at 129 had met and talked about our school before it even existed, before there were rooms or offices. *We* were the school—a principal, teachers, students, and, most important, *ideas.* It didn't matter whether we occupied one whole building or just several classrooms on one floor; we were still a school.

We moved into our new building in February 1958. Four years later Margaret Douglas became superintendent of schools in a Brooklyn district and Martha Froelich took over as principal of P.S. 129. Born into a genteel, German-Jewish, "Our Crowd" family, Froelich had earned a law degree before becoming a teacher and was an outstanding educator as well as a grand lady. After retiring from the school system she returned to the practice of law, often representing those who could not afford to compensate her. It was Froelich who urged me to seek an assistant principal's license. At first I resisted; I loved what I was doing, teaching gifted students from all over Manhattan. "You love teaching now," she responded, "but how will you feel in ten years if you've never tried anything else?" I took her advice and in 1966 accepted a position as an assistant principal at P.S. 146 in East Harlem.

I first came to East Harlem before the decentralization law of 1968, an outgrowth of the sixties' "school wars," which for the first time placed elementary and intermediate schools under the control of elected community school boards. I use the word *elected,* although in most neighborhoods fewer than 10 percent of those eligible actually vote. Their performance since 1968 has been mixed, but it has certainly not been worse than what went before. Previously all schools fell under the administration of the central Board of Education at 110 Livingston Street. And I do mean fell. East Harlem was consistently at the bottom in reading and math test scores.

Even then, however, there were successes, individual schools that were able to resist the tide of mediocrity that had engulfed the system. When I arrived at P.S. 146 it had been designated a "more effective school." The More Effective Schools Program had begun when the United Federation of Teachers (UFT) rejected the idea of "combat pay" for teaching in inner-city schools and insisted that the money be applied instead to developing twenty model schools across the city. Class size in these schools was limited to twenty-two students. An assistant principal was assigned to every two grades, and an administrative assistant freed them from clerical work. My fellow assistant principals and I worked with teachers in their classrooms and provided support that allowed the instructional program to move ahead. We knew every child. The staff worked closely together and got along well. My brother Lee, an outstanding teacher himself, was one of the original supervisors who opened the school and later served several years as an assistant principal.

P.S. 146 became one of the finest schools in New York City. In his groundbreaking study, *Crisis in the Classroom,* published in 1970, Charles Silberman held up two schools that were exceptions to the morass of New York City public education— P.S. 129 and P.S. 146. I am proud to have been a part of both of those schools.

The lessons I learned at P.S. 146 reaffirmed my experience at P.S. 129 and confirmed my conviction that meaningful change can take place even in the most difficult situations. The children of the poor can achieve academic success so long as their schools treat them with respect and establish high expectations.

It is the Pygmalion Principle: People respond to how they are treated. Treat a flower girl like a lady and she will respond like a lady. Treat a classroom full of inner-city kids like a bunch of uneducable future criminals, and they won't let you down. Treat them with love, respect, and dignity, however, and watch them bloom.

Over the past twenty-five years, innumerable studies have been done by countless researchers to find out what makes for truly effective schools, those which, given a certain student body, will do a better job of educating those students than other schools. Despite the investigators' reliance on different methods and different assumptions, a remarkably powerful consensus has nonetheless emerged. There exist definite, pre-dictable ingredients to effective schools, but they are not the ingredients most people have been promoting over the years. The amount of money spent on a school is not the determining factor. Educational methodology does not matter very much either, so long as the method is followed by a good teacher. I realize that this may sound idealistic and fanciful, but the re-search has shown that the most important factor in education is a lot like what used to be called "school spirit."

Overwhelmingly, these studies used words like *leadership, motivation, teamwork, professionalism,* and *commitment to shared educational goals* to describe schools that work. Good schools are good organizations, they found: organizations that get the best out of their people. It is the people that matter, not the money or the methods. And people perform better in organizations that take their humanity into account.

Nearly all these studies, for example, agree that the principal is a crucial factor. Good schools have principals who are good leaders and who use their leadership to focus their schools on real priorities—teaching and learning. Effective schools not only treat teachers like professionals but also provide an environment in which the teachers share in the formulation of the school's goals and show leadership in pursuit of them. They participate extensively in school decisions, and within their classrooms they are free to tailor their practices to the needs of their students. In short, effective schools function like good teams.

By contrast, in ineffective schools the principal thinks of himself as an administrator, and the school is governed not so much by a shared vision as by rules and regulations. Teachers and staff are often angry and dissatisfied, and they view the principal as an adversary, a bureaucrat, a voice of "the system" —and not as a leader. Unfortunately, in most urban school systems, the central bureaucracy is so powerful, and its ethos so pervasive, that individual schools are much more likely to be run along bureaucratic lines, rather than allow entrepreneurial and innovative thinking.

Centralized educational bureaucracies tend not to be concerned with higher motives (among faculty or students), seeking instead to satisfy and reassure their various constituencies —parents, unions, the press, and so on—without exposing the system to failure or ridicule. Rather than promoting new educational strategies or potentially dangerous tactics, schools accountable to a bureaucracy find it more productive to keep the central board headquarters happy by hewing to the tried-and-true line. Even the most well-meaning principal would find it difficult to put his or her energy into leadership when much of the day is spent filling out forms in triplicate and weighing every educational decision against a vast compendium of rules and regulations imposed from above.

The harmful effects of a huge, faceless educational bureaucracy come up repeatedly whenever anyone investigates what's wrong with our schools. In their 1990 book, *Politics, Markets and America's Schools,* John Chubb and Terry Moe examined data from five hundred randomly selected high schools nationwide and found that the most important factor in explaining why some schools succeed and others fail is that effective schools enjoy a great deal of autonomy. In these schools principals and teachers are relatively free of outside control and free to pursue educational goals. Dysfunctional schools, on the other hand, had been found to be ruled by outside authorities to a much greater extent. Indeed, freedom from bureaucratic control turns out to be the strongest determinant of school effectiveness, more important than family background or any other factor. "The message for reformers is very simple," they concluded. "If you want schools to be organized more effectively and to teach more successfully, you must give them autonomy." Chubb and Moe's findings confirm empirically what generations of New Yorkers have long felt in their bones.

The New York City school system is the largest and most complex in the country. It has departments and whole levels of bureaucracy which even it seems to be unaware of. Calls to the central board for information on its operations are invariably passed to two or three or four additional staff members. Even after all that time and effort, the most frequently heard response is, "We can't help you with that."

The central Board of Education headquarters is located at 110 Livingston Street in downtown Brooklyn. The city school system's full- and part-time employees, including teachers, principals, administrators, superintendents, kitchen staff, and bureaucrats of every size, shape, and texture, number over a hundred thousand people. In 1992, the total school budget of the New York City school system was over $7.5 billion, or $7500 per pupil. But like all bureaucracies, the central board tends to be more concerned with preserving its own rules and prerogatives than with the business of educating the city's 940,000 public school children. In his book *110 Livingston Street Revisited,* David Rogers described the entire institution as "a model of bureaucratic pathology," characterized by overcentralization in its chain of command, horizontal and vertical fragmentation, compulsive rule-following, and almost total insulation from its clients.

The system can be purposely byzantine, as John Chubb found out when he tried to get an answer to one straightforward question:

Some time ago I was called by a reporter. In the course of explaining about autonomy, I told him that in New York City they have an enormous central office bureaucracy, staffed by 5,000 people. I contrasted this with the Catholic school system in New York City, which despite the church's reputation for hierarchy has only 50 people in its central office, though the system has fully a quarter of the students the public schools have. After talking to him, I decided to double check those figures.

I called the personnel office of the city school system and said, "I have a question: how many people work in the central office of the New York City school system?" The first person I reached had no idea, nor did the second or third, but they all promised to transfer me to someone who did.

Thirty-five minutes and many transfers later, I got to a person who said, "Yes, I do know the number, but if you want to know, you'll have to put your request in writing, and we'll get the information back to you in a month."

Well, I pleaded and finally I was put in touch with someone who had the authority. And he told me it wasn't 5,000, it was 6,000.

Now I needed to find out the number for the Catholic school system. I got someone in that central office and said, "I need to know how many people work in the central bureaucracy of the Catholic school system in New York City."

She said, "I'm sorry, we don't keep that kind of data."

"Well," I said, "would you have any idea? Is there any way you could get the number for me?"

And she said, "Just a minute—I'll count them." And she counted. There are 25. Twenty-five people running a system that's a fifth of the size of the public school system!

The central board, moreover, is not the only school bureaucracy in New York City. There are also thirty-two local community school districts who share power with the board and very often represent different interests. These community school boards are an outgrowth of the continual struggle in New York between the central authorities, who run the system and considered themselves to be the guardians of the public trust, and the local political powers, who benefitted from the system and wanted a greater voice in the way it functioned. Since their creation in 1968, the local boards have matched 110 Livingston Street in their single-minded protection of their turf, again to the detriment of the students and teachers under their purview.

Professor Nathan Glazer of the Harvard Graduate School of Education has reviewed the history of this vast bureaucracy, which has metastasized through successive cycles of scandal, crisis, and reform. "Whenever a scandal occurred," Glazer explains, "another level of control was added," yielding new rules, new enforcement offices, and new regulations for principals and teachers to follow, whether they wished to put together a lesson plan or buy new erasers, recruit new teachers, or repaint a school. Few New Yorkers who know the system would disagree with his assessment that "there are so many rules and regulations and levels of control that it's impossible to do anything. It is literally impossible to build a new school within the

New York City school system in less than eight years, which was why a law had to be passed creating an independent school construction authority that promises completion in two years. . . . No matter what you try to do, it is too hard to do it in the New York City school system."

As an education major at City College in the spring term of 1957, I had my first run-in with the educational establishment, and I only narrowly survived. After completing a series of intimidating interviews required for taking methods courses, I faced the speech interview, the final step before getting a student teaching assignment. The members of the Speech Department who conducted the interviews were sticklers in the Henry Higgins mode, and in those days before *multiculturalism* had become a watchword, the very fact of my native Bronx accent was reason enough for them to fail me. And for failing the speech requirement, I was denied a student teaching assignment. In effect, that meant I could not become a teacher.

My wife and I were expecting our first child that March. I had enrolled in the City College evening school after my discharge from the Army in 1954 and carried a full sixteen-credit program each semester. I had worked as a waiter during the day to supplement my income from the G.I. Bill of Rights and had dug into my studies, determined to become a teacher. By the end of three years I had accumulated a 3.8 grade point average and I was not about to submit to this arbitrary assessment of my ability to communicate with public school students.

I appealed my denial of a teaching assignment to the Director of Student Teaching, who in classic bureaucratic style ignored my request. The weeks passed until the weekend before the Monday when student teachers were to report to their schools. In desperation, I asked one of my more sympathetic professors, Edward Townsend, for advice, and he suggested that I send a registered letter pleading my case to the home of Harold Abelson, the Dean of the CCNY Education School. On Saturday morning I did just that, though I had begun to lose hope.

That night Dean Abelson called me and said, "We've been giving you a hard time, haven't we? Can you come to my office on Monday morning?" When I showed up at precisely nine o'clock that day, the very first thing he said to me was, "Mr.

Fliegel, before we sit down, I want you to know that I have reviewed your records and spoken to some of your teachers. You will be a teacher." By lunchtime I had my assignment and I was on my way.

I have never forgotten that meeting and the compassionate manner in which the dean cut through the impersonal regulations to address the real issues involved. In meeting with students, parents, and teachers for the last thirty-five years, I have done my best to try to emulate his example.

In 1975, when Anthony Alvarado, the charismatic new superintendent of East Harlem's District Four, asked me to leave my assistant principal's post at P.S. 146 to take on the role of acting principal at P.S. 108, I readily agreed. I spent nine rewarding and exhilarating months at that school, again introducing innovative ideas, treating people with dignity, and making myself available to students, parents, and teachers, with gratifying results. And when it began to look as if I would not get the permanent appointment, quite a few parents and teachers started a movement to lobby the district to give me the job. Their letters and petitions demonstrated just how seriously inner-city parents take their children's education. Today, when I hear people say that public school choice cannot work because poor parents don't care enough to make a good decision, I remember the parents of P.S. 108.

Despite all the support, I did not receive the permanent appointment, which went instead to a Latino teacher from one of the district's bilingual schools. In East Harlem in 1976 that was to be expected. The person selected was connected politically to members on the school board and at that time there was a definite policy regarding the appointment of more Latino principals. I was not bitter because I had been fully aware of the political process involved in the selection of a principal when I accepted the job on an "acting" basis. Indeed, I was lucky; missing out on the principalship at P.S. 108 provided me with the greatest opportunity of my career.

3

Debbie Meier and the Dawn of Central Park East

I n the early 1970s East Harlem epitomized the collapse of the New York City school system. Only 16 percent of District Four's children were reading at or above grade level; morning attendance at Benjamin Franklin High School on East 116th Street was 44 percent of enrollment, and by graduation time 93 percent of the high school's ninth graders had dropped out. But in 1974 East Harlem's predicament began to change with the founding of the first alternative schools. Ironically, it was the severity of the situation that provided us with the opportunity to spark a revolution in public education. School board officials, community leaders, and parents were all desperate; and the central board, embarrassed by one of its most conspicuous failures, was inattentive.

We applied what we called the "judo principle," taking negative energy and turning it into something positive. Discouraging though the statistics were, we looked beyond them to the people—the children and their parents—with whom we interacted. Even in the early 1970s, teachers and administrators in some of the worst parts of the system were beginning to realize that directives from above would not fix what was broken. Twenty years later, the New York State Commissioner of Education, Thomas Sobol, has begun to preach a similar sermon:

Top down efforts have not worked. . . . You can't regulate excellence into a system because excellence is a product of the energies of those most intimately engaged, the kids themselves. It's a product of their hearts and minds. And the only way you can engender excellence in the system is to energize those hearts and minds and create a context of direction and support wherein their energies can be used to the best effort.

I have always believed that it is counterproductive for school professionals to spend their time pointing to poverty statistics, crime rates, and assorted social problems in order to deflect criticism from poorly performing schools. The best way to help solve these problems is to provide a meaningful educational program for the children of the poor, which is what the pioneers in District Four did. Perhaps that was the single most important event to happen in East Harlem, because the courage of those educators and the results they achieved in the face of sustained struggle would inspire others to join them in their cause.

The funny thing is that had I not been passed over for the principalship of P.S. 108 I might never have been a part of District Four's evolution. After the new principal was appointed, Superintendent Anthony Alvarado asked me to come work with him at the district office. The few alternative schools recently established in District Four were facing a number of common problems, and Alvarado felt that they needed a "friend in court" at the community-school-district level, so he asked me to direct the district's new Office of Alternative Schools. For someone whose career had been formed in special schools like P.S. 129 and P.S. 146, this was where I belonged. I said yes.

I started out in an office in the old district headquarters on

117th Street and First Avenue in what had been P.S. 85. The fifth-floor walk-up office to which I was assigned was anything but prepossessing. There was no desk or telephone at first. More important, there was no particular job description, nor any formal announcement of my appointment. Alvarado gave me no specific instructions and he had not even introduced me to the district or school staffs. But I couldn't just sit there waiting for something to happen, so I did what came naturally: I got into my car and started visiting the schools. I learned a fair bit about the district in those early days, which was a good thing, because within two weeks Alvarado did call me with an immediate, urgent assignment.

When I got to his office Alvarado was busy, as he always was in those years. Once I was shown in, the superintendent looked up from his desk and said to me, "I've got a problem in the Central Park East School between Debbie Meier and some of her parents. Go see what it's about."

I went over to CPE, which was then a fledgling alternative school just completing its second year, to introduce myself to Debbie Meier, the school's director. I did not know her at the time, but she struck me as a smart, strong woman. I could tell from the way she looked at me that she didn't trust me; to her I was just another annoying bureaucrat from the district office meddling in her affairs.

Her wary demeanor aside, Meier knew she needed help, because a group of the CPE parents were unhappy with how she was running the school. They had asked the superintendent to remove her from the directorship, and she didn't understand why the superintendent wasn't defending her unquestioningly. "How could Tony Alvarado have so little confidence in me?" she asked. And I really couldn't answer. We talked a little about the school, and I thanked her and went off to see the parents who were complaining. They proved to be a very articulate and angry group of parents. The problem, as they saw it, was not minor: they wanted Meier removed. "She doesn't listen to anybody," one of them said. "She runs the whole place herself," added another. "She's out of control," said a third.

I was on the spot and had to do something. But what? Debbie Meier has since become a nationally known authority on education, the recipient of a MacArthur Foundation "genius" award, but in June 1976 that wasn't the case. Central Park East was a struggling school that might well fail; in fact, it had attracted conflict from its very inception. What was not yet clear to outsiders was that it had been deliberately designed to thrive on conflict.

Before taking any action I decided to acquaint myself more with this upstart school and its embattled founder.

Deborah Willen Meier had grown up in Larchmont, New York, and had attended the private Ethical Culture and Fieldston Schools in New York City. After two years in the cooperative work-study program at Antioch College, she embarked on graduate-level study in history at the University of Chicago, during which time she married and had three children. Soon thereafter Meier began her teaching career, substituting in public schools around Chicago.

Once this product of private education began to teach in the public schools, she was hooked:

From the first moment I walked into a public school I was intrigued. I started teaching kindergarten in the school across the street from my home, but soon I was substituting all over Chicago from grades one to eight. I frequently went into classrooms which had never had a regular teacher. They were forever assigning me to what were called "opportunity classes," which, of course, meant the reverse. Parents were not allowed near the schools. Principals were unbelievably rude, not only to students and parents, but to their own teachers as well. And the teachers passed it on! The way teachers talked about kids in those days was scary.

Meier continued as a substitute teacher after she and her family moved to Philadelphia. Then she came to New York and began to work full time, first in schools and then in the education program at City College, where she worked with public school teachers committed to finding new ways to reach difficult students. "The principals paid lip service to us and our aspirations," she remembers, "but the changes didn't last." By the end of 1973, just as she was becoming disgusted by her lack of progress working within the established system, she got a call from Bonnie Brownstein, a science coordinator in District Four. Brownstein told Meier that Superintendent Alvarado had heard about her work and wanted her to start a new school

34

in East Harlem. Meier, attuned to the ways of educational bureaucracies, was skeptical at first, but when she met with the new superintendent, he convinced her that he was serious.

Debbie Meier had been thinking for some years about what kind of school she would start if the opportunity ever arose. She had worked with Lillian Weber, the director of the City College Workshop, on open education, and she had tried to create "open classroom" programs in District Two on Manhattan's East Side. She had developed an educational method which she believed reflected the cognitive development of children, combining John Dewey's learning theory with more recent psychological investigations of Jean Piaget. In place of the standard system, which emphasized covering a prescribed curriculum, Meier and her associates proposed a pedagogy based on "open classrooms" where teachers would provide children with stimulating materials, observe them working and playing with those materials, and, guided by their observations, offer each child assistance to extend his or her skills and interests. Meier wanted a school that was small and run by the staff, not from above. Now with Alvarado's backing she would have a chance to put her thoughts into action.

It would not be easy. Meier's new elementary school, Central Park East, was to be housed on the second, third, and fourth floors of P.S. 171, a run-down, seventy-five-year-old elementary school on East 103rd Street between Madison and Fifth Avenues. The physical facilities could hardly have been less hospitable to the open classrooms the staff aimed to create. Neither the parents in the neighborhood nor the other teachers in District Four understood what the school was trying to accomplish, and they regarded Meier's efforts with attitudes ranging from indifference to outright hostility. Local educational conservatives, on the other hand, were equally mistrustful of what they saw as the school's "permissiveness."

Debbie Meier was undeterred.

She wanted to start slowly, with just a kindergarten and a first grade. She asked for the authority to hire her own staff, which would develop its own curriculum. There would be one rule: Children would come to CPE because their parents chose that school for them. It was a choice school from the start, and parents were required to visit with their children in order to gain admission. Beyond that, Meier set forth no policies and promised no particular results.

Meier had little difficulty recruiting a group of teachers who shared her dream for a new kind of public school. When CPE opened its doors in the fall of 1974, there were just thirty-two students, twelve each in two kindergarten classes, and eight more in first grade. Nevertheless, those children who walked through the doors for their first day of classes discovered a rich world welcoming them. As Meier recalls:

When we arrived in mid-August we built at least ten storage units, two playhouses, a puppet stage, three writing tables, several book display racks, room dividers, etc. We organized and stored all our personal materials—paints, magic markers, science equipment, art materials, and books. We bought some things—typewriters, a variety of beginning reading books, wood and dry wall for building, paint and brushes, rugs for the reading corners.

As the first school days passed, parents with small children in tow began appearing in CPE classrooms, asking to enroll their children. Within three months enrollment in the kindergartens grew by 50 percent, and a waiting list burgeoned of parents interested in enrolling their children the following year. By midyear, as parental interest swelled, enrollment reached eighty-five students. Some parents were well educated and liberal, others were poor and uneducated. But in CPE they all found a school that seemed right to them and their children. One of the students later described her experience this way:

Where we came from it was all sitting down at a desk and writing at the same time, and doing math at the same time. As the first week went by at Central Park East we were all very excited about the school, and what we were doing was so different from what we had done before.

From the beginning the staff at CPE fought to integrate children who would otherwise be certified as "special education students" into the mainstream program. They resisted giving up any students to the ostracism of a special-education setting, believing that if they could retain slow learners in the regular environment, they would find a way to help them learn. Originally a source of bitter contention, the CPE approach was fully vindicated in time by Meier's receipt of the MacArthur grant and the local families' loyalty to the school.

The CPE staff tried hard not to pressure students to worry about any "normal" pattern of achievement, but by midyear, many of the older children who had entered CPE as nonreaders were reading without difficulty. Meier confessed that their progress was so startling that she suspected that the children already knew how to read, but had been unable or unwilling to reveal it to their parents or teachers.

The school tried to create an environment that was an extension of the children's families, a place where both children and parents knew they would be accepted and cared for rather than judged. In matters of discipline, CPE stressed mutual respect rather than fear. Teachers spent time explaining to students why certain forms of behavior made it impossible for others to do their work; they tried to teach children to empathize with others and to understand the impact of their actions on others. In short, during a decade in which some floundering schools questioned whether any values should be transmitted through public education, CPE strove to instill a moral sense in its students.

CPE especially tried to enlist parents in the learning process, informing them regularly about what was happening at school so they would not see education as a threatening or alien activity. Parents were encouraged to spend time on homework and to read aloud to their children or to have their children read aloud to them. Moreover, there were frequent parent-teacher meetings, at which teachers dealt with parents on a basis of respect: The message was that CPE valued the parents' ideas and contributions.

The essence of CPE was a group of highly dedicated teachers who understood that the child must be the center of education. They believed that educational programs must be built around the abilities, interests, and needs of particular children, fortified by a loving humanism. It was a progressive program of child-centered education. But it required complete commitment, long hours, and many practical innovations to implement effectively.

Meier, for example, organized her own class around the

theme of New York City's natural environment. Children studied New York's geography and visited Central Park often; they observed animal and plant life and noted the rock formations. These trips were supplemented by visits to museums. Meier believes that such outings enabled her children to get to know the world beyond East Harlem and gave them a sense of resources they could return to throughout their lives. She observed that "outside the classroom children tend to observe things more keenly and to ask more questions."

Everything went surprisingly smoothly during CPE's first year, and Alvarado expressed his confidence in the school's success by asking the staff to double CPE's size to 150 students by the next September, adding grades two through five to the program. And yet, in the fall of 1975, CPE's very existence was threatened by deep-seated conflicts. Bedeviled by another of New York's perennial financial crises, the administration of Mayor Abraham D. Beame had forced drastic cuts in the Board of Education budget, which meant that thousands of teachers were laid off. There was a system-wide reshuffling of teachers, as those "excessed" from one school exercised their seniority rights and claimed positions in others. As Alvarado recalled, "We tried a number of creative ways to ensure the kind of teachers that were required to run a program like Debbie's, and it involved a lot of risk-taking."

Bending the rules when hundreds of teachers were defending their rights to their jobs was not always easy. To make matters worse, when CPE opened for its second year in the fall of 1975, two teachers were unexpectedly stricken with serious ailments. Debbie Meier was teaching a combined class of forty-two third, fourth, and fifth graders, most of whom were new to the school, while continuing as director.

As the year went on, strains within the staff began to mount. The democratic staff organization that had seemed to work so well the year before was now breaking down. From the beginning Meier had brought the staff together to function as a sort of teacher collective. "What I was seeking was the kind of ease, trust, and mutual respect that would permit us to avoid absolutely rigid distinctions and fully spelled-out roles." But in practice, the staff's search for consensus consumed more and more time. While the teachers acted as if all were equal, they held

Meier responsible for solving major problems. And while Meier professed a belief in functioning democratically, she believed she had the right to act unilaterally when it came to make-or-break issues affecting the school's best interests.

Opposition mounted outside CPE as well. The central board refused to grant waivers to keep schools open beyond specified hours for those teachers who wanted to come in early or stay late. The new principal of P.S. 171, which housed CPE, waged a series of time-consuming turf wars over who had what prerogatives within the school building. The teachers' union became suspicious of CPE's flexibility. And a small number of vociferous parents voiced misgivings about having their children's education controlled by "a white Jewish lady."

Toward the end of the school year, a group of angry parents brought their complaints about CPE to Alvarado, and this is where I came in. For the next week I made it my business to visit the school every day. I talked to Debbie Meier, to the teachers, to the students, and to the parents. I looked around the school. Whenever I go to a school I observe the children, and if they are involved and paying attention, I know that there is learning going on and that it's a good place for a kid to be. I was not disappointed with what I found at CPE.

I held three meetings with the parents before going back to Debbie, listening attentively to their point of view so I really could understand it. There's a mnemonic I used: AIR, which stands for "acknowledge" (I acknowledged to the parents that their information was serious and important), "investigate" (I spoke to the teachers and observed the students), and "respond" (I met with the parents on a number of occasions to tell them what I had found out).

The truth is, after all my investigating, I determined that Debbie Meier was running a superior school. She regarded kids as individuals, an approach that my own teaching experience had convinced me was essential. She cared about youngsters, about learning, and had assembled a staff excited about education. There aren't enough people like that in the world, so when you find the Debbie Meiers, the people who really try to do something, you have to stand by them. They will make some mistakes, and they will always draw fire. But ultimately, people like Debbie and schools like CPE are always worth protecting.

The dissident parents in this case simply wanted control of the school and would not be satisfied with anything less. They distrusted a white outsider like Meier who thought she knew what was best. I could see how Meier could be too forceful in her opinions, but I also knew that she was the right person for that school. I therefore strongly recommended to Alvarado that we back Meier to the hilt. You support good people, I told him, even when they make mistakes. That's what support is all about. And Alvarado agreed.

So I went to the parents. I told them in the nicest possible way that even though some of their complaints were true, they were far outweighed by the fact that CPE was a really good place for kids. Meier was staying, I told them, but I would do everything I could to see that their children were placed elsewhere if they so chose. In the end fifteen families decided to leave CPE, and I got every one of them into a school of their choice. The crisis was over, the credibility of the new Office of Alternative Schools was enhanced, and a lasting friendship began.

I had learned an important lesson, too. When push comes to shove, you have to support your good people. Debbie Meier soon decided to leave the classroom and assume the role of full-time director. She had come to see the importance of having one person clearly responsible for making sure that staff decisions are implemented, and, taking a page from my book, she told each of the teachers that they were free to leave CPE if they wished. Two of the school's seven teachers chose not to return.

When the air cleared, we saw that the overwhelming majority of parents had decided to keep their children in CPE, and a similar proportion of the faculty had chosen to stay, a vote of confidence that gave the school a newfound vitality. We did not know it at the time, but we had inadvertently discovered the invigorating power of choice. By the time classes resumed the following year, CPE had entered a new phase and had begun to develop its own distinctive culture—and an approach to urban education that would soon spread to other East Harlem schools.

Inside their own classrooms, CPE's teachers were able to realize the dream of virtually all teachers—they could run their classes on their own, without interference or interruption from outside authorities. The result was an astonishingly rich educational program. One year, for example, CPE's curriculum included extensive mapmaking, studies of Native American woodlands culture in seventeenth century Harlem, Egyptian and Roman history, the Dutch settlement of New York, printing and newspapers, the emergence of cities (including a mini-study of the neighborhood around the school), and African-American history.

But children at CPE were not simply presented with a set of facts to learn from a textbook; instead they were given the opportunity to explore unfamiliar territory. They participated in a wide variety of activities aimed at bringing that civilization to life, thus enabling the children to understand and appreciate that civilization more fully. When Leslie Stein's third-grade class studied medieval society, they not only read books but built castles, made armor, and visited the Cloisters in upper Manhattan. Carol Mulligan's kindergarten and first grade developed the idea of building a mythical city, one that might resemble one of the very first cities of the ancient world. CPE's approach taught children how to ask questions and helped them form the proper foundation for critical thinking.

Meier's pedagogical goals have remained clear and constant for nearly twenty years at Central Park East. She aims to create a better informed, better equipped, and more engaged person who can play a greater part in her community.

My ideas on teaching and learning focus on small 'd' democratic values, by which I mean a respect for diversity, a respect for the potential of each individual person, a respect for opposing points of view, and a respect for considerable intellectual vigor. My concern is with how students become critical thinkers and problem solvers, which is what a democratic society needs. If we believe that our schools are failing us and that children can't learn the basic skills, then what we are saying is that democracy is a utopian ideal, an impossibility, and I just don't believe that. There is nothing in the nature of being human that makes democracy an impossibility.

Admittedly, not every teacher would favor adopting CPE's methodology. Debbie Meier is a politically committed, unabashed social democrat, and she and her cohorts were staunch believers in progressive education. In some quarters Meier's agenda provokes substantial skepticism; the average parent may not know much about the educational crisis, but she strongly suspects that it all started with the new math. To a lot of people, "progressive education" sounds like something that has failed already.

Disputes about educational methodology, however, miss the point here. In practice a capable, committed, caring teacher can use almost any method and achieve good results. The really important factor is the energy and effort extended. If the school is doing its job well, it will find a receptive audience, and it will provide quality education, as long as it has a methodology and philosophy. Other District Four alternative schools were to be far more traditional in their curriculum and methodology than CPE, but they would have no trouble attracting students and parents for whom their approach was well suited. A diversity of schools, in fact, is healthy. I have never felt uncomfortable knowing that Debbie Meier considers Manhattan East, an alternative school we established in 1981, to be elitist, because it seeks out high-achieving students in academics and the arts. She is entitled to that opinion, and the students, parents, and teachers who built Manhattan East are entitled to theirs. As educational researchers have consistently found, schools that are given the opportunity to define their own missions are routinely superior to those that have been dictated to from above.

Thus, a second and equally valuable aspect of CPE's "open classrooms organized around a theme" methodology was that it gave teachers an opportunity to follow their own interests, rather than repeat the same lessons year after year. "Curriculum development," as it was called, gave teachers a good reason to read about societies that interested them, to fill in gaps in their education, and to take interesting trips in the summer. It motivated teachers as well as students.

Alice Seletsky, who has taught at CPE since 1977, opens a window on the school's ethos when she says, "What I like best about teaching is that there are no easy answers to anything. Even after thirty-five years, I have to keep wandering, tinkering, changing my mind, learning." Seletsky is an innovative teacher, but her innovation is nothing mysterious. What she does is spend time with the kids who most need her. "I believe

42

I come to know children more fully through their works," she explains, "and they begin to know themselves through producing them." These are the words of a gifted teacher. But her gift does not reside in the fact that she uses a particular educational methodology. It resides in the fact that she is willing to give of herself freely, fully, and lovingly to her students in ways that suited her and her students best. All Alice Seletsky needed to be a good teacher was a system that would let her do just that.

By matching teachers with compatible educational environments, schools of choice enable once-frustrated educators to feel better about themselves. Having teachers participate in curriculum design might improve the curriculum, but it definitely improves the morale of teachers, who sense that they are making a positive contribution. And good morale, above all, makes for a good school. Classrooms like Alice Seletsky's constantly stimulate children to ask new questions and try out new skills. Her classroom reflects her own personality, curiosity, ethical concerns, and educational commitment. Most of all, it reflects her selfless hard work, a contribution no one in any school can absolutely guarantee but which a choice system by its very nature does the utmost to encourage.

When you feel you have a stake in your school, whether you're a teacher or a student or a parent, you're willing to work harder, make sacrifices, and protect and build up your highly personal investment. The sense of ownership that naturally develops is what has energized the students, parents, and staff at CPE for nearly twenty years.

CPE's children came to feel they owned the school, and this is partly because of the enthusiastic participation of their parents. Aurea Fernandez was one of CPE's original students in 1974. Her mother, Josie, began to work at CPE as a school aide, helping out in the lunchroom. Later, Josie worked as a paraprofessional in the classrooms, and ultimately she became the school secretary.

Two of Josie's other children also came to CPE. They were nice kids, and the education they received, coupled with the opportunity to interact with children from other parts of the city, gave them the boost they needed to grow beyond the world they had known in East Harlem. Aurea graduated from CPE and went on to an alternative junior high school in District

Four. Her brother Manuel did the same, and attended Cathedral High School. Both children went on to Brown University on full scholarships.

Then Aurea returned to New York and entered graduate school at Columbia Teachers College. Josie died a few years ago, but not before she had the satisfaction of seeing her kids make it in the world. In the fall of 1992, Aurea Fernandez joined the faculty at the CPE Secondary School.

Teachers at CPE show an extraordinary degree of dedication. In the standard New York City public school, teachers rarely talk with each other informally about what is happening in their classrooms. In weekly grade conferences, teachers may discuss issues, but all too rarely is education the focus; more often it's the overcrowded faculty parking lot or some other utterly superficial side issue. In contrast, at CPE the teachers talk about what's going on in the heads of children—for instance, do they really understand what democracy means when they have to ask permission to go to the bathroom? Such child-centered talk is a constant preoccupation of the staff, whether in the teachers' lounge, in car rides to school, in the hallways, on school trips, or on regularly organized staff retreats. All of this dedication and hard work rubs off on the kids—they reflect it right back.

And the results are gratifying. In a follow-up study of 117 CPE students who completed the sixth grade between 1978 and 1983, David Bensman of Rutgers University found that almost every single CPE graduate had a positive memory of their school and said they would send their own children there. Ninety-five percent had graduated from high school, and 66 percent had begun college. And, not insignificantly, all of the CPE graduates were alive. These are statements that not many schools in the inner city can make.

4 A Handful of Pioneers

Good schools have to be created one by one. But a public school district has the capacity to create an environment that is either supportive of school-building or antagonistic to it. I am not saying that District Four is unique; on the contrary, I believe that there are educators all over the country just waiting to be freed from outworn constraints to set up the schools of their dreams. But the fact remains that a handful of courageous, energetic educators and politicians in East Harlem provided the strong leadership necessary to rise to the challenge of creating effective new schools.

In the early seventies committed teachers in District Four found a champion in the new superintendent, Anthony Alvarado. A young Latino educator who had lived in East Harlem and attended Fordham Prep and Fordham University, Alvarado was the only child of working parents who had given all their energy and disposable income to provide him with a fine education. Growing up, Alvarado was a studious young man who always carried a book in his hip pocket, a habit that would inspire us years later to form the Hip Pocket Book Club in District Four.

Alvarado began his teaching career in 1966 in Junior High School 38 in the Bronx, and later worked for one year as Field Coordinator for the Board of Education. He also directed higher education opportunity programs at New York University and City University of New York before becoming principal of Community Elementary School 235 in the South Bronx.

In 1973, after an extensive search by the community school board committee headed by Tony Burgos (an energetic young Latino politician who today is one of New York Governor Mario Cuomo's closest advisors), the superintendent candidate list was narrowed to three applicants—Nathan Quiñones, Peter Negroni, and Anthony Alvarado. It wasn't a bad list inasmuch as two of the people on it were to later become chancellors of the New York City public schools, and the third, Peter Negroni, is today superintendent of schools in Springfield, Massachusetts. After due consideration, the board appointed Alvarado Superintendent of District Four. He was thirty-one years old.

Alvarado was ready and eager to entertain new ideas, such as allowing teachers to create schools. Coming into the district in the aftermath of the 1968 decentralization, he found, in his words, "a climate in which education was not taken seriously. The schools lacked clear goals and articulate strategies." Alvarado decided to "foster serious experimentation which would provide other ways of educating kids successfully." At an early meeting, his staff was excited to hear that he was willing to try out a dramatically new and different district-wide reading program. But this was just one example of Alvarado's open-minded attitude toward innovation.

Fortunately for Alvarado and the students of East Harlem, the school board in District Four was generally supportive of the new superintendent's initiatives. The president of the community school board, Robert Rodriguez, was only twenty-six years old and had come to the post by virtue of his work locally on an antipoverty program. He and Alvarado brought youth, energy, and savoir faire to East Harlem, which were critical to setting into motion the political and educational processes that transformed District Four.

Ironically, it was Robert Rodriguez who had played a major role in my not having gotten the permanent appointment as principal at P.S. 108. In those days there were few Hispanic principals in District Four, and Rodriguez believed that the East Harlem schools ought to reflect the community around them. The appointment at P.S. 108 was part of his implementing that design; as Rodriguez later explained to me, the decision was nothing personal.

Rodriguez understood that his own job as school board president was to be a politician and not an educator. He saw his role as that of Alvarado's protector, providing political cover before the elected school board while the new superintendent tried to turn District Four around. Under Rodriguez's strong leadership, the board placed its faith in Alvarado, despite knowing little about alternative schools or new educational theories. Rodriguez set himself up as a buffer between the board and the superintendent, channeling all problems through himself, and strictly separating administrative problems from educational ones.

With his board solidly behind him, Alvarado opened a crack in the school system's normally sealed doors, out of which sprang the first six alternative schools. Along with the Central Park East elementary school were the B.E.T.A. (Better Education Through Alternatives) School, Harbor Junior High School of the Performing Arts, the East Harlem Performing Arts School (EHPAS), the East Harlem Middle School, and the Children's Learning Center.

These first schools each had different purposes, in accordance with the different priorities and goals of their founders. CPE was an "open classroom" elementary school, while B.E.T.A. was designed to give chronic problem students not only a new learning environment but a new lease on life. Harbor sought to give students with an interest in the performing arts an introduction to what might ultimately become their career, while EHPAS used drama and music as a tool to encourage learning in other subjects. The purpose of East Harlem Middle School was to extend the educational approach of the elementary school into the adolescent years. And the Children's Learning Center, today called the Creative Learning Community, balanced academics with a humanistic approach to the social and emotional growth of its students, and was an experiment in the use of school co-directors.

These schools hardly constituted a system or a movement,

and neither the superintendent nor the founders of the schools regarded their efforts in that light. Alvarado, charged with running the worst school district in the city, was willing to try new ideas, and the early founders had something they wanted to try. Their first efforts already contained the essence of what District Four would become, vividly demonstrating that if you liberate energetic leaders from the bureaucracy they will try things worth trying and sometimes succeed, and if they fail, instead of hiding their heads and covering up their errors as bureaucrats are wont to do, they will try something else so as to overcome failure.

The pioneers of District Four had very different ideas about what a school should be, but they had a great deal in common, too. They were devoted to their students. They had energy and leadership. They believed that education could change their students' lives. And they proved that they were right.

The B.E.T.A. School

B.E.T.A. is the kind of school that everyone in the educational community supports, even the opponents of alternative schools. Specifically designed for youngsters who are failing in traditional learning environments, schools like B.E.T.A. say, "Give us your troubled youngsters, and we will take them off your hands." I have often thought that such a school could attract students even if it consisted only of a door at the edge of a cliff. Principals from other public schools are only too happy to help schools like B.E.T.A. find students. The hard part is to make such a school work.

There is still a small community of old-line Italian families in East Harlem, perched between Second and Pleasant Avenues, extending three or four blocks north and south of 115th Street and the famous Rao's restaurant. John Falco, the founder of the B.E.T.A. School, grew up here. His father peddled vegetables through these streets from a horse and wagon. He understood life in East Harlem and knew how kids could go wrong. Solidly built and bearded, Falco is in perpetual motion, and has the slightly harried look of someone who is always running twenty minutes late, which he usually is. An imposing man (he was a minor league baseball player before devoting himself to education), he nevertheless warns, "You don't earn people's affection and respect up here by being a wise guy or a big mouth. You've got to be sensitive and strong in the right ways."

From B.E.T.A.'s opening day in 1974, Falco took the most problematic students in the district—"acting out" kids, emotionally disturbed kids—and structured a program that addressed their needs while providing discipline and respect for each individual. B.E.T.A. could give these students individual attention because the school was much smaller than others in the district. Some junior high schools in District Four had 1200 students, while B.E.T.A. began with about 35 and never grew beyond 250. "We had to be the family to these kids," Falco says. "No one else was. They were on the street, and they were often in trouble at home. Many of them had an abusive parent or an addicted parent. Those kids had been really wounded."

The curriculum targeted the children's deficiencies. Emotional problems were identified and psychiatric or social counseling was begun. Then each student began what was intentionally designed as a slow process of learning, with abundant support from the staff—who made a particular effort not to impose undue pressure on psychologically fragile students. As Falco explains, "Interaction with a healthy adult is incredibly important to these kids. They're starved for it. You have to give these kids a sense of their own dignity. Nobody else ever has, but once they're convinced you really care about them, good things happen."

The intensive individual support approach employed by Falco worked slowly but surely. Some students probably could not have been helped by any educational environment, no matter how supportive, but the vast majority did respond to B.E.T.A.'s approach, including one family of three boys who remain vivid in Falco's memory:

The father was in jail and the mother was hopelessly hooked on drugs. The kids were spending all their time on the street. We took them in, and worked with them, and they responded beautifully. For all their problems, the kids had all been blessed with talent in the arts. We worked at directing their energies in this area. Eventually, every one of them got into the High School of Art and Design [a good city high school on Second Avenue and 57th Street], which was unheard of from District Four at the time.

The last time I spoke to the eldest brother, he had gone to work for an architectural firm and was doing excellent work there.

Today John Falco and I are close friends. When we started working together, however, it was not that way. His operating premise, like Debbie Meier's, was that anyone from the district office must be up to no good. When I first went to see him he was polite, but my gut feeling was that he was essentially trying to snow me and hoped I would go away. I was always treated as if I were a visiting superintendent, and John made everything sound *too* good.

It took time for us to build trust and a productive working relationship. What really helped the process was that I visited B.E.T.A. often and became acquainted with its operation, thus making it possible for me to address the school's specific personnel, instructional, and physical-education needs.

B.E.T.A. was on the fifth floor of J.H.S. 99 on East 100th Street. It was quite a hike to get up the stairs, which enabled the school to remain pretty well insulated from outsiders. While other school directors called me up and told me their problems, John Falco tended to keep his problems to himself. That was his operating style. But Falco's curriculum-development director, an older teacher named Ed Allen, realized that the district office might conceivably be helpful in locating superior personnel.

It takes a certain kind of teacher to work in a school like B.E.T.A. Not everyone can stand the day in, day out strain of dealing with such a dysfunctional student population. Falco had recruited good people, like Beryl Epton, one of the finest teachers I have ever known. Epton, who was also from the neighborhood, is today the founder of the Children's Workshop, a one-class nongraded school. But Falco needed more strong staffing, and I was able to help him get an exceptional teacher, Carl Vinci, who had been excessed from another school. He too was of Italian ancestry and had a profound empathy for the black and Hispanic kids growing up in East Harlem's street culture. I knew immediately that he would be able to work well with Falco. Indeed, Vinci became a great asset to B.E.T.A. both as a teacher and as an administrator. In addition to all his regular duties, he ran the evening-school program and the Police Athletic League summer recreation program. A fine tennis player, he set up the first District Four tennis program. Today he is still John Falco's right-hand man, running the attendance improvement program for the district.

Placing Carl Vinci at B.E.T.A. was my great breakthrough with John Falco. Alternative-school directors always test their supervisors. In their minds they think, "He talks a good game, but what can he really do for me, except interfere?" When I showed I could be constructive, I broke through such resistance and moved on to a new level of collaboration. I helped B.E.T.A. with its personnel and programming needs while at the same time protected its unorthodox approach from critics within the district and at the central board who felt Falco had too free a hand. I brought Charlotte Frank, head of the central board's office of curriculum and instruction, to visit B.E.T.A. and three of our other schools; she included all four of them in her list of model schools to commend. That was a great shot in the arm for Falco and his staff.

B.E.T.A. was soon providing support and referral services as good as those provided by any other public school in the city. Falco also started a serious sports program to provide an outlet for the students' energies. And he himself was on call at all hours of the day, for any emergency:

One morning a kid came in with a machete and said he was going to kill his teacher. I took him into my office, and he spent the next five hours with me. I didn't make him give me the machete. I talked about it with him and asked him if he would. For a long time he said no. So we talked about him and his problems and the situation at school, and eventually he realized that his problems really had nothing to do with this one teacher, who had become the lightning rod for all his frustrations. In the end he handed me the machete and said, "I want you to have it, Mr. Falco, and I want to apologize to my teacher." And, believe it or not, because I know it sounds corny, but in this case it was absolutely true, that was a real turning point in the life of that kid.

B.E.T.A. accepted only students recommended by their previous teachers and also insisted that prospective students and their parents visit B.E.T.A. before deciding to attend. But Falco puts an ironic twist on the idea that B.E.T.A. was a school of choice: "It was a school of *last* choice. For most kids B.E.T.A. was the end of the road, an alternative to special ed, suspension, or big trouble. Our first priority was to give those kids some self-respect. Each and every one of our kids was treated with dignity."

This emphasis on dignity underpinned the staff's work at B.E.T.A. Whether it showed up in the way John Falco handled the boy with a machete or in other day-to-day decisions, it sent the message that the students were people whose accomplishments were worthy of respect.

Mary Romer Coleman, an original staff member and eventually Falco's successor as B.E.T.A.'s director, was an extraordinary teacher and director who was comfortable dealing with street kids, while always maintaining a sense of dignity about herself and respect for her colleagues. Each spring she treated her graduating class to a steak dinner, taking them to Hanratty's on 93rd Street and Second Avenue and always insisting on paying the tab out of her own pocket. It became the most talked-about and eagerly anticipated event of the school year. Although I knew her well, she always referred to me as Mr. Fliegel, never Sy. Her untimely death in 1991 at the age of forty-three was a loss to the district and all others fortunate enough to consider her a colleague.

This kind of commitment and concern Coleman and others evinced had a profound impact on the students. George J.,* who attended the B.E.T.A. School from grades four through nine, was a learning-disabled child whose dyslexia went undiagnosed until the seventh grade. George was a troublemaker, the toughest, strongest, most difficult kid at B.E.T.A., and he spent most of his time acting out. But there was something intriguing about him that didn't fit the stereotype. His attendance at school was perfect.

The breakthrough came one day when he screamed at Coleman, "I kill myself here. I'm fifteen years old and I can't read!" With her encouragement and B.E.T.A.'s support, George entered Northside Center for Child Development, a well-known guidance facility on East 110th Street which had been founded by the eminent social psychologist Dr. Kenneth Clark. There he learned to read and discovered a previously hidden aptitude for math. Today he supports himself as a skilled arc welder while he works his way through Rockland Community College.

B.E.T.A. fostered success like this again and again.

---

* The names of certain students have been changed. These changes are indicated throughout by a first name and last initial.

The school started small, with only thirty-five students and seven teachers, working out of the fifth floor of P.S. 109 on East 99th Street. Five years after its founding it had moved into J.H.S. 99 on East 100th Street, where by 1979 it had expanded to 240 kids. As the program grew, students, parents, and the entire community became more trusting and supportive of the school's singular mission. Falco's acceptance by the local community has helped him enormously as an educator, and he will say that one of his biggest advantages is that he actually likes East Harlem.

B.E.T.A. was noticed by the press and began to be cited as a model program. Reporters noticed that in many ways John Falco ran B.E.T.A. like a private school. He prized his autonomy and used it to achieve results that would have been impossible in an orthodox New York City public school setting. At the same time, he managed to have fun and keep up morale, a vital mission often ignored in bureaucratic systems. Falco persuaded his people to believe that if you like what you're doing, and you're doing well, you can have a good time—even in New York public schools. He assembled a colorful assortment of teachers who "hung out" together. They enjoyed the atmosphere of East Harlem, frequented local establishments, and knew the community well. As for the central Board of Education, in Falco's view the less it knew the better (and, to judge by the board's complete indifference to District Four in those years, the feeling was mutual). The community quickly came to know and accept them, too. Precisely because East Harlem has a real street life and people do know one another, news often travels faster than in New York's richer, more insulated highrise neighborhoods. People know who is doing what, and they judge by results.

In the end, though, B.E.T.A.'s success was its own undoing. By helping to inspire the growth of the alternative school movement in the district, B.E.T.A. became the model for other schools. They began to adopt B.E.T.A.'s approach and attitude to troubled kids before they had to be placed in a special situation. Though it once served 240 students, in the early 1980s enrollment evened out at 60. By 1989, when some 26 alternative schools were in operation in District Four, there were only 38 students enrolled, and the district office decided that these children could be better served within the environment of the other alternative schools. B.E.T.A. thus started what was to become a trend in District Four and elsewhere: when schools of choice succeed, they encourage other schools to try harder.

The Harbor School

Colman Genn, the son of Lithuanian immigrants, came to District Four in the fall of 1960 to teach at Intermediate School 117 on East 109th Street. A recent graduate of Brooklyn College, Genn had just gotten married and still lived in Brooklyn. "I didn't even know where East Harlem was," he recalls. In 1965 he became dean of students at I.S. 117, a position that didn't mean much in the way of perks: "I remember one mother asking me, 'I can't find your office. What does it say on your office door?' So I told her: 'Mimeograph room.' "

In his early days Genn spent more time enforcing than he did educating. Kids were in his face every day, confronting him.

I'd say, "your turn," wrestle the next one to the ground, and make him give up. It was like a game. Even outside, I always had to chase the local Italian kids off the playing field so we could use it. If they weren't there, I'd be chasing off a Puerto Rican gang. But I got on well with the kids, spent time in their homes, helped to keep them out of trouble, and learned to love the community.

He also learned how tough a community it was for some youngsters:

There was a small, funny, very dark-skinned boy named Jackson Jenkins, who loved to play the court jester. I took him to summer camp, and he did well. But after three weeks he said to me, "Genn, I have to go to town to see the doctor." I said, "No you don't. We have a doctor here at the camp." But that wasn't good enough for him. He insisted, and eventually, not knowing any better at that early point in my career, I relented, and for the rest of the summer I took him into town every two or three weeks, and never asked him what he was going for.

Two years later Jackson was killed by another kid who dealt drugs in the school yard. It was only then that I learned that Jackson had been addicted to heroin since he was fourteen. The boy had been dying in front of my eyes, and I had never suspected a thing.

Cole Genn learned fast, however, and began to rise in District Four schools. In 1970 he was named an assistant principal. But by then, together with a group of what he now calls "educational wild men and women," he was ready to organize a different kind of school. Park East High School, an alternative school that predated Tony Alvarado's arrival in District Four, was started on the assumption that "everything the Board of Education does is bound to fail." Its specific mission was to set up a racially integrated model of a free democratic society in which kids took part at every level of the educational process.

Genn joined the idealistic Park East team, writing the physical education curriculum, and, though only there for two years, served as a critical member of its staff.

In the spring of 1975, at Alvarado's request, Genn came to the Harbor School, which had been struggling through a difficult birth. Harbor had been started as a collaborative effort between the district and Boys Harbor, the famous inner-city youth program and East Hampton summer camp founded by Anthony Drexel Duke. Additional assistance came from Title VII competitive federal funding and the National Council on the Arts. Along with the East Harlem Performing Arts School (discussed later in this chapter), Harbor was one of two schools founded at this time that were focused on the performing arts, and it was set up on a conservatory model with the goal of training its students for careers in the arts.

Harbor's first months had been a near disaster for a variety of reasons. The four teachers on board had a total of six months experience among them; consequently there was no administrative organization to speak of, and no student discipline whatever, before the arrival of Cole Genn.

Genn accepted the job on two conditions—that he could pick his staff and move the school into the I.S. 117 building. Alvarado said yes to both. Though Genn was required to go through the United Federation of Teachers (UFT) procedure of posting job descriptions and holding interviews, he got the teachers he wanted by unofficial recruiting. This was an early example of what we would come to call "creative noncompliance." "The assignments were definitely not done by seniority," he recalls, "but the whole idea of alternative schools was so new that the union was asleep at the wheel." Like the bureaucracy at 110 Livingston Street, the UFT had been blinded by its own procedures.

Genn himself says he hired some "outrageous characters," because they had what it took to get the material across to the kids. "I wanted to show those kids, living in that hell, that there was something else available for blacks and Hispanics in this country, if they just had the skills and one door open. It was about that time that we began talking about the Harbor family."

That spring Genn toured sixth grade classes in and out of the district to sell the Harbor program to students. Harbor reopened in September 1975 at I.S. 117 with 120 students, eight more than the previous year, in grades seven, eight, and nine. The academic staff was now comprised of teachers who were personally recruited by Genn, teachers with far more experience than the original group. I didn't know Cole Genn well in those early days, but the Office of Alternative Schools did pitch in at Harbor by helping get the teachers he needed and running interference when necessary with the central board. We also helped him get the maximum possible allocation from the district budget, always a crucial function of the office. Every year we would meet with the district superintendent and his business manager and lobby late into the night, fighting to get the largest possible allocation for each of our alternative schools.

Often success was measured only in safeguarding or creating one position, worth perhaps $40,000 or $50,000. But in an alternative school in those years that one position was equivalent to 10 percent of the school staff. It was essential to save those positions. One teacher we saved was Dave Chamberlain, Harbor's excellent band director. The district and the central board saw nothing wrong with a performing arts school cutting its band director, but I was able to convince them that this wasn't a great idea. By doing so and by attending all of Harbor's productions, my staff and I soon became a part of "the Harbor Family" in the eyes of Cole Genn and his school.

Within a few short years the Harbor student body grew to over two hundred. The school stressed group spirit and sharing. The cafeteria was opened at seven-thirty each morning and became a gathering place for students and staff, a safe haven for kids, and a place where they could do homework, observe their role models in an informal setting, and make a friendly transition to the structure of the school day.

Harbor's curriculum had two components—academic and performing arts. The academic program was a traditional junior high school program with some modifications. Teachers were given an unusual amount of autonomy in curriculum, methodology, and decision making. Within a few years students at Harbor were improving their academic performance markedly, which we attributed to the uplift in morale due to Harbor's great sense of community. The performing arts program was based on a conservatory model, with intensive training provided by professional performing artists in instrumental and vocal music, dance, and drama. At a school like the High School of the Performing Arts (of *Fame* fame), most children do not perform until the twelfth grade (although the exceptional eleventh grader may perform). At Harbor, the seventh graders began performing two weeks after they arrived.

A striking aspect of the Harbor educational philosophy is its strong ethical dimension, restated in almost every talk, memo, or communication at the school. The message is that students are part of a world greater than themselves and therefore have obligations to themselves and to society. The spirit Genn sought to inculcate in his students is summed up in the end-of-year message he wrote for the 1977 Harbor Yearbook: "The essence of art, including performing arts, is to create something beautiful. . . . It is our prayer that our students go out into the world with the strength, not only to survive, but to remain beautiful human beings."

Another distinctive feature of the school was the annual tour. During the spring terms of 1977, 1978, and 1979, when there was enough money, a group of approximately forty students accompanied by five teachers and one parent traveled by bus to perform in places as distant as Illinois, Georgia, Florida, Virginia, and North Carolina. This tour was a fantastic motivator for the school's young performers. They performed for small church audiences and to big crowds. They saw other schools, many poorer than their own, and other parts of the country. One of the things that struck everyone as they toured the South was that Harbor was the only school on the tour comprised entirely of minority students. One day, as the kids were eating breakfast in a motel in Atlanta, Georgia State Senator Julian Bond noticed the group and stopped to ask, "Who are you?" He came on the bus and gave the kids a twenty-minute lecture on Georgia, probably one of the best educational experiences they ever had.

Genn remembers the tours as a critical turning point in many students' lives:

The children were beautiful. It was an awakening for those of us on the staff who were there. I used to put this sign up on the wall that said, "Seldom, if ever, do you exceed your expectations." We expected a great deal from these kids, and the truth of it is that they exceeded our expectations. We pushed them and they pushed themselves even further. They were superb. We had kids come off the stage and faint. They were ill. They never told us. It gave them a sense that they were members of a group whose needs became more important than their individual concerns.

One of the Harbor kids who blossomed at the school was Miriam T., a sweet, quiet Hispanic girl. In fact, she was too quiet. When Cole Genn noticed how withdrawn she was he visited her home. There were five or six children by three different fathers there, and one of the fathers had abused the mother and all of the kids. The family was being broken up by the social welfare agency, but Genn interceded in the court process and pulled Miriam's older brother Ricky into the ninth grade and her younger brother, Ernesto, into the school as well.

At first Miriam didn't know what she wanted to do at Harbor, but she soon fell in love with dance. She became the star of "A Salute to Black Performers" show that Harbor performed in New York and took on its road tour. Later she also starred in a dramatic production of *A Raisin in the Sun.*

With continuing outreach by the Harbor staff, Miriam's family was kept together. Genn got Miriam's mother involved at Harbor, sewing costumes and serving as chaperone on the tour. Later he found her a regular job. He also secured a court order that kept the abusive husband away, and became a second father to the children. Today Miriam is happily married with kids of her own, Ricky is managing a McDonald's, and Ernesto is also doing well.

Another successful turnaround in the Harbor family was Robert R. He used to hang around outside the band classroom, just listening. Realizing he was extremely interested in music, Genn approached him. They started to talk, and the director discovered that Robert had been classified as a special education student and was attending an unrewarding program in Washington Heights. After several conversations, Genn came to believe that Robert's emotional disability (he was an aggressive, acting-out youngster at the time) could be much more effectively treated in a mainstream school. He arranged for Robert to come to Harbor, where he became an enthusiastic member of the band. Little by little he was also able to tackle complex subjects such as musical theory, social studies, and mathematics. When the central board discovered that Genn had admitted Robert to Harbor, a guidance counselor at the placement office summoned Genn and berated him for breaking regulations. Over the central board bureaucrat's objections, Genn quickly persuaded the hearing officer that he had acted in Robert's best interest, and that to return him to special ed would be counterproductive.

End result: By the end of the ninth grade Robert was completely mainstreamed and entered a college-prep program at Seward Park High School.

Ronnie H.'s mother had been married four times, and when Ronnie came to Harbor he suffered from low self-esteem. Performing gave him the self-confidence he needed, and Harbor's support system gave him a solid grounding in values. In a citywide spelling bee at Madison Square Garden during his last year at Harbor, Ronnie came in third. He continued on successfully from that point and today is majoring in economics and political science at Howard University.

In New York City one of the most telling measures of a junior high school's success is its ability to get its students into the city's selective high schools. In 1974, only one student from District Four was admitted to the High School of the Performing Arts or the High School of Music and Art. Between 1976 and 1981, Harbor alone placed a total of forty-two at

Music and Art, thirty-four at Performing Arts, and fifteen at private high schools through the ABC (A Better Chance) program sponsored by a consortium of private school people located in Boston.

Some of these students went on to perform professionally—though Genn always said that he'd rather have his students turn out to be attorneys who perform as a hobby than have them be waiters and waitresses waiting to make it in the performing world. Others, like Laceine Wedderburn and Peggy Ruffin, became teachers. Today Laceine teaches dance at Harbor, while Peggy Ruffin teaches music right across the street at P.S. 83. Laceine is also a professional dancer and is working on her master's degree.

In many ways Genn became the prototype of the alternative school director, immersing himself in every aspect of the system. Because of his prior experience in alternative schools, he was able to approach his task at Harbor with very clear ideas as to what he wanted to accomplish, thereby creating a strong educational program while still allowing for significant input from staff members and parents. He observed that humanistic education is not achieved by telling people to teach humanely but by treating people humanely, teachers and students alike. Genn's commitment also encouraged students to grab a hold of their dream and then hang on even when times were tough. A key difference between Harbor and regular schools was the intensity in the air, the all-consuming effort to make that school succeed, whatever the odds.

In the alternative schools the issue of second generation leadership was often problematic, as it always spelled a difference in focus for the institution. Cole Genn's leadership enabled Harbor to prosper even after he left the school in 1981 to pursue other challenges in the New York City public school system. There was an orderly transition as another highly effective educational leader, Bill Colavito, took the reins for four years, until he left to become assistant director of the Office of Alternative Schools. Whereas Genn had believed in taking in the most uneducable kids in the district and then working countless hours to rehabilitate them, Colavito brought with him a talent for administrative detail and a different focus on academic achievement. Of course he also had the same warmth and empathy for kids that his predecessor had had.

60

Still later when Leslie Moore, a member of the original staff, became Harbor's director, she introduced yet a different emphasis. Unlike either Genn or Colavito, Moore came from an arts background, and she made raising the standards of Harbor's performances her priority. The school began putting on an annual musical, and it also added a highly successful circus arts program in conjunction with the Big Apple Circus, whose members teach circus acts to the youngsters. In fact, one Harbor graduate, Carlos Guity, took a year off after school to join the circus before deciding to make his career as an accountant. The Big Apple Circus currently employs him in a bookkeeping position while Carlos completes his accounting degree at night school. Thus the Harbor curriculum offered Carlos a toehold in a field that he otherwise might not have had.

As our network of alternative schools grew, District Four attracted about a thousand kids annually to its schools from other districts. But when the money from the federal Emergency Schools Assistance Act that had started Harbor off was replaced by the New York State Magnet Schools grant program, the continuing preponderance of Hispanic and black students was the reason Harbor became ineligible for competitive funds in the 1980s—it wasn't sufficiently racially integrated! Nevertheless, Harbor School for the Performing Arts is still thriving today, with 240 students in grades seven, eight, and nine.

East Harlem Performing Arts School

A slightly different approach from Harbor's conservatory-oriented curriculum achieved great success at the East Harlem Performing Arts School. EHPAS integrated the arts into the entire curriculum on the theory that inculcating artistic values would draw students deeper into the learning process. Students were accepted based on their interest, not their proficiency, in the arts. They applied and auditioned, but the school was not trying to appeal to an elite group of super-talented youngsters. EHPAS accepted kids for what they were and then helped them grow.

The driving force behind EHPAS was Ellen Kirshbaum, a tall, sturdily built woman with strong convictions, who had previously employed an arts-based curriculum in her work with emotionally handicapped students. This experience convinced her that the arts—particularly the performing arts—could be used as an exciting motivational force for underprivileged minority students. She had tried doing just that in her work at P.S. 108, where she and a colleague who shared the same class, Nancy Goldman, achieved outstanding results motivating students and raising math and reading scores. Having come to love their students and to respect their aspirations and talents, Kirshbaum and Goldman feared that their learning progress could be impaired or even destroyed in East Harlem's overcrowded, unruly, and ineffective junior highs. They wanted to save their students from that fate, and to give them the time and the skills they needed to nourish their artistic dreams. Their principal agreed and encouraged them to meet with Superintendent Alvarado, who in turn encouraged them to proceed.

Kirshbaum and Goldman decided to recruit 150 students and 14 teachers, a number which could not be accommodated in P.S. 108, so they moved their new school to the Church of St. Edward on East 109th Street. The Shubert Foundation, run by one of New York's leading families of theatrical producers, provided a $15,000 grant to help defray the start-up costs. The recruited teachers met all Board of Education requirements but also had the right abilities for a performing arts school.

The school had no difficulty attracting students, for they and their parents shared Kirshbaum and Goldman's apprehension about the traditional junior highs. The school opened in September 1974 with five seventh-grade classes.

Though the arts were integrated into the academic program, EHPAS emphasized public performances, as Harbor did, and students and teachers devoted a major part of their energies to making these memorable. I must say that there is something wonderfully impressive about walking into a hall and hearing two hundred kids singing, and over the years I brought many first-time visitors, who by the end of those shows were overcome with tears.

A talented coterie of faculty members helped assure the school's success. Members of the performing arts community visited frequently and talked to the students about careers in the arts. Kirshbaum and company scouted out free tickets to take the kids to Broadway and off-Broadway shows. In later years EHPAS experimented with annual curricular themes, such as black culture or the arts in Asia.

Not that there weren't problems. Some teachers were inexperienced and did not understand the connection between arts and academics. The school's success quickly caused it to outgrow its site at the church, and for its second year EHPAS moved into P.S. 50 on East 100th Street, the Vito Marcantonio school, where it is still located today. Sid Schwager, with whom I had been an assistant principal at P.S. 146, was the principal at P.S. 50, and my close relationship with Sid enabled me to smooth out a lot of problems Kirshbaum had regarding space, daily routine, use of the lunch room and gym, and so forth when she moved the school.

I got along fine with Kirshbaum. She was a passionate and creative teacher, but organization was not her strong point. Neither day-to-day administration nor effective staff management came easily to her, and she had personality conflicts with her staff and with three successive co-directors. Some critics called her style of administration ad hoc, others called it chaotic. But these were problems of growth and innovation, symptoms of an excess of energy, not the frustration and despair found in schools doomed to fail because they are forbidden to change.

In the fall of 1975 Kirshbaum had not only moved the school, but had also married Superintendent Alvarado, causing further political conflicts within EHPAS. Indeed, over the next several years rifts developed between Kirshbaum and a number of her teachers. I was often called in to mediate, and the usual result was that I found the aggrieved teacher a placement in another school. Kirshbaum's last co-director was Maryanne Coleman, an excellent teacher who fortunately had a great talent for administration. In March 1978, however, the two of them had a major dispute over the suspension of some youngsters. Kirshbaum had summarily sent the students home, a move that Coleman opposed. Parents and teachers got involved, and the EHPAS community became sharply divided. I spent countless days trying to repair the rift, to no avail. Nor could I recommend in good conscience that Coleman be transferred. When I refused to do so, Kirshbaum never spoke to me again.

The matter of a possibly incompetent teacher-director married to the Superintendent put the Office of Alternative Schools in an extremely delicate position, but we tried to play the role of honest intermediary without unnecessarily offending anyone. Alvarado was in a tough spot, too, and he asked Deputy Superintendent Barbara Barry to look into the matter. An Alvarado loyalist, Barry ruled that Coleman had to leave EHPAS, and she was transferred to J.H.S. 99 across the street.

However, management and personality problems persisted at EHPAS until Kirshbaum finally took a maternity leave in the fall of 1978, and a new director, Elaine Fink, took over. The whole matter had been painful for all of us, but we had learned some important lessons. Not only did we find that co-directorships of alternative schools are extremely tricky things, lending themselves to personality conflicts, but also that it is important not to lose sight of the primacy of learning as the focus of a school.

EHPAS prospered anew, with increased stability and more sensitive leadership under Fink and her successors Roberta Long and Jon Dresher. A better balance was struck between arts and academic activities, and the kids were the principal beneficiaries of this new harmony.

Richard L., for example, was a difficult student who performed poorly and was prone to frequent emotional outbursts. EHPAS used dramatic role-playing to channel his energies more constructively. Through an interdisciplinary approach that allowed him to study areas of science and the humanities through the performing arts, his academic performance improved dramatically. By the time Richard graduated his average was up in the eighties, and he had become an outstanding member of the EHPAS community. In 1991, he graduated from LaGuardia High School for the Arts, the specialized high school formed by the merger of the High School of the Performing Arts and the High School of Music and Art.

Carleton Anderson is another example of how the EHPAS approach can yield unexpected dividends. Carleton came from lower Manhattan to attend EHPAS over the objections of his local superintendent, who charged that we were "stealing" students from his district. Carleton's motive for coming to EHPAS was simply that he could not find the same level of education in his area. He worked hard at performance but also showed an interest in the technical aspects of production which led him in another academic direction. When he left EHPAS, Carleton Anderson went on to the Manhattan Center for Science and Math, and eventually received several college scholarship offers.

Savion Glover is the kind of success story we all dream of having. Savion came to EHPAS as a sixth grader. He was already a talented tap dancer and singer, but he had fallen far behind in school. His dance teachers pushed him to perform while at the same time the school designed an academic plan for him that helped him to develop other talents. With the help of his mother and his teachers, this effort paid off handsomely. Because his dance teacher employed his talents in repertory situations, Savion developed a strong feeling for teamwork. Since leaving EHPAS, Savion has gone on to appear in many movies and shows. He is currently a cast member of *Sesame Street* and a featured performer at night on Broadway in *Jelly's Last Jam*. Savion is also a great, great kid.

In the end the lesson we learned from EHPAS's growing pains was a profoundly important one. Alternative schools are free to change. In real life, outside the warped reality of bureaucratic systems, nothing is forever; in fact, a change of leadership is often a good thing in the evolution of an alternative school. Not only is such a school an exhausting enterprise, but the person with the vision and entrepreneurial spirit to start a new school may not always be the right person to maintain it as a mature institution.

Today EHPAS, with 240 students, has become one of the largest alternative schools in District Four and is recognized as one of the outstanding performing arts schools in New York City.

The Children's Learning Center and East Harlem Middle School

There were two other pioneering alternative schools in the early days of District Four's transformation, both of which experienced their own growing pains. Like EHPAS, the Children's Learning Center (which was founded at P.S. 171

in 1975) wrestled with the problem of co-directors. The founders, Mark Wallach and Mary Anne Marripodi, were hardworking and cared a great deal about children. Their idea was to take the concept of child-centered education, which they had used successfully in elementary schools, and apply it to youngsters in grades six through eight. But the co-directorship arrangement was complicated in this case by the fact that the co-directors were involved in a personal relationship outside of the school. When that broke down, the strained feelings carried over into the everyday running of the school.

The Office of Alternative Schools was again in a delicate position. But finally we decided that Marripodi should remain as sole director, while Wallach was transferred to another of our alternative elementary schools. Marripodi later moved up to math and computer sciences director at the district office, and from there went to the chancellor's office under Anthony Alvarado.

East Harlem Middle School, the sixth of the original schools, was founded in 1974 at P.S. 155 on East 117th Street. It was the brainchild of Jeffrey Hansen, a young man with a Ph.D. from Columbia, an M.B.A. from Harvard, and experience in New York's Teacher Corps. He was always a serious young man, but he and I were able to form a close relationship. I even promised to teach him how to dance and enjoy life, but like many of the other alternative school directors, he was single-minded in his devotion to learning and to his kids. Hansen's curriculum, based on a caring, intensive learning process, rescued many students from underachievement. One of these was Albert Graziosa, a poor student from a family of non–English speakers, who was two years behind grade level in both reading and math.

I remember arriving at the district office one cold winter morning and seeing Hansen and Albert outside. When I asked them what they were doing, Hansen said he was taking Albert to an interview at the George School, a private boarding school in Newtown, Pennsylvania. I later received a telephone call from the headmaster of the George School, who told me how impressed he was that an alternative school director would take an entire day to drive one of his students to an interview. "If he believes in him that much," this gentleman told me, "we are more than willing to give him a chance." Albert's acceptance into this prestigious private school—on a full scholarship—was the turning point in his life. Thereafter he was accepted into Carleton College in Minnesota and today is a successful physician.

East Harlem Middle evolved in the course of its existence into the Writing School. Under former teacher Fran Boren, the school made writing exercises, so often ignored in traditional public schools, a major part of the curriculum. Later it became Northview Tech under director Maria Bonet. Northview Tech (so named because its building faces north) emphasizes the teaching of communications arts through computer technology.

Jeffrey Hansen went on to work with me in the Office of Alternative Schools, as my assistant in charge of curriculum and later in the budget office, and is now superintendent of schools in Ridgefield, Connecticut.

The six pioneer schools begun in 1974 and 1975 had a tremendous impact on the educational landscape of East Harlem, generating excitement not only among the kids who attended them but throughout the community. They formed the nucleus of what was to become an entirely new franchise in public education. These early alternative schools demonstrated beyond any doubt that significant, beneficial changes could take place in the educational performance of District Four. Their success emboldened us to push forward with other alternative schools and helped to highlight the importance of our work in the district. The educational and political leaders who made the first steps forward in District Four—Robert Rodriguez, Tony Alvarado, Debbie Meier, John Falco, Colman Genn, Ellen Kirshbaum, Mary Anne Marripodi, Jeffrey Hansen, and others —were fully vindicated.

Up until this time I had been functioning more or less alone in the role of the alternative schools' "friend in court." It became increasingly apparent, however, that the alternative-schools movement in the district would need enhanced support at the district level if its growth was to continue. I set out to provide that support.

5 Gathering Steam

As the alternative schools in District Four began to multiply, the work of the Office of Alternative Schools evolved. Increasingly, I came to see our role as a buffer to protect the alternative schools from the system so as to encourage them to take advantage of their new freedom. The central board, the district office, and the union all sought to control the schools, or tried to exert the maximum possible leverage on them. Our job, you might say, was to "un-control" them.

Part of un-controlling people is to get them to know and trust you so they can accept help and not feel like they're taking orders. I held regular meetings of the directors of alternative schools, who reported directly to me. At first, some of them were reluctant to let me know too much; they were afraid I might try to take control myself. So my staff and I had to reassure them. Our approach was always the same; we asked, "What do you need?" Whatever the response—personnel, curriculum enhancement, secretarial help—we gave the message that we were there to help them. I worry today when some advocates of choice invoke the free-market principle exclusively to advance their educational argument. Good schools need so much more than the functioning of a free market. They need love. They need courage. They need commitment. And they need time to grow.

Two major areas of our involvement were in personnel and curriculum development. For all schools, but particularly for alternative schools, the personnel process is crucial. Alternative-school directors always want to hire particular teachers, whom they think are unique and well-suited to the environment they hope to create. These teachers are often working in another school district, making the entire process far more complex.

The transfer process mandated by the UFT contract is the only transfer plan in effect in New York City and it works in the following manner: Each spring a list of vacancies is promulgated. Teachers throughout the system may apply and are transferred solely on the basis of their seniority. The receiving school principal, staff, and superintendent have no say whatsoever in who will join them; they don't even know the names of the teachers being transferred until the first day of school. Sometimes a teacher will put in for a transfer just to avoid a threatened "unsatisfactory" rating in his or her old district.

Besides being unwieldy, this transfer system is contrary to the spirit of school-based management and shared decision making. How can a school have autonomy if the principal doesn't even know who his teachers will be, much less have any say in choosing them? If there is one thing in the UFT contract that needs immediate changing, it is this provision. At any rate, recognizing the inadequacy of this system, we invented an improved version of the "administrative transfer," a temporary transfer mechanism that few in the system knew existed. It required only four signatures, those of the principal and the superintendent of the releasing district, and in District Four, my signature and that of the superintendent. We printed up our own form, and the central board's Division of Personnel accepted it without question.

Strictly speaking, such a transfer was valid for only one year, after which we would have to declare a vacancy. At that point, according to the UFT rules, a teacher with more seniority could take the place of the teacher who had been transferred in. We simply "forgot" to declare the vacancy and so kept our own handpicked choices. Like Cole Genn's system of staff recruitment at Harbor, this was another early example of what I like to call "creative noncompliance." We didn't break the rules outright or challenge the central bureaucracy head on when we could avoid it. We always tried to operate in a way that permitted people to save face. Our goal, after all, was not to humiliate anyone. We were trying to build better schools, and by resorting to "creative noncompliance" in certain key areas, we were able to do so.

The tactic worked extremely well for us in getting the personnel we needed into the district. If, on the other hand, we wanted to remove someone inappropriately assigned to an alternative school, we tried to do so gently and constructively. We would call him in, tell him he was a fine fellow, but he was obviously not doing well in his work. We offered to find him a more suitable placement.

It is hard to overstate how important it is to school directors to know that someone is fighting the personnel battle for them. Principals and directors appreciate that kind of assistance more than any other. They have trouble merely getting through to the central board, let alone successfully managing the traditional procedures.

We also worked hard to improve instruction and curriculum development. After running East Harlem Middle School for three years, Jeff Hansen joined my staff, supervising an outstanding team of curriculum specialists. Etta Proshansky, a fine teacher-trainer, who spent most of her time working with teachers and students in their classrooms, was our staff development person for early childhood education. Helene Steinbuck, an expert in writing instruction, was our director of communications arts. She and I organized Superintendent Alvarado's Hip Pocket Book Club in order to get hundreds of kids interested in reading. While the New York school system is often concerned only with raising reading test scores, we sought to instill in our kids a love of reading and learning for their own sake. We also introduced a successful district-wide writing program called "The Writing Experience." To introduce the program we encouraged the alternative school English teachers to take the course themselves. I took it, too.

In math and computers, Mary Anne Marripodi from the

Children's Learning Center and Bob Gyles, who holds a doctorate in math from New York University, set up the first computer instruction program for teachers in the city. Gyles, who had been named "Teacher of the Year" in District Five in West Harlem before coming to the B.E.T.A. School as assistant director in September 1981, systematically installed a math program that earned the respect of teachers and supervisors throughout the district. He appointed a math liaison in every school and brought them into the district office for training. This created an esprit de corps among the alternative school math faculty. They began to work together, building up their curricula. Gyles was so enthusiastic about what we were doing that he twice refused offers from the central board to become director of mathematics for New York City. Today he is still in District Four, as director of curriculum and instruction.

Typically, the alternative schools occupied some small portion of a regular school, in accordance with our maxim that "a school is not a building." We made every effort to work productively with the principals and other staff of the regular schools that housed them. But the alternative schools were run by their directors, who reported not to the buildings' principals but to the Office of Alternative Schools. Our office and the individual schools jointly controlled staff selection and recruitment of children. These unorthodox reporting arrangements created friction with principals who felt that their authority was being eroded, but it permitted us to support our people.

And the arrangements had interesting side effects. Teachers from both types of schools learned from one another, helped one another, took heart in one another's successes, reassured each other in times of failure. And over time they came to see that a network of alternative schools could have an impact on all the schools in the district. While it is true that in the very beginning the staffs of the regular schools saw the alternative schools as a threat, before long the alternative schools began to spur the traditional schools to improve.

The principals of the regular schools learned that they, too, could have a vision. They learned that their schools would be better if they were smaller. They began to upgrade their operations, in some cases even outperforming the alternative schools. A notable example of this was P.S. 50, where Principal Sidney

Schwager emulated EHPAS, which was housed there, by developing his own outstanding arts program in the traditional public school.

There are, of course, many examples of cross-pollination between the alternative schools as well. The two performing arts schools, Harbor and EHPAS, competed against each other and benefitted from insights into each other's approach as they developed and refined their curricula. In the early 1980s, the School of Science and Humanities in P.S. 96 at the very northern end of the district grew directly out of two alternative schools, Isaac Newton and the Academy of Environmental Sciences, which had been set up at the southern end. Yet all of these science schools retained distinctive cultures, which were outgrowths of their directors' passions and teaching philosophies.

Another example of cross-pollination was the creation of The Children's Workshop, an alternative elementary school. It was begun and is still presided over, strictly but lovingly, by Beryl Epton. Born in West Harlem, she started her career as a substitute teacher at P.S. 80 on East 120th Street. When P.S. 80 closed during the budget cuts of the 1970s, Beryl Epton moved to B.E.T.A., where she taught the fourth and fifth grades. "I learned a lot there," she says, "about non-book-oriented teaching."

In 1980, ready to try something new, Epton came to me to ask for a change in assignment. When I asked her what she wanted to do, she was silent for a moment and then asked me what would be the limitations. "None," I answered, "just dream your dream." Epton soon returned with her concept. Believing that some District Four students were in need of the earliest possible intervention in order to succeed in school, she proposed what was in essence a one-room schoolhouse for youngsters in the second, third, and fourth grades. The Office of Alternative Schools helped Epton bring her dream to life. We located space and got her a telephone, more important than you might suppose for running your own school. (Isn't it amazing that in a time of such technology when we can communicate instantaneously by satellite to the other side of the world, a teacher cannot communicate with a parent when something especially bad or especially good happens in a class!) We also found her an invaluable paraprofessional colleague trained in bilingual education, Ramona Gorbea, with whom she has worked ever since. The following year the school set up shop in P.S. 96 on 120th Street.

The Children's Workshop is a small school, uniquely small. In the 1992–1993 school year it had an enrollment of only fourteen: three first graders, four second graders, and seven third graders. The children are referred by the district office, or from within P.S. 96. Epton does not like the label "slow learners" attached to her kids. She prefers to say that her children need a special learning environment, which she supplies. Her children often have some academic deficiency, and she works with them so that they can reenter mainstream education successfully.

Epton's pedagogy is based on building self-esteem. She emphasizes individualized help and emotional support for all of her students. She likes having a mixture of different age groups in her classes. As she says, "My second grader's strength may be my fourth grader's weakness." One typical student, Johnny F., was a left-handed boy who was slapped and upbraided by his brothers and sisters whenever he tried to use his left hand. He became sullen and withdrawn and performed poorly at school. Epton's approach was to discuss his situation with the boy's parent and to let him use his left hand as she gently brought him back up to speed for his age. "Not all children learn at the same rate, and it is pointless to pretend that they do," she says.

Her classroom is filled with special learning projects that accommodate her students' sense of individuality. When asked what she hopes for her children's academic future after they leave the Workshop, Epton says, "that every teacher in their future will see them the way we did, so that they don't fall through the cracks of the educational system. I want them to grow up capable of meeting their responsibilities to themselves and to others.

"One thing that is often left out in discussions about good schools is how much the children change us. In a good school, when we are really alive and alert, that should happen as much as we change them."

Today Beryl Epton is still going strong at the Children's Workshop. She is one of the original corps of innovators in

East Harlem who have continued to build on solid, hard-earned success. She has also made a lasting impression on her students. One of her alumni from P.S. 80, now a lawyer in Texas, still writes her regularly. Others have turned to her when their own children were having trouble in school. The younger generation of students in the Children's Workshop have responded anew to her gentle, caring, yet determined approach by becoming active learners and achievers.

As time went on, the alternative schools began to acquire a collective identity. They were not just discrete educational entities but an incoming tide of new ideas and fresh approaches. As the alternative schools grew and diversified, this sense of community had a profound effect. There was a buzz in the air in the district. People were charged up and excited about learning. A sense of momentum developed in the process of creating new schools that became unstoppable.

Because of the growing enthusiasm for creating additional alternative schools, I could no longer spend the greater part of my time visiting existing schools. I still went around as often as possible, but much of my day began to be taken up by teachers who began coming to see me who were not yet part of the movement. We would talk, and at some point I would always ask them, "Tell me the truth, if you could do anything in education, in starting a new school, what would be your dream?" They would be surprised or even startled, but most of them did have something on their minds. Otherwise they would not have come to see me. They would outline their vision, and if I thought it made sense and their credentials checked out, I would say, "Fine. Put something down on paper. Let's do it."

At first each was stunned. They could not quite believe that a school administrator had just told them, "Sure, start a school." Such things just weren't possible. But by working together we made them possible. The willingness to say yes, and the willingness to un-control people, soon led to the building of a whole network of alternative schools in District Four, generally run by the hardest working, most imaginative people in the district, the people who wanted to do things, which is what had brought them to my office in the first place.

Throughout this early period no one ever mentioned the

word *choice,* though the alternative schools were choice schools from the start, in that no one was drafted into them. But the intellectual groundwork for the choice philosophy was being laid as early as 1977, when a policy statement and guidelines for the alternative schools were first issued by our office to the entire district.

We proclaimed our purpose to be the provision of alternative school environments that would meet the needs of individual children better than existing schools. We further announced our intention to work toward reducing the size of *all* schools in the district. We encouraged all members of the district staff to come forward with their ideas. Finally, we signaled our resolve to fight for greater parental participation and involvement in education.

As the years went by we developed many different methods of involving the parents, though in the beginning all we knew was the simple fact that parents were an important part of the choice process. We developed parent advisory councils in each school. We attracted parents into the schools, to performances by their children, to workshops, to parent-teacher dinners. We got teachers talking to parents when their children were doing something right, not only when they were doing something wrong. We opened a "parent center"—a centralized parent organization where parents were trained (by other parents) to become activists in their schools. And we considered ourselves successful when we made our parents into "troublemakers," ready to fight for the schools their children needed.

The Block School

In an effort to get parents involved, we sometimes found parents who had too much power. Take the case of the Block School. One of the first of the new schools to be included in the embryonic alternative-school network, the Block School, at 108th Street and Madison Avenue, had been founded in 1966 by a philanthropist, Larry Benenson, a teacher, Tony Ward, and the East Harlem Block Schools Association as a private school with private-foundation support. In its early years it was a successful experiment; it gave parents a major role in decision making and was able to raise sufficient foundation money to operate a kindergarten-through-eighth-grade school. By the time the Block School first approached District Four for public funding in the mid-1970s, however, it had deteriorated academically, the foundation money had dried up, and the school was in danger of closing.

The Block School was allowed to enter the public school system intact in 1975 and was given space in P.S. 108, where I was still serving as acting principal. I did my best to accommodate the new alternative school by providing space for its elementary grades while the seventh and eighth grades remained in their own building on Fifth Avenue.

It was clear to me, as the principal of P.S. 108, that the Block School needed a major renewal. A small group of parent activists controlled the school and were involved in all kinds of counterproductive day-to-day administrative details. At job interviews teachers were humiliated by some parents who acted inappropriately. One teacher, for example, was asked to take down his trousers as part of an "initiation process." With this kind of selection process, it is not surprising that the school had important pedagogical deficiencies. In addition, funds were being misused and there was little accountability. In successful alternative schools or schools of choice, parents play an important role, but they do not run the school.

The transition from being a private school to becoming part of the public system was difficult for the Block School, which remained under my supervision once I had assumed my new responsibilities at the Office of Alternative Schools. In a period of two years the Block School had three directors, each of whom had serious problems trying to run the school effectively while still satisfying the demands of the Advisory Board. The third transitional director, Larry Munitz, was able to fight and win the battle of establishing his authority, but only a year later he decided to leave education and return to the practice of law. We then had to select a new director.

A selection committee was formed comprised of parents, a teachers' representative, and members of the Block School Association Advisory Board. Jeffrey Hansen and I joined the committee. Immediately there was another struggle, as "community representatives" tried to steer the appointment to one of their political cronies in the district, a teacher named John

Chin. (Years later he would emerge as the central figure in the scandal that would force the resignation of Tony Alvarado as the chancellor of the New York City public school system.) Chin had nothing to recommend him for the job except his political connections. It was shameful that such a man was even considered as a potential director, but regrettably, in many poor inner-city neighborhoods the schools are a major source of political patronage regardless of educational priorities.

Chin was presented to the selection committee as a *fait accompli*. He had the support of an important school district official and a member of the community school board. After his interview, the committee was ready to select him without even interviewing the next candidate, Harvey Newman. Newman, a licensed guidance counselor, was the director of a successful drug program in District Four for at-risk youngsters. Jeff Hansen and I insisted that the interview process continue and, after considerable debate, Harvey Newman was indeed selected as the new director of the Block School. This broke the back of the cronyism at the school and was a turning point in its history.

Under Harvey Newman's leadership, the Block School became one of the finest elementary schools in New York, and the Office of Alternative Schools supported Newman in many ways. Hansen found funds to improve the curriculum and to "liberate" instructional materials. Etta Proshansky, our early childhood expert, was assigned to assist in staff development and in the creation of a child-centered, developmental approach to learning. The partnership that Newman and Proshansky forged was an interesting example of cross-pollination, too. Harvey had had a traditional education background, whereas Etta (like Debbie Meier) was a proponent of "open classrooms," yet they had no problem finding a common ground in which the best aspects of both approaches were incorporated in the Block School's curriculum. They recruited outstanding teachers, including Lorraine Shapiro, one of the finest classroom teachers I have known. Etta convinced her to transfer to the Block School from her school in Brooklyn. Her teaching technique worked so well that the early childhood faculty at the regular school in P.S. 108 as well as the other Block School teachers began sitting in to observe and learn from it. At the same time, on the second floor, the Schomburg bilingual elementary school was developing its own open education approach, which was also based on the Central Park East and Block approaches.

One of the youngsters who came to the Block School was Andre Hampton, a sixth grader from a single-parent home. He was a lovely boy with middle-class values who simply could not read. Then the Block School sent its sixth grade on a class trip to the Manice Education Center in the Berkshires. Andre displayed an immediate affinity for the outdoors. He was a fine athlete and loved hiking in the woods. He also became expert at plant and tree identification. The people at Manice were so impressed that they invited Andre to spend a month with them that summer. Newman arranged for a full scholarship for Andre, and it was at Manice, discovering his love of nature and environmental studies, that Andre began to read. In time, Andre went on to get his high school diploma and became a park ranger for the United States Department of the Interior.

On a later trip to the Manice campsite, Newman noticed that these city kids, who were quite outgoing as they left the city, became quieter and more nervous as they got further out into the country. As they approached the camp, the bus was silent. Until one of the youngsters cried out, "Yo, there's a black dude." It made the kids feel good. And counselor Andre Hampton gave them a warm welcome to the great outdoors.

Harvey Newman supported his students in every way he could, and we did all that we could to support Newman and the other alternative school directors. When you get a reputation for supporting people, you tend to get capable people to support pretty quickly. By 1979 there were ten schools in the network, and we had attracted as directors many of the people that would make up the real leadership of our movement in the coming years. One of those people was Mike Friedman of the Bridge School; and although Friedman was later to experience serious personal problems, the program he developed at Bridge remains a model of effective inner-city education.

The Bridge School

One morning Mike Friedman called me and said, "Sy, you've got to come over. I just looked out the window and saw some drug dealers slit a guy's throat."

My idea of a good time does not include inspecting such

scenes, but I did go over, so that Friedman and I could discuss the situation and see if there was anything the Office of Alternative Schools could do to help him and his remarkable creation, the Bridge School.

As a fifth-grade teacher at P.S. 101, Friedman had been frustrated seeing kids get lost when they went on to an overcrowded, combative junior high school. In East Harlem, the lure of "the streets" often extends right into the schools, particularly the junior and senior high schools. Friedman's idea was for a special school for sixth graders only, that would prepare them to meet the challenges and resist the temptations, not only of junior high and high school but of the drug culture of East Harlem.

Friedman was an activist at heart: when he saw kids heading toward trouble he intervened—fast. Most mornings found him standing on the street in his trench coat in front of the Bridge School, looking to nip would-be problem cases in the bud. He would tell the mother of one of his students that her son was ruining his future with drugs. He was not showing up for school or for the job Friedman found for him. Friedman would get angry. He had been through all this before. He'd say he was through cutting deals for this kid. At six feet, four inches, Friedman made an imposing figure, especially when he habitually pounded his fist into his palm to make a point.

The mother would plead excitedly; the boy asked for one more chance. Friedman gave it, with several provisos: Show up for school on time, drug free, and prepared to work. Those were the terms for remaining at Bridge, a middle school with grades six through nine and approximately 275 students, founded in 1978 after Friedman came up with his idea for a school that would bolster citizenship, self-reliance, and self-confidence.

In the midst of East Harlem's chaos, Friedman saw a school that would be an oasis of order. His hard line on school attendance was part of that effort to create a stable, disciplined atmosphere. If the kids didn't get to school on time, he argued, how will they ever get to work on time?

Friedman spent over twenty-five years in East Harlem—long enough for anyone's idealism to slip. But he and his staff still helped their kids combat their surroundings:

When you step into this school you leave that street stuff outside. We understand that to survive you have to do certain things. But here, we're going to protect students, defend them, and deal with life in a rational way.

These are average East Harlem kids. A lot of them are two years behind in school. Many of them have serious guidance problems. They're not all going to be the most brilliant kids in the world. That's not our goal. But we will graduate kids who are hardworking, who come to school on time, don't curse at the teacher, and who, once they leave us, will get their high school diplomas *despite* what's happening in their high schools.

Friedman ran the school in a strict but nurturing way. Preparing a group of giggly and excited adolescents for the annual student trip to Williamsburg, Virginia, Friedman would tell the kids to be on the bus by six-thirty a.m., to bring two handkerchiefs, enough clean underwear, comfortable shoes. "And don't—absolutely don't—pack more than you can carry. No one's going to be lugging your suitcase around for you."

Not at the Bridge School, dedicated to the idea that people have to be able to carry their own weight in this world. The lesson is a hard one to teach in a community beholden to welfare. Still, teachers are instructed never to give their students pens, paper, or anything else they need for class. If they come unprepared, students must buy supplies from staff members. Prices are good—a penny for a sheet of paper—but the message is clear: You pay your own way.

Friedman believed in frugality. For many years he drove a Chevy with over 250,000 miles on it, which he kept in perfect condition. He treated his school and his students the same way. On school trips, for example, he taught the kids how to order food in a restaurant, even to send back orders that had not been correctly filled. "You have a right to get what you order," he told them. It may seem like a small point, but it's one of many ways in which Friedman instilled self-confidence and the sense that his kids have a part to play in the larger world.

Alternative schools attract diversity in educational attitudes and philosophies, and not everyone would underline the need for independence and self-sufficiency the way Friedman did. Some people might even object to his emphasis on these values. But the students and their parents who choose to go to Bridge are attracted by its philosophy. Friedman, a wholehearted believer in choice, would say, "Because they have choice, they're buying into the school, and that eliminates a lot of the problems that you could otherwise have."

The Bridge School opened with sixty students. Parents, teachers, and students liked it from the start, and the school soon grew to four grades. The school gives kids encouragement, attention, and support many of them cannot get at home. But that support is focused on one strictly enforced goal: learning the discipline to look life's problems in the face and to overcome them the best you can. Students take a required performing arts class which invites them to act out unpleasant situations with their parents. If they are having a problem with a teacher, they can talk it out with a sympathetic staff member at a crisis intervention session. The Bridge philosophy does not simply support children but supports them in the process of becoming adults.

Under this character-building regime, kids begin to increase their self-esteem, and, in turn, do better academically. Unfortunately, the challenges of East Harlem become harsher every year. "All the alternative schools are facing a growing problem with at-risk kids," according to Friedman. "The growing crack problem and the diminishing support from parents makes things tougher and tougher." There is a "drug supermarket" on Lexington Avenue and East 110th Street a block from the school, and Friedman's kids sometimes get sucked into that lifestyle. The lure of easy money and peer pressure capture too many of them. Boys too young to hold driver's licenses have shown up at school driving a Mercedes or a BMW or bragging about the new condos they just bought their mothers.

Today, Bridge's large enrollment threatens the individual attention that made it work. A victim of its own success, the administration is still reluctant to turn kids away.

There are other problems, too. As we shall see, in the late 1980s a jealous bureaucracy began to close in on District Four, making personnel regulations more restrictive and "creative noncompliance" more difficult. With the particular challenge that Friedman took on at Bridge, he especially needed to hand-pick his staff, but sometimes he was forced to accept teachers he never would have chosen himself, or other badly needed assignments went unfilled.

The Bridge School is packed into the mustard-colored fourth floor of a seventy-eight-year-old building on East 111th Street between Park and Lexington Avenues. It has no art or music teachers, no library, no foreign language program, no health class, and no nurse or full-time counselor. There is no clerical help unless you count the director's "secretary"—the dusty answering machine with the throbbing red light beside his desk. Friedman called Bridge the "no-frills school" and made it work by doing a lot of wheeling and dealing. To do so he relied on New York City's resources—public libraries, museum-enrichment programs, health-agency referrals, guidance programs, and whatever else he could use. Like all the successful people in District Four, Friedman was a nonconformist and a maverick. He made no secret about bending rules that keep him from helping kids.

Friedman and his students knew how to develop and keep support. A number of years ago Friedman had students from his graduating class send letters to forty celebrities in New York City asking if they would be the guest speaker at their graduation. The one affirmative response came from Ernie Anastos, then the popular anchorman for WABC-TV's "Eyewitness News." Anastos spoke at the graduation and since that day has been an active friend and supporter of the Bridge School. When, a few years later, Anastos was dropped as anchorman, Friedman and the students of the Bridge School led a grassroots fight to save his job. They printed "Save Ernie" bumper stickers, picketed the ABC building, and helped organize a massive letter-writing campaign. Anastos kept his job, and later became the anchorman at WCBS-TV. In 1990, Friedman and Anastos had dinner with Warner Wolf, the energetic and voluble former sportscaster for WCBS-TV. During dinner Friedman told a sad story about a student at the Bridge School who was ashamed to come to school because she didn't have any decent clothes to wear. Without hesitating, Wolf reached into his pocket, produced a hundred-dollar bill, and insisted that Friedman see that his student buy some new clothes with it.

These stories say something about the loyalty Friedman and his students felt for those who have tried in whatever way to help them, and the way that shared loyalty attracts new supporters who sense that the kids at the Bridge School are trying to do something important.

Sometimes Friedman got discouraged. I could always tell when he needed a break. At such times, like the day the drug dealers slit someone's throat outside the Bridge School's doors, I would insist that he join me for lunch to discuss his school's needs. Our office sought special funding for the Bridge School's programs and assisted Friedman in locating top-notch staff. Sandy Rinaldo was one of these, an extraordinary woman who was Friedman's assistant director for over a decade.

The point is that capable people have to be supported in many different ways. I made it my business to attend Bridge's graduation ceremonies each June, and I continued to do so for four years after I left the District. In 1991 I led a workshop for Friedman and his staff at a school retreat, and it was like coming home.

Despite all the problems, Friedman was committed to sticking it out in East Harlem. As he put it:

A few years ago I got a letter from one of my kids, Luis R. After school he fell into the street and went away for grand larceny. Luis earned his high school equivalency while in jail, and he wrote to assure his old principal that he was now trying to acquire skills that would help him on the outside. Now Luis is working, married, living in Queens, and doing volunteer work in his spare time. He's come by here twice to tell us that our school was the best thing he ever had.

As I was completing the final editing of this book in December 1992, the District Four community was shattered by the news that Mike Friedman had been arrested for sexually molesting a student and had been removed from the directorship of the Bridge School. Parents, students and colleagues expressed disbelief, shock, and concern for Friedman and for the school. In March, Friedman pleaded guilty to charges that he had molested two students, surrendered his teaching license, and left the public school system after a twenty-seven-year career.

The easy out for me would have been to delete the story of the Bridge School from this book. However, the contribution Mike Friedman made to the thousands of students he helped and the strength of the program he built made this option impossible. It is difficult to conceive of a good end to this story, except to observe that the Bridge School goes on under its new acting director, Jim Sanders, doing good work and making a difference in the lives of its nearly three hundred students.

These were not the only schools we started in those early years. The East Harlem School of Communications and Health Services was opened in 1976 with a grant from Polytechnic, the agricultural school in Farmingdale, Long Island, and focused on the health and communications fields in its curriculum. The East Harlem Career Academy was also opened in 1976, to emphasize career awareness in a neighborhood suffering from chronic unemployment. We regularly invited members of the community who were successful in a broad range of fields to the school to serve as role models in the development of self-esteem for the youngsters. The East Harlem Maritime School, which opened in 1979, offered courses in navigation, oceanography, and marine biology, and after-school programs in rowing and sailing to motivate students and teach them teamwork and leadership skills.

By 1980 we had opened up no fewer than fourteen alternative schools in District Four. What had started out as a desperate response to a crumbling school district, dwelling in the cellar of city-wide test scores, had turned into a vigorous and vital renaissance. We had begun to build momentum. We had created a climate where constructive change was welcomed and highly prized. And we were now beginning to see the seedlings of a second generation of innovative educational institutions. In 1980, for example, we opened Central Park East II, the second of Debbie Meier's highly acclaimed schools. Other outgrowths of our work in the alternative schools of East Harlem were also beginning to take shape.

But even as we made impressive strides forward we found ourselves becoming embroiled in battle after battle just to defend what we had already built.

6 Fighting Battles, Finding Friends

W hen the difficulty with administration at East Harlem
Performing Arts arose, and one of the personalities involved was Superintendent Alvarado's new wife, Ellen Kirshbaum, the educational bureaucrats in the district took the
opportunity to attack the growing alternative-school network.
Deputy Superintendent Barbara Barry and the district division
heads complained to Alvarado that the alternative schools were
out of control. What they meant was that a growing number of
successful autonomous schools made them especially nervous.
It would only be a matter of time before people began asking
why the traditional public schools in District Four were not
improving at a similar rate.

After applying sustained pressure, the deputy superintendent and division heads convinced Alvarado to call in a consultant from the central board to assess the operations of the
district's management procedures and the Office of Alternative
Schools.

This was an unwelcome development, though perhaps not entirely unpredictable. We thought we had demonstrated the validity of our approach to schooling, and that our occasional resorting to "creative noncompliance" had been fully justified in light of our results. We had obviously underestimated to what degree we had stirred resentment in the entrenched bureaucracy. But we had come too far and worked too hard to allow our own district's bureaucracy to stand in our way.

The consultant from Livingston Street carried out his assignment to study the district management structure and submitted a report. His recommendation was that I should no longer have direct access to Superintendent Alvarado but should report to Deputy Superintendent Barry. Unfortunately, Barry was responsible for the regular schools in the district, and was notably hostile to the alternative schools; we feared that under her supervision we would be walking down a very rocky road.

This was a classic bureaucratic squeeze play which could have had a killing impact on all that we were trying to do. But I knew that Superintendent Alvarado was still entirely in favor of creating successful new schools, notwithstanding his acceptance of the consultant's report, the political maneuvering going on around him, and the delicate personal conflicts involved. So we adopted a strategy to deal with the new reporting arrangements.

The Office of Alternative Schools informed Barry of everything we were doing. In fact, we saw to it that we overloaded her with a constant stream of information, little of which she ever read. The result was that whenever we scheduled meetings with her, she inevitably canceled. In this way we outmaneuvered the district bureaucrats while still following the letter of the law. Whenever I spoke to Alvarado, as I still frequently did, he would ask, "Does the Deputy know about this?" And I would answer, "Of course." Procedure had been followed.

After this first skirmish we made extra efforts to earn and to receive the superintendent's support. And that support made a crucial difference in program development for the alternative schools. Our office was able to gain access to district monies to pay for worthwhile school trips and projects. In District Four we bought laboratory equipment for science classes, instruments for school bands, and copy machines. We also funded an after-school basketball league in order to create a sense of collective identity and to give the kids something better to do than hanging out on the streets.

To start a series of alternative schools we needed not merely a certain energy and a certain spirit, but also a keen political sensibility. There are administrative procedures and policies that can help to foster the growth of innovative and effective new schools; there are also sensitivities of which those breaking new ground must always be aware.

The first step in getting and keeping Superintendent Alvarado's support was to create a sense of excitement about what we were trying to do, both among our professional staff and in the community at large. Superintendents are politically astute, and if they sense something popular and positive happening, they are going to get behind it. We provided good publicity in the press and in the community for our superintendent, and he couldn't help but be grateful. The fact that *The New York Times* devoted an editorial to District Four's alternative schools in 1982, for example, was a substantial factor in Tony Alvarado's eventual selection as chancellor of the New York City public school system.

When opportunities for good publicity came along, we felt it was best to give our superintendent the credit. After all, when the time came to ruffle someone else's feathers, we knew it would be the superintendent who would have to defend us and absorb the blame. We were generous to him, and it paid off. What we were doing was worthwhile, and there was plenty of credit to go around.

I was once approached by a very fine gentleman, Jack Osander, who worked for the Fund for the City of New York. The Fund is an old-line organization which annually singles out outstanding public employees for prestigious public service awards. Osander spent some time following me around, wrote a very flattering report, and asked if I would permit my name to go forward as a candidate for that year's awards.

I demurred. Instead, I convinced Osander that it was Alvarado—with whom I had a close and fruitful working relationship—who deserved the award. He was a young man on the move, I said, and if he received such acclaim it might result in his one day attaining higher office, for which the Fund for the

City of New York could rightly claim credit. Osander agreed and Alvarado became the first educator to receive the Fund's public service award (which included a tax-free $5,000 prize). That, too, was a big step on his road to the chancellorship.

We considered it important, likewise, to keep the superintendent fully informed about exactly what it was we were doing. We let him take the full share of the glory for whatever results we achieved, and never left him out of anything good or did anything that made him look bad. At the same time, we felt we had a right and an obligation to demand access to the superintendent—despite the consultant's report—whenever a critical question arose with regard to an alternative school, be it from the community, from an obstructive entrenched educational bureaucracy, or from a hostile central administration. He knew that we expected him to back us up, and he came through for us. The bureaucracy can always persevere; since it is used to doing nothing it can hold on and wait an innovator out. It is the quintessential immovable object, and the challenge we faced was to become a sufficiently irresistible force.

As soon as we began to experiment in District Four, it semed as though a countermovement arose to squelch any new ideas. Established school officials spoke of "reining us in," and the budget people at Livingston Street complained of "special treatment." Our cardinal rule at this time was, "Don't organize the opposition." In other words, don't give them an excuse to start a movement that will end up with us out the door. Don't ever embarrass them. Don't let them know too much about what we're doing in other areas. And keep the superintendent's support of our enterprise uppermost in their minds.

Another potential obstacle to change was the UFT. The union was one of our most serious concerns, and we always subscribed to the principle that we must never embarrass the union. We were so successful in this approach that for the first few years of the alternative schools' existence not one teacher filed a grievance! The UFT representative was consequently receptive to our aspirations and did not stand in our way. Of course, friction developed over time, but by then we had the toehold that we needed. The union district representatives could stir the pot by raising the question of a director's status. "She's really only a teacher, right?" they would say, and this could cause problems because, technically, teachers cannot supervise other teachers.

When these difficulties developed we would sit down and talk. Some horse trading would ensue. The union was happy to be told in advance of impending changes; the chapter chairperson was glad to be invited to some of the meetings of the Office of Alternative Schools. In exchange, they would look the other way when we asked teachers to attend lunchtime meetings, or when our posted job descriptions were only pro forma announcements of spots available.

In time, our understanding with the union bore fruit. Once, I remember, we asked Albert Shanker, the president of the UFT, to address all our teachers at our staff development-day program at the Alternative Education Complex. That proved to be a productive way of opening lines of communication between us. Since that time, I have gotten to know Shanker on a professional level, and he has lived up to his reputation as a bright, articulate, and tough union leader. Yet we were able to change the district dramatically and he never stood in our way. He now has publicly endorsed teachers starting "charter schools" that are based upon the District Four alternative-school model.

Because we had started small, usually with only three teachers per school, nobody even noticed us at first. By the time our potential opponents had targeted alternative schools, we had turned out a number of classes, set up schools in several sites, and built a constituency of satisfied customers. In order to stop us, the union—or any other opponent—would have had to bear the burden of trying to foil a good thing.

From the beginning we positioned the new schools so that they were not a threat. For example, it made strategic sense to start with B.E.T.A as our first alternative school, because it was a school everybody could see the need for, and many traditional- school principals could actually benefit from it, getting problem kids out of their hair. It may sound like a cynical strategy, but, human nature often warranting cynicism, it worked. It also benefitted many, many youngsters.

Sometimes the enemies of change become its advocates if you give them a chance to do something innovative themselves. When Debbie Meier sought to expand CPE to the seventh and eighth grades, Bill Hall, the union representative at J.H.S. 13, led the fight against allowing the alternative school into the building. Years later, however, Bill found the right path to channel his energies and skills productively. He was an expert chess player and coach, and, when he was given the opportunity, he transferred to J.H.S. 99, where he organized a chess team that became so successful in tournament play that it eventually competed in the Soviet Union. He changed the lives of those kids, giving them self-esteem and a goal to work for, when many of their peers saw no alternative but to go to the street.

Besides the district bureaucracy and the union, one of the most persistently difficult groups we have had to deal with is the central Board of Education. The complexities of the central board's operations and the general inertia at its headquarters at 110 Livingston Street posed perennial problems for us in getting what we needed. We used to spend a good deal of time trying to piece together the byzantine situation behind the scenes at the central board, on the theory that if you understand the problems being faced by your adversaries you will often come up with a better negotiating position than if you merely rush in with your own needs uppermost in your mind.

I remember one meeting in 1985 when we in District Four were pressing our argument for a fair share of the school system's resources, particularly the State Magnet School monies that we were entitled to but not receiving. We argued that since the Magnet School funds were supposed to be promoting racial integration, and our district accounted for 10 percent of the racial integration in the city, we should be receiving 10 percent of the Magnet School funds.

After we had made our point Chancellor Nathan Quiñones turned to Steve Schwager, the chief financial officer of the central school board, and asked him where the money had gone to which we were entitled. "We supplanted it and gave it to the High School Division," Schwager replied. Why? It turned out that the Office of Budget and Management had cut funding from the high school budget and the central board had used the magnet monies to make up for the cut.

The budget officials at the central board often resisted our requests for funding—even when we were just asking for District Four's fair share of the pie. We had to do something to thaw out this cold war, and so I invited Steve Schwager to come to East Harlem and see our schools. No one had ever thought of inviting the chief financial officer of the central school board anywhere. He was delighted to come, and he loved what he saw. But in all likelihood it was simply the invitation itself that made the difference. The gesture helped to humanize what could otherwise be a perennially antagonistic relationship. Deputy Chancellor Jerry Posman also visited our schools and he and Schwager became great allies of ours at 110 Livingston Street.

To the extent that we could, we also brought political pressure to bear on the central board from the board members whom we knew and who liked what we were doing, and from our own local politicians. For example, on a number of occasions Robert F. Wagner, Jr., the central board president from 1986 to 1990, visited East Harlem and toured our schools, enabling us to get to know him.

Further, as a gesture of support, Wagner dined with me twice at Gage and Tollner, the fancy restaurant near the Board of Education headquarters in Brooklyn. Well, this may not seem like much, but, as Wagner himself told me recently, at the time the budget office at the Board of Education wanted to kill us! And sometimes the perception of support is more important than the action. The budget office people felt that the board president was our ally, and it helped. Frank Macchiarola, who served as chancellor from 1978 to 1983, consistently and strongly supported District Four's innovative practices. Bernard Mecklowitz, acting-chancellor in 1989, came to see our schools unannounced during that time, and let it be known around the system that he was willing to help us in every way he could. This was despite the fact, as we learned recently at a conference of former chancellors, that the district was at that time under heavy attack and the chancellor was being urged by the budget director's office to cure District Four's budget shortfalls by closing District Four's alternative schools.

Having such friends helped us. Inevitably, it also caused resentment among those at the central board's Office of the Budget who felt we were getting more than our fair share of resources and credit. But it served notice that we were serious about what we were trying to do for our young people, and we wouldn't be satisfied with an obstructionist, business-as-usual attitude at the central board. We would fight.

Closer to home, another group of potential problem makers were what we called the "building principals." As explained earlier, each autonomous alternative school was housed in a portion of a regular school building and was overseen by a school director, so we called the traditional principal of those host schools the "building principal." None of them liked it.

Principals are proud people who have achieved a certain amount of respect and stature in their educational careers. One can readily understand how they might feel jealous or uncertain as how to deal with an alternative school newly installed in his or her building in what they thought of, in fact, as his or her school—and often reacted negatively and caused severe problems for the school directors. Sometimes these matters were trivial, regarding the times of day in which the alternative school could use the lunchroom or the playground. Other times, the building principal tried actively to intervene in the curriculum and functioning of the alternative school. Even when it appeared to be a trivial issue, however, such conflicts were a drain of resources and time on the school director involved, and the Office of Alternative Schools would get involved to try to resolve conflict and create a productive atmosphere. And when we succeeded in building good relations, the result was a better environment for everyone.

This was essential, especially in the early days, when, to conform with central board regulations, an alternative school's budget had to be submitted in a somewhat covert fashion, as part of the over-all "school building" budget. Needless to say, this only reinforced in building principals' minds the notion that they controlled the entire building, an area of contention we often revisited. One of the early changes I made when I formed the Office of Alternative Schools, in fact, was to take responsibility for negotiating alternative-school budgets directly with the district.

When principals in District Four complained about the alternative schools in the early 1980s, after I became deputy superintendent under Superintendent Carlos Medina, our approach was to say to these principals, "Don't you worry about them.

Tell us what *you* want. What's your vision?" If there was anything to help them achieve a vision we did it, whether it was implementing an experimental program or simply taking a school trip. We impressed upon them how it was really in their best interest that the alternative schools succeed, because then they, too, would have far greater latitude in the planning and implementation of their curricula.

In District Four, in addition to administrators and principals, we even occasionally found teachers who opposed any effort to upgrade educational activities. It was a turf battle! They did not want to cede any of their authority or seniority in a given situation. Often, however, it was something more. People are naturally apprehensive about others doing something new because it could make them look bad, and no one wants to look bad. Even so, we decided it was advisable to avoid the "consensus trap." If we had had to get every teacher at P.S. 171 to agree to every detail of the school's operation, Debbie Meier would never have started Central Park East. They'd still be discussing it. At some point every school needs a leader to assert and implement its educational style.

Our experience has been that so long as one took the time to communicate what was being done and created an atmosphere in which people felt that they, too, could share in an educational experiment, most teachers joined in enthusiastically. With teachers it is also productive to ask them what they need and want the most in order to help their kids. Often it is so little yet it means so much to them. And we found that they had never been asked that question within the system. Again, it is not so much a question of what people are as how they are treated. Treat people well, and you will bring out the best in them. Some teachers, it is true, simply could not adapt to the special demands posed by alternative education, and where this was true we worked with them to find assignments that they could undertake with enthusiasm and success. And we did it from a starting point of respect, which they appreciated.

With some building principals we had no problems. We got along beautifully and worked together to solve problems or address areas of mutual concern. It was as if "turf" never existed. But, regrettably, there were a few principals with whom we always seemed to be in the middle of a pitched battle. We could never get beyond the question of who controlled what to engage in the more important and ultimately more fulfilling work of educating youngsters. And in such cases, of course, there was no way that the Office of Alternative Schools could transfer principals. They had more power than we. But here again, access to and support from our superintendent helped us to fight the good fight. Given the myriad ways in which the system can wear you down, tire you out, and knock the last ounce of fight out of you by tying you up in a bureaucratic knot, I know we could not have achieved what we did except for that wonderful support from Tony Alvarado and his successor, Carlos Medina.

You see, the superintendent's support was crucial in fighting the annual allocations battle at district headquarters. There are warring fiefdoms in every local school district, and these compete aggressively for the limited resources available. Our job at the Office of Alternative Schools was to act as lobbyist and advocate for our constituency, just as the special education people or the bilingual people did for theirs. Getting what we needed for our own schools came first, of course. But we mollified the regular principals and teachers by backing them in district budgetary matters and helping them get the new facilities they so badly needed for their own schools.

In the end, though, these fights over the alternative schools' autonomy were so sharp that to maintain our hard-won position we had to arouse the alternative-school community, even to getting them to come to school-board meetings to present our case. By "the alternative school community," I mean of course the parents, mostly mothers, aunts, and grandmothers, some uncles, a few fathers, in this inner-city, low-income district. It should come as no surprise that they cared about their children. How we mobilized their love for their kids, their support for the work we were doing, and their outrage at the way New York City schools are usually run, is the story of the next chapter.

7
A Community of Parents

I n the early days in District Four, we didn't talk much about choice, we talked about creating good schools. The first item on our agenda was to create schools that were at once stronger and more flexible, schools that were more alive and inspiring, schools that better fit the needs of the district's children. To do this we harnessed the energy of teachers—committed teachers with dreams of new types of schools, who did not balk at running their own alternative schools despite almost endless problems with the district's and the central board's bureaucracy. And the more schools we started, the more we noticed that the parents and the kids were all making choices and that this act of choosing was crucial to the success of the school. So we started to talk about taking it even further.

Other educators saw what was happening in East Harlem, and they came forward with their own ideas, which we embraced whenever we thought they were valid. In that sense teachers could now choose where they wanted to teach as much as students could choose which school to attend. But it would be dishonest for us to say we understood choice's power from the moment we began to introduce it—we didn't. Our purpose, our vision, our dream was to start schools we could be proud of, where young people could learn. It grew organically out of our educational priorities, transforming us and District Four in the process.

At first, our school directors recruited their students in a laissez-faire fashion. They visited other schools; they let word-of-mouth fill their incoming classes. We encouraged parents to pick a school in the same way that they would pick a doctor, an idea they embraced with enthusiasm.

As the alternative-school movement blossomed, we had to establish more systematic recruitment procedures. As the popularity of the schools swelled so did the competition to get in, and this posed new problems. We had to devise a system that allocated kids to schools in an equitable manner. When we went to an all-out choice system in 1982, it was a complete departure from the past. It is important to understand that from that time on there was no such thing in District Four as a zoned junior high school; students were no longer automatically assigned to a school based on where they lived. Today, District Four's twenty-four junior high schools accept applications from all interested parents and children from across the district. Some of these schools are organized around particular themes while others are run as traditional junior highs. On the elementary level choice is optional: there are twelve alternative elementary schools that parents may choose from in addition to the sixteen zoned elementary schools.

In a typical New York City school district the process by which students move from elementary to junior high school is automated and impersonal. In June of every year, each junior high school receives a computer-generated roster of students that have been assigned to their entering class. The roster contains some rudimentary information about the students, such as their latest standardized test scores and attendance records. A detailed record of the student's performance and abilities will arrive some time in the fall semester, but the records of some students never arrive. The student has no interaction with his or her new school prior to the first day of classes in September; students are given no choice regarding the junior high school that they will attend, nor have they been asked to reflect upon their interests and abilities to determine the type of school that is best for them.

In District Four, by contrast, the process by which students move from elementary to junior high school is an important part of the student's education, an opportunity to teach lessons about decision making. All students in District Four must make a conscious choice about the junior high school they will attend, because they are not assigned to junior high schools based on the location of their homes. Each parent is given an information booklet that describes the program offerings of the district's junior high schools and is invited to orientation sessions and to school fairs. Every sixth grade teacher in the district is also briefed on the various junior high school programs, so that they can advise their students in the choice making process. Throughout this process the junior high staff speak not only of their curriculum offerings but also of the work-load requirements they expect from their students. In essence a social contract is formed: "This is our school, these are the rules. If you choose our school, you accept these rules."

Parental interaction is seen as an important part of the application-choice process. Each student, with the help of their parents, completes an application form. Students must rank their choices (up to three are allowed) and explain in writing why they made the choices they did. Every sixth grader's teacher must also provide information and recommendations on their student.

The schools themselves retain control over the selection process and many of them require a personal interview. In the Central Park East Schools, for example, parents and prospective students are invited to spend a day at the school in order to understand the different methodologies at work in open education. In such a school you will seldom find a teacher standing at the front of the classroom lecturing. To the contrary, small groups of children tend to be involved in different activities while the teacher interacts with them, acting as facilitator. Many parents do not at first see the connection between these techniques and learning. Given their own classroom ex-

99

perience, it takes some time to appreciate and understand the value of what is going on. Such insistence that the parents become acquainted with the school prior to their child attending helps to broaden the base of potential students and parents. We wanted our parents to know what they were selecting for their children and why; that way they could be more supportive.

As time went on and our process was refined, the children learned how to make better decisions, and so did their parents. We taught parents how to recognize a good school by discussing with them the following criteria for making a decision:

- Are learning and teaching the focus of the school? To me, nothing is taught until something is learned. Good schools focus on what the students come away with, not just what the teachers supply.
- Does education take priority over the teachers' convenience, contractual disputes, maintenance schedules, and other peripheral matters?
- Do all the constituencies of the school share a clear vision of what that school is about?
- Is everyone made to feel that they are an "owner" of the school and that they are involved in the planning and implementation of the school's goals and programs?
- When you walk around the school do you get a sense of excitement, and that things are happening in a purposeful manner?
- Do people care about one another and treat one another with respect?
- Do teachers talk about their students' work and their rate of academic achievement knowledgeably?
- Is student work displayed?
- Is the school's leadership strong enough to keep the school focused on its goals while allowing flexibility in selecting strategies to attain those goals?
- Are students given opportunities to work in small groups?
- Do people outside the school recognize it as a good school?
- Do district personnel bring visitors to the school?

- Do the children of teachers and administrators attend the school?
- Do other teachers want to transfer into the school?
- Does the school have a school improvement committee involved in the decision-making process?
- Does the school seek out resources other than from the district office?

These are the kinds of questions we taught parents to ask and to investigate for themselves. And once we did there was no holding them back. They loved sending their kids to the school of their choice and came to respect what District Four was trying to do.

Yet when we implemented the idea of district-wide choice in 1982, there was opposition from many quarters. Had the central Board of Education known more about it, they undoubtedly would have objected. Nor were the local school district staff and the building principals at all enthusiastic about the district-wide choice system. And, ironically enough, some of the opposition to choice even came from the teachers and directors of the alternative schools themselves. They had put their necks on the line, having created their schools in the face of great obstacles; when they saw other people wanting to jump on their bandwagon and share in their success there was at first a very human reluctance on their part to lose their position as pioneers. But they got over that when they realized that the institution of choice legitimized their efforts, brought recognition to their schools, and put them in good stead for promotions in their careers. After an initial hesitation they pitched in wonderfully to help us create the next wave of alternative schools.

A frequent criticism that we heard at the outset of implementing district-wide choice was that choice—especially in a poverty- stricken district like ours—may lead to elitism. School directors can select whom they want, the argument goes, so they will of course take the cream of the crop, choosing the best possible students. In fact, from the very beginning our strategy was to avoid any charge that we were skimming off the brightest students. The truth of the matter is that we were always against elitism, whether at B.E.T.A., CPE, Bridge, Harbor, or anywhere else. The directors had admissions criteria, to be sure, but theirs was not an elitist agenda. We were opposed to the practice of "tracking" as it had been historically practiced in New York City, creating one tier for the "academic" students, one for the "commercial" students, and relegating the rest of the students to an unchallenging environment under the heading of a "general" program. Our intention was always to match students' talents and interests with the diverse schools' specialties, not to select high-scoring students routinely for elite schools.

Another criticism we heard of our performance in District Four, chiefly from professionals in the neighboring, more well-to-do districts, was that once we began to receive federal funds for Magnet Schools, and began to attract kids from outside the district into our schools, we were in effect altering our student mix so as to guarantee better performance. The truth is that during the years of District Four's decline many of our students had fled the district and had begun going to schools in District Two, downtown, or in District Three, on the West Side. They submitted false addresses and were accepted by those districts, so in fact we were to a large extent merely recovering what we had previously lost. Later, as our schools began to be become well known throughout the city, there was a significant migration to East Harlem, but even then it was not a skimming-off-the-cream process. We did not seek to lure away the most outstanding kids. In fact, we always gave priority to students from District Four over all others, regardless of ability. To this day, almost every District Four school has fewer than 8 percent of its entering class from outside the district boundaries. (The only two exceptions are Manhattan East and CPE, our federally funded Magnet Schools, which have to attract white students to qualify for funding!)

When the superintendents of the neighboring districts complained to Chancellor Frank Macchiarola in 1982 that District Four was taking their best students, he wisely replied, "You are asking the wrong question. The question you should be asking is not why District Four is admitting your kids. The question you should be asking is why do your kids want to leave their district?"

Before we implemented our full-scale choice system, our

staff in District Four had spent eight years on program development in existing schools and had helped to open seventeen new schools. Once the system was in place, it seemed obvious to us that the very nature of alternative education requires choice. One simply cannot develop schools that are designed to meet the needs of a diverse population and then assign seats based on addresses.

District Four was unique because it did not stop with a few magnet or alternative programs. We adopted high standards and high expectations for the entire district and for all our students. We were not elitist; in fact many of our schools were heterogeneously grouped. At the same time we did not shy away from raising standards in our regular schools as well. Our motto was always that we had never seen a school that could not be improved. As discussed in chapter 5, the establishment of small alternatives in regular school buildings acted as a spur to those traditional schools to improve. Principals and teachers across the district looked at what we were doing and began to develop and implement their own educational visions. A number of the mainstream schools improved so markedly that they began to outperform the alternative schools. P.S. 206, a regular elementary school, for example, was recognized by the U.S. Department of Education in 1987 as a national "model of school excellence."

And the parents understood and appreciated what we were doing.

Here is an example of how we met with and talked to the parents on a level they understood. A very bright and committed mother from District Three, on Manhattan's West Side, approached me one day to get her daughter placed into one of our alternative schools. "Let's try an experiment," I told her. "Let's try to do this according to the system." She agreed and went to the District Three office on three separate occasions without being able to meet with the person in charge of granting waivers to transfer into another district. On the fourth occasion she succeeded in meeting him. He told her that District Three's policy on waivers (this was some years ago) was not to give any waivers. She appealed such an arbitrary and mindless ruling to the central Board of Education, which has an appeals process for precisely such abuses. After three or four weeks the decision came down from on high. The central board upheld District Three's ruling, the rationale being that District Three already had a program for intellectually gifted children. But neither the daughter nor the mother wanted to attend that program. The girl was interested in art and had an aptitude for it, and her mother wanted her to go to a school with an arts orientation as well as a strong academic curriculum. Manhattan East in District Four prided itself on just this combination.

So, despite the bureaucrats, we arranged for her daughter to enter our district by simply forgoing the transfer of previous records. As I have said, the transfer of records from elementary to junior high schools is sometimes spotty; in this case they were just nonexistent. No one ever noticed in District Three or at the central board. And that young lady did very well at the school of her choice.

We had followed the procedures that were supposed to guarantee a fair shake for parents and students, and we had seen that they did no such thing. Again, our creative noncompliance left everyone better off. The student and her mother were happy. Speaking selfishly, I felt much better getting that girl placed than I would have had I only been able to tell her that she had to stay at her failing school.

Cole Genn remembers a local community activist with whom he had had bitter battles on the streets in the 1960s over school control and who came to Harbor in the late 1970s and asked him to take in a certain young man named Raul P. The boy was deeply troubled and was then institutionalized upstate, but he had written one musical skit. Cole decided to gamble and took Raul in, and by the end of the second year Raul's life was changed. He was part of a team and had become a regular member of Harbor's southern performance tour. Although this selection process was completely irregular, the story illustrates how people in the community who had always distrusted the East Harlem schools were now beginning to look to the alternative-school network to solve their problems. And in a large number of cases we were able to respond successfully.

It could, of course, be argued that while it makes for a nice story, you can't run a system that way over time. Maybe, maybe not. In our experience in District Four, one of the most underestimated sources of strength for a school and a child's educational development is family support. When a student and his teacher have an ongoing dialogue with the student's parent, chances are the youngster is going to do much better than if the parent is left unengaged. But the longstanding practice in New York City's public schools has been to keep parents at arm's length. Teachers and principals do not want to be bothered by parents, who are too often considered difficult.

In my opinion, given the quality of the education a lot of those kids were getting, the parents had every right to be difficult. Furthermore, it seemed to me an attitude of the most incredible arrogance that teachers and bureaucrats could look down their noses at parents and consider their concerns insignificant. I had an entirely different perspective.

When I was growing up and attending the public schools, mothers in the poorer sections of town, often immigrants of many different ethnic origins, used to come to the school doors at the end of the day with milk and cookies for their kids. When I first came to East Harlem in 1966, I saw Hispanic parents doing the same thing. The custom made a lasting impression on me. Many, probably most, of those mothers had received little formal education of their own, but they wanted more for their children. And by coming over to school to greet them, give them some simple nourishment, and walk them safely home, they were manifesting their care and concern and love.

Times have changed in the schools and the neighborhoods of New York, and this practice has largely come to an end. It's too bad. My colleagues and I have watched changes take place in the sociology of the school parents. There are far more single parents today, most of whom are the sole breadwinners for their families, whether that means holding a job, dealing with the welfare system, or some combination of both. Drug use, especially of crack, has grown among mothers in Harlem, straining the entire social fabric. Often my contemporaries and I ask one another, "What will happen when all the grandmothers are gone?" In the past, when a family broke up, there was always a grandmother to take the children in. That doesn't seem to be the case anymore.

In the past, the school system's attitude with regard to parents was to say, "Let them come to us. (And with any luck they won't bother.)" That wasn't good enough for us in District

Four. We viewed parents as a greatly underutilized resource. We wanted them involved. We didn't wait for them to come to us. We went to them, fought for their attention, and got them to fight alongside us. And they were delighted that we did. However bad the neighborhood, however serious the social conditions afflicting a population, we never underestimated a parent's love for his or her child. In District Four, once they understood that their input was welcomed, the parents became valuable partners in their children's education.

We often went directly to the parents when we wanted to start a new school. For many other of our alternative schools, our first move, long before the schools opened, was to approach the parents. We started out with orientation sessions. We went to people's homes for coffee klatches with interested parents and described the schools we were trying to start.

Later, when we had a network of alternative schools of choice up and running, these orientation sessions developed into School Fair nights once or twice a year when all the alternative schools would give presentations to prospective students about their schools. The students and their parents would ask questions and decide for themselves which schools they wanted to attend. Up to a thousand students and parents would come to these fairs, living proof that parental choice fosters and demands parental involvement.

Even for a hardbitten veteran of the New York City public schools like me, these School Fairs are a marvelous sight to behold. Twice a year the Office of Alternative Schools takes over a campus in the district for an evening. Ideally, each alternative school is given its own classroom where it raises a banner with the name of the school, posts the name of the current director and sets up a display explaining what its school is all about. The director may bring in slides, or even videos, to tell the story of the alternative school in question. Student projects and a detailed description of the curriculum are available. Most important of all, both teachers and students from the school are on hand to discuss and demonstrate in detail what their school is like, and why prospective students should want to attend.

At the appointed hour, after each school has set up its exhibit, the kids who will be entering junior high the next year begin walking through the fair, most often with their parents. Some of them may already have a very good idea of which junior high they wish to attend; others are still undecided. Often the parents are a bit intimidated at first and hang back. But when they get the message that they are really welcome at the School Fair, and that the schools are actively soliciting them and their children to attend, they get into the spirit of the evening. They begin to get involved, to ask questions, to imagine different possibilities. Even those who have fairly fixed preconceptions of what they want to do educationally browse through a number of alternatives—and that is a good thing.

I have seen many wonderful scenes at the District Four School Fairs. A young lady will walk up to a school director and say, "I see from your literature that you are currently on an IBM computer environment, but will you be Macintosh-compatible next fall?" A young man will inquire, "I see that you have very strong offerings in basic science, and your sports are good, too, but what do you provide as far as enrichment is concerned?" Youngsters from the performing arts schools will sing musical numbers that they have written, and shy but enthusiastic parents will try to talk to them about commercial possibilities.

At another booth, or in another room, or in a corner of the gym, or even outside in the cold, a fifth grader may ask a teacher in the Computer School if they have Lotus. Another young potential "buyer" asks the director of an academy to go into greater detail about its core curriculum. A twelve-year-old student asks an assistant director, "I know your school specializes in math and science, but what do you offer in history and government?" Two or three students may be handing out copies of a school newspaper or literary magazine and being questioned as to whether or not it is a play and might be performed. There is laughter. The parents may or may not accept such a document.

In my day as a student in the public schools it would have been unthinkable that anyone would have dared to ask such questions. You just kept your head down and did as you were told. No one was so brazen as to question teachers and principals. At the School Fairs, however, the directors not only welcome such inquiries but answer them in great detail. After all, they have to. They want to enroll students in their school, and if they aren't willing to compete for kids they'll lose out to others who are.

Besides setting up a mechanism for school accountability, a significant benefit of the School Fairs is the tangible way in which it lets the parents know that we educators respect and value them. Parents are used to being paid lip service, but a School Fair is far more than that. It shows that we believe in empowering parents, and that we want them to be co-owners of their schools. I cannot tell you how many times I have had parents come up to me in the middle of one of our fairs and say, "Until tonight I have always felt that we weren't really wanted or respected by our children's schools. Now I know that you really do regard us as an important part of our children's education."

When they try to thank me, I say, "For what? This is your right. And you have a very important part to play." But I would be guilty of false modesty if I did not acknowledge that such remarks are deeply gratifying. They are yet further testimony to the profound interest and care that parents, no matter what their social status, take in their children's well-being. And we educators are criminally negligent when we do not try to mobilize that energy for the greater good of our students.

Finally, in late spring, comes the application process. Kids apply and list their top three selections. This admissions process serves an important purpose in addition to placing kids: It also acts as a clear-cut monitoring system on the quality of the education being offered by the individual junior highs. The continued existence of the alternative schools is predicated on their ability to attract a student body. A school that experiences a dip in applicants must reassess its "product" and make revisions where necessary. Over the years, the district has discontinued those schools that could not attract a clientele. Some of these failed experiments are discussed in the next chapter, along with other apparent failures that we managed to redeem.

We found, however, that we never had to discontinue a school we considered successful. We have found that the choices made by parents and students are generally in concert with the administrators' own perceptions of the relative quality of the program offerings. The open classrooms of the CPE group of schools, a favorite with our office, were also a favorite with parents and children, increasing in popularity through the years. And, as might be expected, our more academic and scientific programs, which are discussed in chapter 12, were always in demand. That is further proof that even poor parents are capable of determining which schools are best for their children.

In general, we were able to give students their first choice 60 percent of the time. We were almost always able to give kids one of their top three choices. And if there were three or four percent left over who did not get into any school, the Office of Alternative Schools stepped in and acted as the ombudsman to help place those students.

In the course of administering this system, we found that the Office of Alternative Schools had another, delicate role to play. If a student seemed to us to be better qualified for a different school from the one he or she had chosen, we tried to make the match for them. We were, in fact, forever making matches, for teachers coming into our schools, for teachers going out, for students going in, for students going out. But it was this personal attention that helped make the District Four experiment work so well in the end. And in those individual cases where we felt that the student in question had been inappropriately denied admission to the school of his or her choice, we said so and worked with the school director to secure the child's admission. It didn't always work out, though, as sometimes the school director knew something we didn't or had observed a potential problem we were unaware of. Other times, however, the director had concerns that we were able to satisfy, and the student was then admitted. So the system we devised often did produce desirable results. Our basic assumption was and remains that there is no one best way to learn, and that there's no one best school.

In all my years in District Four I can't recall a director of an alternative school turning down our repeated request on behalf of a youngster whom we felt could make it in his school. We were always honest with the directors. We did not sugarcoat the facts to get them to accept certain students, and we also made it clear that a school did not have to feel it was chained to a particular student. If the marriage between student and school did not work out, we would try something else. Invariably this approach worked, and at the end of the year I usually got a call from the school director letting me know how well that student was doing.

From the very beginning we sent a signal that parents would have to be involved, giving priority to those students who visited the school of their choice with a parent along. Today it is commonplace to talk about parental involvement as a critical component of school improvement. The key word is *involvement.* In ordinary schools the principal and teachers take it to mean that the parents are there to reinforce what the school wants the students to do. The school wants parents to see to it that youngsters do their homework, come to school on time, and are respectful of their teachers. They also want parents to support school functions and fund-raising activities.

What most school leaders most certainly do not want is for parents to raise troublesome questions about the quality of instruction, or about how well their children are learning what is being taught. The concept that there is a link between teaching and learning is one many teachers resist. "Oh, I taught them that, but they didn't learn it," is a phrase heard all too often in schools. Well, the truth is that if the students didn't learn it, then the material wasn't properly taught. And if that is happening to one of your children, you as a parent ought to sound the alarm to your child's teacher and principal, loud and clear.

Most principals get along very well with four parents—the members of the executive board of the Parents' Association. Their children usually have the best teachers in the school. The principal treats their kids with respect and a pleasant, slightly chummy sort of informality. As to the other parents and their kids, well, they get considerably less attention. But in successful alternative schools the base is broadened, and the parents feel they have a true, democratic voice. Parental involvement really means giving all the parents the opportunity to bring pressure on the school system to make changes that are beneficial for their children. Although the genteel, limited parental input sought by most teachers and principals will influence some aspects of school life, in District Four we strove to give parents a more fundamental role.

An unappreciated aspect of a choice system is that it has its own built-in accountability mechanism. If parents don't like a school they let you know quickly. And if the school doesn't succeed or adapt, students and parents vote with their feet and find a place that meets their needs. In 1983, Superintendent Carlos Medina instituted the Parent Training Center, a program that gave parents the opportunity to play a part not only in their children's schools but also in forming the educational policies of the entire district. Of Puerto Rican background, Medina understood that the mostly Hispanic parents in District Four have a culturally derived reticence to question their children's teachers. This built-in reluctance was exacerbated by the desperate economic and social deprivation in East Harlem. Medina correctly saw that parents needed to be empowered by some outside impetus. He assigned a very capable parent advocate, Ray Rivera, the job of running the center. Rivera's task was to train parents to become effective advocates for their children. Most districts try to mollify or co-opt parents with as little expenditure of time and effort as possible; we did the reverse.

We identified the leaders among the parents—the ones who were most willing and eager to come to the schools for their children's sake—and then did our utmost to develop parent networks, bringing the parents together and inviting outsiders to come and talk to them. Especially during hard times, we felt this created a sense of community and interdependence.

I briefed our principals on what we were doing and told them to be prepared to respond constructively to parental inquiries and criticisms, no matter how discomfitting they were. I helped the principals to understand that, in the long run, having parents become active agents in their schools would be very much to their advantage. Eventually parents would become the strongest supporters of their schools. We set up two-day retreats in rustic camp environments where parents and teachers could voice their concerns. Later, with the help of an outside grant, we took parents and teachers to the even posher Hudson Conference Center in Ossining. Besides improving teacher morale, these conferences sent another message to the East Harlem parents that we cared about them and that we took their concerns seriously.

One of the workshops we held was a role reversal exercise

111

in which parents played the principal and the principals were parents. What an eye opener that was! The parents, acting as principal, pretended to ignore the parents; while the principals, acting as parents, couldn't stop saying "Why? Why? Why?" This was particularly enlightening and brought about a closer working relationship between principals and parents.

Another of our outreach efforts focused on The Friendly Place, a cross between a community resource room and a public library branch on First Avenue, between 100th and 101st Streets. It started out as a place where kids could go after school and read. There were storytelling programs for the younger children as well. Julia Palmer of the American Reading Council, who was the driving force behind The Friendly Place, joined forces with us when we saw an opportunity to use the facility in a related way. Together we designed a program to improve the literacy skills of our parents. The Friendly Place donated its space and resources, the district contributed trained personnel, and the program was a great example of how different community groups can work for the common good.

Finally, we created the district-wide Alternative Schools Parents Council, to address a host of distinctive issues which never arose in the conventional schools. The Council became a great force for the expansion of the alternative-school network, lobbying effectively with the District Four board as well as with the chancellor himself. Later one of our parents, Minerva Warwyn, became a school-board member and served on the selection panel to name the new chancellor in 1989. Another, Evelyn Pacheco, became a member of the District Four community school board.

Once we got the parents on our side, they became staunch allies. They supported us not because they liked our politics or because we were promising them jobs down the line but because we took the time and the trouble to explain to them what it was we were trying to do for their kids, and because we listened to their ideas and suggestions in return.

And we got back more than we gave. In 1981 there was an extremely contentious dispute between the alternative-schools network seeking autonomy for its schools on the one hand, and the entrenched regular-school principals, their allies in the district office, and some members of the local community school board on the other hand. The principals were maneuvering to win back control of the alternative schools in their buildings, with the tacit support of Barbara Barry and others in the district office, who had indicated privately that they wanted "to rein us in." Acting through their union, the Council of Supervisors and Administrators, the principals sought to legitimize a process by which they would take control of the alternative schools.

Our response was to take the offensive, organizing the parents in each alternative school to come forward. Until then we had always been satisifed to take the route of creative noncompliance or, as we also called our tactical style, "dancing in the dark." Now, however, the very existence of the alternative schools was being threatened, and we realized that a more frontal counterattack was necessary.

We called a district-wide alternative-schools conference to mobilize our forces. I myself appeared at over a dozen meetings of the Alternative Schools Parents Council to explain why the time had come for us to press for the autonomy of their schools. At the same time, being a member of the C.S.A. myself, I attended their meeting and brought Cole Genn with me. There we dealt with the proposed takeover of the alternative schools by the principals in a very subtle way. We elected Genn to be the C.S.A. representative to the school board. There was a minor flaw to this strategy, which was that Genn was not at that time a member of that union. But he promptly signed on.

Meanwhile, our office was meticulously organizing the timing and agenda of the alternative-schools conference. At this point, the common perception was that the District Four school board was leaning against us. We made certain that members of the school board were invited, and several came.

For a while our future looked bleak. But that was before the Alternative Schools Parents Council set to work. They organized the parents into a unified block and stormed the meeting en masse. There were over five hundred parents there in the auditorium of P.S. 117 on that cold winter night, demonstrating and demanding that recognition and autonomy be granted to the alternative schools. Parent leader after parent leader stood up and proclaimed that the time had come to recognize the autonomy of the alternative schools. Bob Sancho, a politically astute board member and supporter of Superintendent Alvarado, immediately grasped the potential power of the alternative-school network, not only in changing the schools but for his own reasons, including gathering support for the next school-board election. He was instrumental in getting the community school board to pass a resolution recognizing the alternative schools as autonomous institutions.

When the night came for the District Four board to consider that resolution, we saw to it that our parents were there again to urge its approval, and they did not let us down. Faced with such an unprecedented and overwhelming show of support in their midst, the board shifted directions and passed the autonomy resolution!

Immodest as it is to say so, we deserved the parents' magnificent support. The system we had installed worked well. Our schools had taken off, and the performance of the youngsters in them did too. You could almost say that we became too successful, because until then we had been laboring in relative obscurity. Once we began to succeed on a large scale, the central board finally roused itself and noticed what we were doing. And while we tried our best to turn even that to our advantage, it was clear that more fights against their big guns still lay ahead.

8

Freeing Schools to Overcome Failure

W hen a school is free to pursue its own educational vision, and has the support of its major constituencies, good things will happen. Principals and teachers will be invigorated by their heightened opportunities and responsibilities. Students will be inspired and motivated. Parents will invent new and ever more constructive ways in which to become involved in their children's education. And everyone involved will have a good time. To call it "the joy of learning" may sound hopelessly clichéd, but once students, teachers, and parents get that feeling—that spirit—it builds from one plateau to the next. The students' self-esteem grows, and they begin to achieve at levels that surprise even themselves.

In a school that is functioning freely, you can sense the excitement in the air. The kids want to get to school early. They stay late. The teachers are involved in a dozen different projects, large and small, often giving up their weekends to help

115

stimulate their students. Parents take an active role in contributing to and assisting the success of the school's mission. A "can do" attitude pervades the school. If an idea is right, if a certain project will help the students to realize the goal of a given course curriculum, the project is undertaken. If a school trip is desirable to drive a point home, the trip is taken. If community support is necessary to fund an enterprise, it is solicited and received. Questions may be asked later, permission may be received after the fact—the point is to do what needs to be done today without waiting around rationalizing inaction while some distant bureaucrat delays making a decision about what you can and cannot do. When schools are free they do what they have to do, and in the overwhelming majority of cases they do it well.

Contrast that, for a moment, to the atmosphere in a restricted, failing public school, where authority is handed down from above, and there is never any room to maneuver. Classes are sullen and largely silent. The only excitement is from bored students letting off steam in the halls or the playground. Morale is poor. Kids come late if at all. Teachers take sick days so often that marginally qualified temporary teachers accumulate as many teaching days as regular staff. Parents seldom bother to visit. And children don't learn. Or, to put it more accurately, such schools fail to teach. Regrettably, there are far too many public schools failing to teach across America today.

Failure occurs in all walks of life, and this is equally true in education. The difficulty with failure in the public sector is that centralized bureaucracies try to deny that failure ever takes place. My daughter Sharon is a clinical psychologist, and she tells me that one definition of insanity is doing the same thing over and over but expecting a different result. Rather than acknowledge failure, bureaucrats continually try to cover it up. Rather than remedy it, they take a few half-hearted measures, merely muddying the waters so as to obscure the dismal reality. Constructive action in such an environment is practically impossible, because the central authorities render those people who might be able to energize a demoralized system utterly incapable of having any positive impact.

The ways in which the bloated bureaucracy of the New York City Board of Education has managed to perpetuate failure are

116

far too numerous to discuss in a single chapter, but an illustration or two can give some idea of how gargantuan the problem is.

According to the board's regulations, the proper way to hand out books to kids in class is for both teacher and student to fill out inventory cards, and for the teacher to give official notification to the students' parents that such books have indeed been distributed. The board's Standard Operating Procedures manual drones on for twenty pages on jury duty alone. It has another chapter called "Cash Funds," which, for forty-six pages, recites all the contingencies and corollaries and rules and exceptions which have to be mastered before you can write a check for ten cents.

It is enough to make the mind go permanently numb. After reading such masterpieces of misguided regulation, it is easy to understand the commonly expressed sentiment of many within the school system: "If you followed all the rules of the central board all the time, there's be no time left for teaching or anything else." The school system's shortcomings in these matters may appear almost laughable, but the accumulation of incompetence seriously injures young people's lives.

One of the most disgraceful failures, which remains uncorrected after more than twenty years, is New York City's handling of special education. I am reminded of the story of the two city slickers who go deer hunting for the first time. They drive out to the woods, park their car, and trek into the woods. As luck would have it, they bag a buck and start dragging him by his legs to their car. The buck's antlers catch in the underbrush making it difficult to move quickly. An old farmer who is watching advises them it would be a lot easier to put down the legs and lift up the antlers. They follow his advice and, although finding it much easier, they notice that they are moving farther and farther away from the car. The moral? You have to know what direction you really want to go in.

Special education is like that: It has lost its vision, its goal, and needs to be seriously rethought if it is to make any sense. Youngsters needing special education are certified into one of a number of categories: brain-damaged, neurologically impaired, mentally retarded, emotionally handicapped, learning-disabled, and multiply handicapped. After bruising legislative and court conflicts, New York's special education programs have turned into a quagmire from which young people are rarely saved. Long waiting lists for evaluation and for placement, a disproportionate percentage of minorities in special ed, and an extremely low return rate to the regular system (5 percent) all suggest catastrophic failure, despite expenditures of over a billion dollars a year.

The problem is, some people like it that way. It serves their purpose. A regular student brings in only six thousand dollars of New York State funds to the system, but a special ed student brings in twelve thousand dollars. Because of court orders and state mandates, a whole system has developed around the special ed entitlement: more teachers, supervisors, social workers, psychologists, and guidance counselors—a whole interest group fighting to maintain its position. These people are not even working directly on amelioration but are spending enormous amounts of time testing for certification. Furthermore, deliberately hanging on to a problem set of children keeps the total school budget higher, and that's what central bureaucrats like. It's a terrible, cynical strategy and deeply unfair to the youngsters victimized by it, but this is how the system perpetuates itself.

In District Four we tried to look at failure as an opportunity. As the special-education morass grew worse in the late 1970s we refused to stand passively on the sidelines and decided instead to take strides to break through the inertia. In 1982, two innovative teachers, David Goldwasser of District Four and Steven Axelrod, a special ed teacher, created a program called Project Mainstream, whose goal was to get kids decertified from special education programs so that they could learn, at least part-time, in a traditional school setting. They felt that there were many kids who had become imprisoned in special ed who would really be much better off in ordinary classrooms. They came to the Office of Alternative Schools with an intriguing idea. They wanted their program to be assigned to an alternative school where they could have adjacent rooms. They specifically did not want their students to be identified as "special ed kids," and went to great lengths to see that they were treated and perceived as full members of the school community. Project Mainstream also took pains to brief and train teachers on how to deal with the kids who were mainstreamed into regular classrooms, so as to cut down on the excessively high number of kids who were mainstreamed and then failed.

This approach was tremendously successful: 30 percent of Goldwasser and Axelrod's students were decertified from special ed, versus the 5 percent average throughout the system. Moreover, once the program began to succeed, Project Mainstream went back to the regular teachers and offered to supply remedial services to some of their regular education students as well, helping to save some marginal students who were teetering on the brink of being placed in special ed. They recognized that some kids take their placement in special ed as a sign that they are destined to fail, and they need a mechanism to get out. Project Mainstream gave them that, providing all its students with support and counseling, and its founders' conviction proved to be absolutely correct. Goldwasser and Axelrod got some kids out of special ed programs and all the way into college! Axelrod recalls that one of their students graduated from Lesley College in Boston, and another now attends the Borough of Manhattan Community College.

As might have been expected, the central board didn't see matters as we did. District Four carried the expense of Project Mainstream for five years, and all that time 110 Livingston Street refused to acknowledge what we were doing despite our demonstrable success. The administrators of special ed even refused to fund the extra position out of their budget. They would talk endlessly about the need to mainstream students, but when we began to do it they refused to support the program—because it wasn't theirs. The fact that someone else was doing it made them look bad, and they wanted it to go away. But the point is that there are individual teachers who, given the right environment, will do wonderful things for kids.

Goldwasser and Axelrod subsequently moved into new positions in District Four: Goldwasser, an experienced teacher and a registered nurse, started a traveling health class using Sesame Street puppets, and Axelrod became a supervisor of education under the district's new special ed director, Steve Kahn.

Kahn had actually served time at the central board as assistant director of the Bureau of Emotionally Handicapped from 1974 to 1978. But when he was asked to curtail his programs, he told the Chancellor, as he demurely puts it, "to do something biologically impossible." He saw how poorly the system was being run from 110 Livingston Street, and he believed that the best way to handle the problem was to organize a data base for the special ed kids, showing what each one had done and was capable of doing, allowing the teachers to work with more compatible groups.

In the spirit of learning from previous failures, we set him up in 1985 with a small staff and left him alone to build a special ed learning environment, as he said, "kid by kid." In the next five years he did it, with the help of staff-development programs and the involvement of the district administration and the community. He reached kids who would otherwise have been left out in the cold. He designed and managed innovative programs for all the categories of learning disabled. When Kahn took over, 23 youngsters were mainstreamed; today over 250 youngsters are mainstreamed in an appropriate educational environment.

Moreover, thanks to Kahn's on-line and up-to-date management-information system, a parent can come into his office at any time and they can talk meaningfully about the child's current performance. Kahn can call up the records of every child and the comments from all of their advisers. He can see their progress in class, their grades, attendance, and other relevant data. In other words, he and the system he has designed can track every kid and provide the services that that child needs. In contrast to the black hole that passes for special ed at the central board, this is no small achievement.

We had other kinds of failure in District Four besides those for which the central board was responsible. Some of our own alternative schools did not work out as we had hoped, and they had to be redesigned or restructured before they finally succeeded. The point is that we weren't perfect, and not everything we tried worked; but unlike a centralized bureaucracy, hiding its head in the sand and pretending not to see obvious problems, when our schools got into trouble, we did something about it.

An early example of our own failure was the School of Communications and Health Services, where, despite many good teachers, there was not sufficient discipline, structure, or leadership. It is not enough to say, as the co-directors did, that if you love kids, do your thing, and let them do their thing, somehow it will all work out. Loving children is not enough. In a successful school, "love" is demonstrated by making the students into learners. The kids in the School of Communications and Health Services were in continual riot, and pretty soon the teachers' morale had also broken down entirely. More than once, groups of teachers called our office, begging for help. I raised the subject repeatedly with the school directors and with my district superiors, but the school developers, in the district Office of Funded Programs, kept telling us to "leave it alone" and saying that they would straighten out the situation.

I stayed away awhile, until finally I got a call from Eddie Rodriguez, the principal of the regular school housed in that building, who suggested politely that there was a serious problem. I made another visit to the school. I walked in at eleven o'clock in the morning and in one classroom two kids were playing handball on the blackboard while all the others just watched. Finally, even district office supporters who had defended the school repeatedly said that they could no longer support it. It was a fiasco, a clear-cut disaster.

We brought in Linda Lantieri as the director, a woman who today is recognized as one of the leading experts in conflict resolution, and she succeeded in bringing a certain amount of stability and order to the classrooms. But even she felt that the school as it stood was incapable of achieving success, so we merged what was left of the school with another alternative school, the Creative Learning Community.

The Maritime Academy was another alternative school that at one time was sinking under the leadership of its director. He was a very nice guy, but whenever a difficulty arose he would always brush it aside, saying, "I'll handle it." One time, just to test the limits of his optimism, I said to him, "Say you are in your office at P.S. 96 and surrounded by homicidal snipers. How will you respond?"

"Don't worry. I'll handle it."

Despite all the best intentions, things were not working out there, so we saved Maritime by transferring control of it to our new friend, Izzy Bernstein, the principal of J.H.S. 45. Izzy had been an antagonist in the early days of the alternative schools, but as we moved forward he himself saw the potential of what we were doing and became a convert to the concept of mini-schools and schools of choice. Bernstein assigned one of his staff members to run Maritime, and the school stabilized. Then a young man came to my office who wanted to work in District Four. In talking to him about his interests outside of school, he impressed me with his love of boating and the sea. He was perfect! Today, Paul Pennoyer has built up Maritime to an entirely new level, upgraded its boating and sailing curricula, and vastly improved the school's academic performance. His is a great example of the benefits that flow from someone "taking ownership" of an institution.

Another bumpy transition to the second generation of leadership occurred when Shelley Price, the director of our third CPE elementary school, River East, decided to leave New York. Price had been a forceful and dynamic leader in the mold of Debbie Meier and Esther Rosenfeld, the director of CPE II. A conflict arose over the succession, because the CPE schools felt that they should have the right to name the new director. Their choice was the then assistant director, a fine person and a dedicated, hardworking teacher, whom I knew and admired. Unfortunately, I felt in my gut that this person was not quite strong enough to follow in Shelley's footsteps, and would not work out as a school director. I suggested another teacher, Marilyn Calo, who had been doing excellent work at one of the alternative bilingual schools.

To complicate matters, the acting interim director of River East, Bill Reilly, fell sick and died while still in office. We thus had to resolve the issue of succession as soon as possible. Debbie Meier did not hesitate in our conversation on this subject to reiterate the issue of school autonomy to me. If I was so much in favor of independent alternative schools, she was saying in effect, where did I get off trying to ram a new director down River East's throat? It was a good point, made all the stronger by the fact that she now had River East's parents totally on her side. The Office of Alternative Schools therefore acceded to her wishes—that's the price you pay when you extend autonomy to others! Regrettably, however, although the director who was appointed worked her heart out, within two years the parents and teachers came to me asking for a change. We made it, and River East prospered anew.

I like to call the Sports School an honorable failure; though, by the time we were through, we had turned it into a success. Its founder, John Elwell, was a young and idealistic teacher who had grown up in Scarsdale where, he says, "good public schools were taken for granted." After college he spent two years as a Peace Corps volunteer teaching English in Nigeria, before entering the New York City public school system in 1968. The Third World, however, had not prepared him for the realities of inner-city education. His first posting in District Four, J.H.S. 13, nearly exhausted his idealism. "It was a very bad school," he recalled. "Nothing worked, and it was never possible to make any kind of progress. I felt like I was becoming a bum."

Distraught, Elwell went to see Superintendent Alvarado, who encouraged him to start a school of his own. Elwell went home and wrote up his idea that night, and made arrangements to meet with Jeff Hansen and me in the Alternative Schools office. Elwell's idea was to create a school that would put acting-out youngsters into a program of serious athletic training and physical education. This curriculum would teach them to appreciate the value of discipline and hard work. And this, in turn, would influence their study habits. I didn't like the name, but I thought this was a good idea. For one thing, it has always been my belief that doing anything serious would have to be an improvement over what was being replaced. For another thing, in our country, sports is truly a focus of learning. It seemed only logical that motivated young athletes would learn concentration, discipline, and teamwork, and that this might carry over to their other studies.

The Sports School was opened in September 1978, with about sixty students, on the fifth floor of P.S. 102 on East 113th Street. Within a few months, however, serious problems had developed, threatening the school's mission. One major problem stemmed from its original strength: Elwell's youthful idealism. It's one thing to set high standards, but the Sports School had unrealistic expectations of its students. Many of them were coming out of sixth grade many years behind their grade in reading; and, instead of realistically expecting them to improve one grade level within one year, Elwell and his staff seemed to want them to come all the way up to their own grade immediately. Elwell and his staff had trouble coming to terms with this.

Many of the kids in the Sports School had been kept back repeatedly, and so were older and bigger than they should have been for their grade. As one eighth-grade teacher told me when I visited, "I didn't expect to be the biggest guy in my class. But the smallest? And not only that, I was the youngest!"

Elwell himself admits having made poor hiring decisions. One of the mistakes that a beginning director sometimes makes is in not distinguishing between friendship and teaching ability. This is a critical factor in the success of an alternative school, especially since in a small school with perhaps only four teachers, mistakes are magnified tenfold.

When the Sports School seemed to stumble during its second year, Elwell had the presence of mind to look at the situation objectively. "This is a lousy school," he said to himself. The school was just not reaching its stated objectives. It did a great job of making the students feel that they belonged, but in terms of academic achievement it was falling short. Elwell brought his problems to the Office of Alternative Schools, and together we searched for answers. We assessed the problems of the existing curriculum and joined the staff at the school in searching for the best possible solutions. We pinpointed the failure in concept: The kids that Elwell had specifically wanted to attract had proved to be more of a problem than anticipated. Morale was on the decline, and enrollment would soon suffer as well. Most important, the school's teachers were simply not doing the job to get those kids where they had to be. The staff was informed that the school was not performing up to city-wide standards, and they in effect replied that they didn't care. In such a situation one has no choice but to act. Over the next three years these inadequate teachers were replaced. This was a particularly wrenching experience for Elwell, who recalls, "I had to transfer out four or five friends of mine who just weren't performing, and they still hate me for it to this day."

An entirely new ethos was introduced as well. Instead of being the Sports School, the school was renamed New York Prep, and a concerted effort was made to give the place the atmosphere of a private school. The academic emphasis was returned to curricular basics and strengthened. Parents and students loved it, and from that time on the school has done well. The staff there does a good job placing students who want to go on to similar learning environments in preparatory schools under the auspices of such programs as A Better Chance and Prep for Prep. One of our Sports School alumnae is now attending John Jay College at night and working during the day as a paraprofessional in special ed at J.H.S. 117 in the district.

Part of the reason for the success of Sports School is that we protected John Elwell when he needed help and gave him enough time to turn the school around and promote its new orientation to students and parents, so that it could succeed. This was an important element in the approach to alternative schooling taken by District Four. Anything that sounded good was worth trying, but it had to work. If it failed, something had to be done to take our problems and turn them into opportunities. We converted our weaknesses into strengths by transforming the Sports School into New York Prep, and it worked very well. We did the same thing with special ed and with the School of Communications and Health Services, Maritime, and River East. We changed them around until they worked. And we didn't stop working on them until they were working well.

One of the least appreciated principles of starting a choice system is that you have the freedom to fail. Because the new schools we had started were small there wasn't too much invested in terms of money, manpower, or morale. By contrast, a traditional public school costs tens of millions of dollars to start in New York City. No matter how bad it may be, no one on the central board will dare admit it's a failure because there is too much at stake. Everyone must pretend it is doing well so as not to look bad. Our schools started with as few as sixty students in two classrooms with four teachers. If we decided to change direction it wasn't the end of the world. We were able to take a harder line on defining failure. When we said a school failed it wasn't because the teachers weren't competent or the students didn't learn; it meant that the school was not reaching its objectives or attaining the high standards that we had set for it. We insisted on schools of quality, and we would not settle for less.

Anybody can start some schools and call it alternative education, but that's meaningless unless those alternative schools are also good schools. Choice is not about choosing among bad schools. As I have said before, the crucial thing about choice is that there have to be good schools before there can be a meaningful choice system. And while at first it may sound a little difficult to master the principles behind the day-to-day, school-to-school problems that arise, the District Four experience suggests that in order to build a network of good schools, one also has to be willing occasionally to fail.

9
New Chancellor Downtown, New Superintendent Uptown

By 1981 District Four's initiatives and successes—and even
its failures—had brought the alternative schools in the
district to a new plateau. In the previous two years we had set
up five new schools and all were oversubscribed. Kids from
around the city were clamoring to gain admission to District
Four's alternative schools. A formula had been created for improving public education, and it could now be applied on a
significantly larger scale. This was a remarkable turnaround
from the days just a few years earlier when concerned parents
falsified their addresses in order to escape the district. Now the
district's work had begun to be noticed by the community. The
word on the street was that the most exciting place in the New

York City schools was East Harlem, and parents and students from other neighborhoods wanted in.

Of course, in New York, until *The New York Times* says something, it isn't so. The Gray Lady discovered District Four and editorialized in favor of expanded choice programs in March 1982:

SCHOOLS THAT DARE TO COMPETE

New York's School District No. 4 has done it again. For nearly a decade, the East Harlem community district has been a fount of innovation, offering "alternative" junior high schools that give students unusual choices. Now it will take the further step of allowing seventh-graders to attend whatever district school they like. . . . Teachers, taxpayers, and, above all, children stand to gain a great deal if East Harlem's daring experiment is validated.

At Manhattan East, one of the outstanding schools we opened at this time, we demonstrated that middle-class white and black parents are willing to send their kids into a poor, inner-city neighborhood if they believe that a quality education is being provided.

Even though Manhattan East was to be one of our greatest success stories, its early development was difficult. Jackie Ancess, then a teacher working in District Ten, in the northwest Bronx, came to me in 1980 with the idea of starting a middle school which would emphasize aesthetic education. There was to be a rigorous arts and academic curriculum based on the theories of Maxine Greene, a philosopher of education at Columbia University and the Lincoln Center Institute summer session. Greene believed that direct involvement with art, music, drama, and dance should increase student academic achievement. Ancess and I had a long meeting in which we discussed the idea and the educational philosophy behind it.

Originally Ancess wanted to staff the school with a group of teachers from District Ten. But because there was a year's delay before the school was opened, her group of teachers made other commitments. That could have very well been a fatal blow to the fledgling school, but Ancess was not one to give up. I encouraged her to join forces with Marcia Lipsitz, an extraordinary arts teacher at I.S. 44 in District Three on the Upper West Side. Lipsitz had a strong following among her sixth-grade students and their parents, who were eager to follow her en masse to a new school. When the school opened she would bring eighteen youngsters into Manhattan East.

Ancess, Lipsitz, and I set up a series of coffee klatches in the teachers' apartments, where we met with small groups of parents and sold them on the idea of sending their children to the first class at Manhattan East. Through this process we were able to interest over one hundred families, sixty of whom were from outside the district. These included the children of John Johnson, a senior newsman for WABC-TV, who had previously been attending parochial schools. The site selected for the school was less than ideal—the fifth floor of P.S. 109, a ninety-year-old building on 99th Street between Second and Third avenues, which had a leaky ceiling and plaster falling everywhere. We could fix the building up, but that was going to take some time. Not wanting to lose prospective students before we even started, we held our first enrollment meeting in the more auspicious surroundings at Fordham University's Lincoln Center campus. At that meeting alone, more than sixty youngsters chose Manhattan East. A fine staff was recruited, and the school was off and running.

But not without one additional, potentially devastating obstacle. At one point during the planning process, Superintendent Alvarado assigned one of his in-house arts curriculum experts to evaluate Ancess's proposal for Manhattan East, and this expert promptly concluded that Manhattan East could never work. We argued our position doggedly and determinedly. After all, risk-taking requires perseverance, and both are fundamental elements of change. I had to convince Alvarado that Manhattan East could work, that a large group of parents were ready to join us, and that we had an outstanding staff. I gave Alvarado my guarantee that I would personally make sure that the school did work. He gave the school the green light.

Within a few years of its opening, Manhattan East had become one of the finest middle schools in all of New York City. It led the city in terms of the percentage of its graduates admitted to the most prestigious public high schools—Bronx High School of Science, Stuyvesant, LaGuardia High School for Music and Art, and Brooklyn Tech.

Many educators sent their children to Manhattan East.

Harvey Newman, the director of the District Four's Block School, enrolled his daughter, Michelle, who today remembers it as her favorite school, more beloved than Spence or Brandeis University, which she later attended. Manhattan East, she says, "created a tremendous support system which permitted me to be myself, and to take risks, while feeling comfortable in so doing."

David Rogers, a severe critic of the New York City school system and the author of *110 Livingston Street* and *110 Livingston Street Revisited,* sent his son Paul to Manhattan East. This year I got a call from Paul Rogers, now a graduate of Brown University. He wants to come back to East Harlem—as a teacher. Patricia Redd Johnson, a former teacher in the public schools and admissions counselor to the prestigious Dalton School, sent her daughter to Manhattan East. Christina had gotten poor grades previously, but at Manhattan East she became an honors student. We gave Christina her first A's; she went on to be accepted at Brown and Sarah Lawrence and to attend Connecticut College. Today she dances in Merce Cunningham's company.

Some of our alternative-school pioneers continued to invent new and successful schools in the early eighties. In 1979 Cole Genn left the performing arts environment of the Harbor School to start an entirely different kind of school, the Academy of Environmental Sciences. This was funded in part by Title VII Civil Rights legislation under the provisions of the competitive "Neutral Site" planning grant. Located on the border of Districts Two and Four, AES was jointly operated by the two districts and thus served to promote racial integration. An environmental center was opened in an old fireboat house at 90th Street and the East River where the students could study marine specimens, put their hands in touch tanks, and work with interactive exhibits of the heating and water systems of the city. Central Park and the East River were used as laboratories, and students had internships in the public and private sector in environmentally related offices. Because the school was small, personalized, and integrated, students' reading and math scores soared.

The Academy of Environmental Sciences was set up to be open to students of all backgrounds. Kevin M. had been labeled emotionally handicapped and learning disabled, but he was accepted by Genn into AES nonetheless. Kevin commuted downtown daily from Washington Heights. Initially, he was very defensive and had limited socialization skills. Genn knew that special education would not solve Kevin's problems and decided instead to involve Kevin with all kinds of students at AES through both schoolwork and extracurricular activities. Over two years Kevin became progressively better at establishing and working through relationships. Had he been relegated to special ed, he would have been separated from other students as soon as he began to manifest signs of aggression, and no such progress could have taken place.

Kevin went on to high school at the Manhattan Center for Science and Mathematics. After that he attended junior college, and today he has a good job with Xerox.

As success stories like these came to be known, the school's reputation quickly spread, and by its second year AES's enrollment had doubled to 120 students. Soon enough, AES graduates also found themselves being accepted into the most prestigious public science high schools in the city.

There was a dynamism spreading around the district that inspired teachers. People really liked teaching in District Four. Professionals like Manhattan East's Adele Gittelman, Jack Monahan, and countless others were committed to giving the kids of East Harlem a superior education, and the kids responded to their enthusiasm by becoming more concerned and active learners. In this atmosphere of shared adventure and educational excitement, people put their own individual concerns aside to work for the common good. The teachers felt that the Office of Alternative Schools was on their side, and that they would be protected from the mindless regulations of the central board as they tried to work out their new programs. District Four was one place in the city where someone with a dream could make it come true. And once teachers proved that they could make dreams come true and provide superior educations in the process, other teachers began to come into the district, and so did many other students.

There was a growing feeling of optimism in the district in the early eighties. We began to think that what we had accomplished in East Harlem could be done in other places, all over the city. The fact that we had won accolades from the *Times* and that Tony Alvarado had won the Fund for the City of New York award all contributed to our own set of heightened expectations. In fact, the idea that Tony might one day become the New York City schools chancellor was talked about informally among the district's staff.

From 1978 to late 1982, Chancellor Frank Macchiarola served in his post more effectively than anyone before him. He raised academic standards and revitalized the system. He refused to grant principals automatic tenure, shook up the bureaucracy, and supported innovative superintendents.

When Macchiarola announced his resignation effective February 1983, the air was immediately charged. This, we all knew, was Alvarado's opportunity. The very next day Alvarado and Carlos Medina, a deputy superintendent in charge of Funded Programs, Liaison, and District Operations, flew to Albany for a meeting that had been scheduled earlier with the Hispanic Caucus in the state legislature. At the meeting they met Tom Minter, a black deputy chancellor who, they learned, would be seeking the chancellorship himself.

There was a feeling around the district that Alvarado had a good shot at becoming the chancellor, or at least a deputy chancellor. We decided to start a campaign of phone calls around the city talking up his prospects. Alvarado's supporters got on the phone. We made an enormous chart with all the contacts we had in every borough. The conversations were always casual, chit-chatting back and forth about this and that. Finally the caller would mention as nonchalantly as possible, "By the way, have you heard they're considering Tony for the chancellorship?" Within two weeks the word began coming back to us from every constituency in the city—religious groups, social service folk, educators, government officials. "Have you heard," they wanted to know, "that Tony Alvarado is being considered for the chancellorship?"

"Really," we said. "That's interesting." It was then we knew that Alvarado had a fighting chance.

Seven people sit on the New York City Board of Education, two of whom are appointed by the mayor and one by each of the five borough presidents. Alvarado needed four votes to get elected. We set out to influence people throughout the city, whether they were union officials, teachers, the mayor, or the chairman of the mayor's educational finance committee. We wanted to assure them that Alvarado was a worthy candidate. Some raised doubts about his managerial skills. Among other things, they pointed out that he had found it necessary to call in a management consultant from the central board to help him upgrade his administrative skills.

But we presented Alvarado as "the education candidate," the one person running who was really going to focus on an improved educational product for the city's children. It also didn't hurt that Alvarado was Puerto Rican. He would be the first Hispanic chancellor in the city's history, a fact that the politicians could use to their advantage. For our part, having worked with Tony and having achieved what we had, there was no question in our minds that he was the best-qualified candidate.

For all our campaigning, however, a stronger candidate emerged. Deputy Mayor Robert F. Wagner, Jr., the son of a former mayor and the grandson of a former senator, was put forward with Mayor Koch's political support and, despite all our efforts, suddenly looked like a shoo-in. He was named chancellor-designate and began to tour the city's classrooms. We smoothly changed course and began positioning Tony for the deputy chancellorship. An important turning point came when Gabe Pressman, a reporter for WNBC-TV, wanted to put the three leading candidates—Minter, Wagner, and Alvarado—on his show to discuss the selection process. Minter declined, but Carlos Medina arranged for a meeting between Wagner and Alvarado in the make-up room before the show aired, and, in those improbable surroundings, the two of them hit it off. Wagner, in fact, asked Alvarado to have dinner with him, during which he invited Tony to become a part of his administration.

That is undoubtedly what would have happened if the Governor of New York State had not intervened. Mayor Koch had recently fought a losing, bloody battle with Mario Cuomo in the gubernatorial primary, and Cuomo was not in a mood to forgive and forget. Meanwhile, political machinations were cranking up around the city as everyone who had a reason to oppose Koch began looking for a way to keep Wagner out.

Word was leaked to *Village Voice* columnist Jack Newfield that Wagner lacked the necessary course credits to qualify for the top education spot.

Normally, in such a situation a waiver could be granted exempting a candidate like Wagner from the requirement. But Cuomo had researched the question legally and concluded that he could use this deficiency to embarrass Koch. Cuomo found that resolution of the issue came under the jurisdiction of state education commissioner Gordon Ambach, who appointed a commission of fourteen people to study the question. The commission ruled that Wagner was disqualified, and the campaign reopened.

There were several public forums thereafter where Tony Alvarado, with his evident sincerity and considerable skills as a speaker, clearly emerged as the best candidate. The only charge his opponents could raise against him was that he was fiscally irresponsible, proof of which was that District Four had run a deficit for years. We tried to justify this by saying that in order to sustain the extraordinary growth in East Harlem's schools, we had no choice but to overspend at certain times. After all, the most instrumental factor in Alvarado's favor was the renaissance in District Four and in the schools themselves. They were the best campaign literature any candidate could ask for.

Despite the district's sometimes creative stretching of union procedures, Shanker and his United Federation of Teachers supported Alvarado. Mayor Koch also threw his support behind our man, another crucial endorsement. When the Board met on May 2, 1983, it decided to take a chance on Alvarado, and he was voted into office by a vote of six to one.

Tony Alvarado's elevation to the chancellorship marked the end of one bright chapter in District Four's history and the beginning of an exciting new one. Of course with Alvarado now so far removed from the day-to-day management of the schools in East Harlem, there was understandable apprehension about the future leadership of the district. Would the schools continue to innovate? Would they slide backward into bureaucratic inertia? Though people tend to have an innate fear of change, it is nonetheless a constant in life, bringing opportunities and rewards of its own. And with the election of

Alvarado as chancellor, we continued to build on our previous successes and to dream of new and better educational programs. With the election of Carlos Medina as our new superintendent in 1983, those dreams began coming true more quickly and more often than ever before.

Like Alvarado before him, Medina was a relatively young man when he became superintendent of District Four at the age of thirty-five. His father, born in poverty in Puerto Rico—known in those days, before the island had its own elected government, as "the poorhouse of the Caribbean"—came north to work in Pennsylvania in 1947 as a welder under the public works and jobs program known as Operation Bootstrap. In 1954, when Medina was only seven, the family moved to Hell's Kitchen on Manhattan's West Side, where he attended the local public schools. In 1959 his father died suddenly, and the family faced disaster. Medina's mother worked long hours, never earning more than eighty dollars a week, and Medina himself went to work in the fifth grade, selling hot dogs in Clinton Park at 55th Street and Twelfth Avenue. Even so, he kept up with his studies, graduating from Aviation High School in 1966. Somehow Mrs. Medina scraped together the money to send her son to college in Puerto Rico, where he majored in political science, and after graduation he returned to New York to get a master's degree from Columbia Teachers College.

Medina entered the New York schools in 1970 as a teacher in District Nine in the Bronx. In 1975 he came to District Four as the assistant director of Public Affairs, reporting directly to Superintendent Alvarado. In this initial function he used his political skills to focus public opinion on the district's educational agenda.

A key activity was raising funds for new programs. Medina and Terry Baker created an Office of Funded Programs in District Four, in which the responsibility was to write grant proposals, solicit funds from various federal and state agencies, and energetically lobby everyone possible for the successful funding of innovative programs. Medina's and Baker's primary source of funds was federal money supplied under the Emergency Schools Assistance Act and, later, under the Magnet Schools grant competitions. These grants funded schools that, in Medina's words, "helped build families" within the district.

In other words, the schools strengthened the sense of community in their respective neighborhoods.

In 1979, Medina became Alvarado's deputy superintendent, and continued to concentrate on fund-raising and liaison activities in both the public and private sectors. Other districts in the city interviewed him for their superintendencies (he was a finalist for the job in District Three), and when the District Four job became open upon Alvarado's promotion, the support for Medina on the community school board was overwhelming. Not only had Medina worked with the board members extensively and demonstrated his understanding of both the educational and political nuances of the job, but one of his most prominent supporters was Alvarado himself. On the first day of Alvarado's chancellorship he came to East Harlem and publicly announced that he supported Medina to succeed him, in effect anointing him.

Medina also received an enthusiastic endorsement from the Parents' Advisory Council. When the actual selection was made, the District Four community school board elected him by a unanimous vote.

Carlos Medina was an unusual selection for superintendent because he had not come up through the ranks as a principal. But those who dismissed him as a political appointee came to understand over the next five years how seriously they had underrated him. Medina had always been an extremely effective advocate and fundraiser for the District Four schools. Upon becoming superintendent he immediately demonstrated two qualities for which he had not previously been given sufficient credit. First, he was highly intelligent. Second, he knew what he wanted to see happen in District Four. He also understood the meaning of leadership.

In one of his first acts as superintendent, Medina promoted me from head of the Office of Alternative Schools to deputy superintendent. It was a controversial decision, as he remembers:

I proposed Sy to the Board for deputy superintendent, and they immediately objected. "We want a Hispanic deputy," they said. "What do you need an Hispanic deputy for?" I yelled back at them. "You've already got me. I'm not naming [an Hispanic or a Black or a Jew or an Italian] to this job. I'm naming the best educator."

When I brought Sy in I sent a very clear message: District Four would not be run on the basis of ethnicity, but on the basis of what was best for educating students. It was well known in the district that Sy Fliegel had an outstanding knowledge of and experience with curricular issues. He was the best person for the job, and I said so. And once I took that stand, there was a tremendous groundswell of local support.

It was not completely smooth sailing for Medina as the new superintendent. There was a natural, reflexive apprehension on the part of some administrators and principals. People who knew Alvarado well were anxious that Medina would not be so approachable. There was the usual uncertainty when those who had been outsiders were now suddenly insiders, and vice versa. Whereas Alvarado could do no wrong in the eyes of many, Carlos could do no right, until he demonstrated otherwise. To his credit, Medina hit the ground running. He went out to the schools, he invited key district personnel to his offices, he staged public meetings, and he fought hard for District Four at every level. He did everything he could think of to win the district's confidence, and he did so with surprising speed.

His labors paid off. Under Medina's leadership, District Four was unified in a way it never had been before. Until his appointment the alternative-school office had been administering its curriculum separately from the curriculum of the traditional schools, the bilingual schools, and the special-education programs, all of which were separate fiefdoms within the district. There was little interaction among them. Medina brought these diverse communities together to make the entire school system function better.

Medina encouraged us all to reach out to one another. For the first time we made a positive effort to invite bilingual education students into our middle schools of choice. We also devoted a great deal of time and energy to upgrading early childhood instructional programs in all the district schools so that youngsters applying to middle schools would be fully able to take advantage of the available options. We also made a huge effort to build up our math and science curricula, in which the district had previously been weak. Finally, and perhaps most important, we made the traditional schools part of our network as well. We formed the Principals Leadership Council and met with them regularly to let the educators of District Four know that we considered ourselves to be their partners, not their superiors. We changed the way the district office functioned, making it more democratic by involving all the departments into a policy-making group, and giving them more say in the decision-making process for all the schools.

One particularly gratifying development of these years was how we won over one of the district's most powerful and effective opponents of the alternative-schools network. Izzy Bernstein, the highly competent principal of J.H.S. 45, was the local chairman of the principals' and supervisors' union; we made a point of making him an important member of our Principals Council. At these meetings I did away with the tedious traditional agenda of administrative issues. "We trust you to read through the rules and regulations in your own offices," I said. "Here we are going to focus on the role of the principal as an instructional leader." The principals felt that, for the first time, the district office was treating them like educators, not bureaucrats, and they responded magnificently. One day Izzy came to me and said, "You know, for a long time we've been on opposite sides. But I want you to know that I respect what you've done with the alternative schools, and I want to work with you." Izzy became a supporter and trusted adviser of ours, and he later introduced four mini-schools in his own school.

At the same time that we were reaching out to the entire district, however, we were also formalizing the status of the alternative schools. Alternative-school directors, who had been working for regular teachers' salaries, were now promoted to assistant principal compensation levels if they had the appropriate license and credentials. We wanted them to know that we recognized all of their dedication and commitment to struggle forward over the years. We wanted them to know they counted. Ironically, the principals' union originally opposed us on this issue, but we convinced them that it was in their long-term interest. After all, more supervisors meant more dues-paying union members down the road. Eventually they got the point.

Unifying the principals of the regular schools behind the alternative-schools movement assured the district that we would no longer have to staff separate teams for curriculum development and personnel development for the alternative and traditional schools. There was a consolidation and concentration of purpose. This freed up funds and time to pursue additional programs, such as math teams, chess teams, school health centers serviced by Mount Sinai Hospital, and a parent training center.

One of the most beneficial outgrowths of the expansion and consolidation of the alternative schools was that the regular schools began to respond to what we were doing with innovative programs of their own. The regular school principals became our biggest supporters. They even asked for the creation of an office to support innovative programs *they* wanted to initiate. Choice made them try harder.

Carlos Medina understood that part of the role of leadership is to hold on to one's vision even when that means taking a good deal of heat in the short term. Medina proved himself ready and willing to take more than his share of pressure. If someone had a serious idea, and we had agreed to support it, Medina would back that person to the hilt, no matter how powerful his or her adversaries were. Oftentimes, these teachers and directors were not even aware of how much protection they were being given.

Debbie Meier was a frequent target of board member opposition. Part of this sprang from the fact that she was tough-minded, strong-willed, and seldom willing to back down. Regrettably, there was another factor, which was that Meier was white, female, and Jewish, and some board members resented her running an East Harlem school, no matter how capably. But since such critics were seldom willing to vent these criticisms openly, they attacked Meier's methods and not her character. They claimed not to understand open education. They objected to a hands-on, "search and discovery" approach to learning, which they called "play." Basically, they favored a return to a more conventional classroom situation, where the teacher stood at the front of the class and lectured the students.

When such criticisms surfaced, Medina joined us in spending hours with the critics trying to get at the heart of their concern. If the motive was essentially rooted in racial or religious intolerance, we rejected it. When the motive was based on instructional approach, we explained the open classrooms philosophy as best we could. Then we offered the critics in question a list of schools where their children or any children might find a different teaching philosophy. In this way Medina deflected criticism constructively and provided his principals and directors with a degree of protection they seldom recognized. And Medina liked it that way, because he knew if his teachers did not have to worry about politics and bureaucratic squabbling they could concentrate on what was most important—letting children learn.

In addition to practicing individual protection, Medina also tried to practice what he called "institutional protection"—the art of protecting fledgling schools and programs from their antagonists until they could stand on their own two feet. This practice gave the staffs of the start-up schools the confidence they needed to see their dreams transformed into reality. In the words of Leslie Moore, for many years director of the Harbor School and now the principal of the Alternative Education Complex at J.H.S. 99:

Being protected means getting a fair allocation of funding, supplies, and key staff. It means staying out of the surrounding politics so that teachers can stay in the classroom and teach and have the energy they need to do that well.

Harvey Newman of the East Harlem Block School described "institutional protection" like this:

When you're protected you can create classes of twenty-two instead of being jammed up with thirty. You can get something done, even with the worst problem kids. When the school directors feel protected by the district office, they can make their teachers feel protected. If, on the other hand, you don't feel protected, you begin to veto yourself, to avoid the risk-taking necessary to providing a stimulating educational environment. When you do feel protected, you can begin to express yourself creatively.

Protection, of course, can take many forms—financial, curricular, individual, institutional, political, and so forth. It's a funny thing. When you're being protected, you hardly notice it. But as soon as you are exposed to the meretriciousness of the system, as soon as you are suddenly "unprotected," you know something is deeply wrong. The Debbie Meiers and Cole

Genns and Beryl Eptons could never have succeeded as they did without some protection. As Harvey Newman put it so well, when you are unprotected and under constant pressure, you begin to veto yourself. And this act of self-vetoing has negative implications for the performance of the entire school. You cannot get the teachers you want or implement the programs you feel are most important. You have to spend much of your time responding to questions from the central board. If you are dedicated to doing something innovative or in any way pursuing a path of creative noncompliance, you are unlikely to get promoted. All of these things wear one down and diminish one's ability to teach.

We made it our goal in District Four that no teachers would veto themselves, and no school would sell itself short. Our instructions to our alternative-schools people was not to talk to the central board when their representatives called, but to refer such calls to the deputy superintendent. When I got a call from the central board I would listen politely to the complaint and say, "I want you to know that I was aware that the XYZ school was instituting that policy, and I personally approved it." In ninety-nine cases out of a hundred, that settled the issue.

Thus the freedom to teach across a wide range of disciplines using a variety of methodologies was taken for granted by our teachers and directors. We shielded innovators from interference on the part of school board members with personal agendas and let the teachers do what they were there for—to teach students and let students learn.

In this the students and teachers of District Four succeeded. By 1983, we had created twenty-four alternative schools in just nine years. Thousands of schoolchildren were having an altogether different experience of education than they possibly could have had a decade before. They were able to choose their schools and study what interested them. More important, they were learning at a rate that would have seemed impossible in 1974. Reading scores and math scores were rising, and our charges were entering excellent prep schools and the city's specialized high schools by the hundreds. Their schools were running admirably well and their futures looked promising. We felt as though we had reached right into the streets of East Harlem and successfully rescued generations of children.

The key to dealing with success, of course, is to keep building on it. This we set out to do, and, despite some devastating disappointments, our five most fulfilling and triumphant years still lay ahead. Tony Alvarado had given his heart to the Board of Education at 110 Livingston Street in Brooklyn, but Carlos Medina had shown himself to be squarely on our side. Now we had a couple of high schools to build.

10 Triumph and Tragedy

For too long New York City educators have labored under the Great Man fallacy. If only we had such and such a person, they say, our school would succeed. If only Ms. X were the superintendent, everything in the district would get better. If only we believed in the chancellor, the entire school system would improve.

Life doesn't work that way. People in authority have great ability to foster constructive change, but change must take place from the bottom up; it cannot be imposed from the top down. There can be no better illustration of the Great Man fallacy than what happened to District Four when our superintendent, Anthony Alvarado, became chancellor of the New York City public schools.

As Alvarado took his new office, District Four's educational experiment began to mature. There was turnover at some of the schools as the original directors went on to other challenges.

Bill Colavito replaced Colman Genn as the director of the Harbor School. John Falco left B.E.T.A. and soon assumed my old post as the director of the Office of Alternative Schools. Jon Drescher became the director of East Harlem Performing Arts. Brian Spears took over New York Prep.

Some people feared these changes, thinking that a school's energy would dissipate once its original director left. Happily, this was not the case. In some instances the school's focus may have been altered slightly, but a new generation of leadership often infused the schools with new ideas and new energy. As we have said before, change is inevitable, and it is often good.

Alvarado's tenure at Livingston Street, by contrast, was a heartbreaking ordeal.

Our first inkling that a chancellor has only limited influence came as we perceived a continued hostility from the central board despite the sentiments of its new boss. Because of our attitude, energy, and still growing success, District Four had become known to the entrenched bureaucracy at 110 Livingston Street as the "cowboys."

Envy and resentment arose anew. To Livingston Street's way of thinking District Four was out of control, especially because we were beginning to gain attention in the media for our students' progress. This was threatening to the entrenched bureaucracy. Soon people would begin asking why they couldn't achieve the same results system-wide. Livingston Street responded by mounting a sustained, relentless attack against District Four. Even Alvarado began to distance himself from us. "You have a problem with your budget," he'd say when we came to see him, and when we tried to explain to him what enormous benefits we could produce with just another 1 percent of our allocation, he'd respond, "That last $500,000 is always the hardest to cut." This wasn't the Alvarado we had known.

Experiences like these taught us not to be seduced by the Great Man theory. In District Four good things happened, not because the superintendent or the chancellor decreed them but because there was a groundswell of activity at the local level which the district office then encouraged. This created a distinctive esprit in the district in which teachers, administrators, and parents all worked to develop better schools.

144

By the early 1980s the strides we had taken began to show up clearly in the numbers. It was not merely an isolated success story of one school but a broad-based improvement that was breathtaking in its scope. Whereas in 1974 District Four students had averaged twenty percentage points below the total New York City average on reading achievement, by 1980 the gap had closed to ten percentage points and by 1984 the margin was only three. And we were still improving. Math scores, traditionally a weak link in the district, were also improving, as was English language acquisition. And as discussed in chapter 9, we were also beginning to see a significant rise in the percentage of our middle school graduates placed into the city's elite high schools.

With such results behind us, and recognition of what we had achieved growing steadily around the city, the district looked to the logical next phase of our development—the high schools.

In New York City, the individual community school districts run the elementary and junior high schools, while the central board retains direct control of the high schools. And no one could deny that our local high schools were in sad shape. Julia Richman High School on East 68th Street was an unmanageable facility with four thousand kids running wild. But closer to home was Benjamin Franklin High School. Located in the heart of the district on East 116th Street and the East River Drive, Franklin had been built by Mayor Fiorello LaGuardia for the East Harlem Italian community in the 1930s, but forty years later it had become the worst school in the city.

What constitutes a worst school? The fact that only 7 percent of its entering students graduated. The fact that the average morning attendance was only 44 percent of the enrolled student body. The fact that no one had the nerve to take attendance in the afternoon. The fact that in 1982 even the Board of Education noticed, and decided to shut it down!

At this point District Four jumped in and asked to be a partner in revitalizing the school. When the idea was first raised, Superintendent Alvarado was in favor of installing what he called "a bilingual performing arts school," but he soon was convinced that the idea was not sufficiently focused. Our kids would have to compete in a technologically advanced society, and that required a high school education that would prepare them for college. I told Alvarado he could "include me out" of a bilingual performing arts school.

To fill a need for a more technically oriented school, the Office of Alternative Schools proposed the creation of the Manhattan Center for Science and Math. The executive director of the Board of Education's high school division, Nathan Quiñones, had reservations because traditionally the city's high schools were the sole responsibility of the central board, not the districts. The decentralization law of 1968 had actually provided for district control of the high schools, but it had never happened. But Frank Macchiarola was still chancellor in 1982, and he gave us the go-ahead after a lengthy meeting in his office in Brooklyn. Once the decision was made, Quiñones became a very cooperative and helpful partner.

Macchiarola and Quiñones also gave the district the opportunity to name its own principal. We called upon Colman Genn once again to take up the challenge of building an entirely new alternative school whose academic emphasis lay in an area outside his own specialization. And, true to form, Genn responded magnificently.

When the Manhattan Center opened for business in September 1982, it positioned itself as a place that could attract students with a good aptitude in math and science but who were not among those capable of gaining admission to Stuyvesant or the Bronx High School of Science. The targeted population were those in the fortieth to eightieth percentile. Anyone could apply for admission, though preference was given to students from District Four.

As he had done at Harbor and at the Academy of Environmental Sciences, Genn was given permission to select his own staff. At first the staff wanted to admit only those students of specialized-school calibre, but we encouraged them to take the students we gave them and treat them as if they *were* gifted youngsters. We believed that if the teachers treated them that way, the kids would respond in kind. And we were not disappointed.

We hired a number of teachers from District Four who had junior high school licenses and who eventually received high school licences. Our concern was not with their credentials but with their performance as teachers. They were a variegated group, but they would work well together. Dusty Miller, an attractive African-American woman who had been a successful English teacher at J.H.S. 45 in District Four, taught English for us. Thano Schoppel, also from J.H.S. 45, taught social studies. Byron Stukey, a former college teacher who had worked with Genn to create the Park East High School, also taught social studies. Rosemary Agosto, who was brought up in the neighborhood, taught math, as did Herb Rosenfeld, whom we recruited from Bronx Science's outreach program. Sandy Gelertner, formerly ombudsman for high school students at the central Board of Education, became our science chairman. Harvey Kaye, formerly with Brooklyn Tech, was our industrial arts teacher. Other teachers included Paul Weeks, from the Maritime School, and Bea Ramirez of the teacher corps project in District Four, formerly an English teacher at J.H.S. 99.

All had demonstrated excellence in their previous positions and yet were eager to join the staff. All understood that this new venture would demand extra time, energy, and an ability to work as a team to create a sense of community and school spirit.

The Manhattan Center was set up to run from kindergarten to the twelfth grade. We brought in River East, the open-classroom, progressive elementary school on the Central Park East model discussed in chapter 8, and started with grades kindergarten through two. Within four years, under Shelly Price's leadership, we had built it up so that it ran through the sixth grade.

We also moved over Isaac Newton Junior High, an alternative school based on science, into the Manhattan Center. Thus we had an elementary school, a junior high, and a high school under one roof: a truly comprehensive educational center.

From the beginning the entire project was regarded skeptically by the educational bureaucracy. We would meet with representatives from the principals' union, the UFT, and the high school division of the central Board of Education, who were, for the most part, incredulous of our achievement. They would try to undercut us in many different, sometimes contradictory ways. Concern for the education of young people did not appear to enter into their thinking. One bureaucrat stunned us by referring to our older charges as "savages." Ten years later, remembering that idiotic remark still makes my blood boil.

At one large meeting, a representative from the principals'

union suggested that we turn the high school into a sports school. After all, he reasoned, the year we closed Benjamin Franklin High School, its team had won the New York State basketball championship. The logo on the school's handbook, in fact, was two crossed size-thirteen sneakers. And, as Cole Genn often pointed out, the laces weren't even tied. Some local community activists also advocated such an orientation. "What about Franklin's proud tradition?" they asked.

That was too much for me. I stood up and asked angrily, "What tradition are we talking about, the seven percent graduation rate or the forty-four percent attendance?"

Eventually we won all those battles. With the help of Donna Shalala, the president of Hunter College (now the U.S. secretary of health and human services), and Dean Robert Pollack of Columbia University, we got started.

We had a close working relationship with Hunter's School of Education. A few years earlier, we had initiated Hunter's Triple-T Program for "training tomorrow's teachers." That meant that Hunter education students were assigned to one of our schools from their freshman year to their senior year. They actually held some of their methods courses at the school, and were supervised by two fine Hunter College professors, Mae Gamble and Dick Smolens. It was recognized by the United States Department of Education as a model program.

On her first visit to the Manhattan Center, President Shalala was stopped in the hall by a tall, older-looking youngster who sensed she was someone important and wanted to know who she was. When she told him and then asked who he was, Donna was impressed by how clearly he articulated his own goals. "I want," he said, "to be an athlete, a scholar, and a mathematician."

On the spot, Shalala promised him a place at Hunter College if he completed the requirements for a Manhattan Center diploma. (Shalala did this without prior discussion and it surprised us as well as the student.)

"Put it in writing," the student said.

Shalala did. And then she extended her promise to every student at the Manhattan Center, sending a resounding message to the students that, if they stuck with their studies, they were going to get somewhere.

148

Another message was sent to parents. Shalala let us use Hunter College's Anna Roosevelt House, an elegant townhouse in the East 60s, to interview children for admission to the Manhattan Center. Our link with Hunter was made more real in parents' eyes when they came there, and they realized that the Manhattan Center, however new, was going to be a worthwhile operation.

Dean Pollack of Columbia also encouraged the students of the Manhattan Center to apply to his university. To make sure admissions to Columbia would be done without respect to ability to pay, Principal Genn set up an impressive consortium of corporate and foundation supporters, including IBM, General Electric, and Bell Labs. G.E. helped by establishing its "Elfund" for prospective G.E. Scholars. IBM sent computer teachers. Bell Labs provided robotics teachers. And the Manhattan Center was able to locate a half million dollars from foundation donors to give scholarships to its graduates.

The Manhattan Center's curriculum consisted of four years of mathematics, four years of social science, two years with computers, one and a half years of technology education, three years of science (biology, chemistry, physics or general science), and three years of a foreign language. A ninth period was added to the class day to provide the necessary time for teaching so demanding a curriculum. That helped to make an impression on people that this school viewed itself as different from the rest. Just as Debbie Meier had created a whole new kind of school, Cole Genn wanted to do the same. He wanted to show the neighborhood that times had changed at Franklin, and that this was a serious operation. So every morning he stood outside the school between eight and nine. If he saw someone arriving without books, he told him to go home and get them. Most of the Manhattan Center students were from District Four, but many commuted from Brooklyn, the Bronx, and downtown Manhattan. So Genn greeted them at the subway stop at 116th Street and Lexington Avenue.

Genn brought in an assistant principal with whom he had worked for years in Harlem. He was a big man named Gene Brown, a wonderful, unforgettable character. In addition to supervising an innovative lunchroom program that treated youngsters with respect by offering three different choices for

lunch—which he dubbed the "Franklin Energy Factory"—
Brown acted as Genn's right-hand man in and out of school.
The two of them would patrol the streets to make sure there
was never any trouble. They got the word out that violence was
unacceptable. At Friday-night dances they had six hundred
teenagers in the school building, and they both made sure that
everyone got home safely.

One day I was meeting with Genn in his office at three p.m.
when a frightened freshman ran into the office and said that
some local toughs were beating up on kids outside the school
door. Genn and I ran outside to find these two big twenty-year-
olds, strutting around in what Tom Wolfe called "the pimp
roll" in *The Bonfire of the Vanities*. They were intimidating everyone and started in on Genn, who simply leaned forward to one
and softly said, "Where I come from only girls walk that way."
The guy stopped. He looked at Genn, completely confused.
Then he said to his friend, "Let's get out of here." And the two
of them disappeared.

Genn and Brown were always having to face down that kind
of nonsense. One time some older kids harassed a student and
stole his coat, so Brown and Genn took the youngster into
their car and began cruising the streets. They finally found the
assailants walking along 125th Street. Genn jammed the car up
on the sidewalk and pinned them against a building. Then he
and Brown jumped out and told them to return the coat, and
that they were taking them to the police. They scared the day-
lights out of the would-be thieves in the process. The word
soon got out on the streets: Don't mess with the men from the
Manhattan Center.

There were other important aspects to building the new high
school. Taking advanced seminars at the Columbia Teachers
College was part of the way Genn approached his job. Eating
lunch with the president of General Electric, trying to interest
him in the Center's needs, was part of it too. Years later, in a
meeting with Vice President Dan Quayle, Genn explained it
this way:

We used to look at the [Metro-North] trains bringing executives from
their Connecticut homes through East Harlem on their way downtown to work for the most important financial institutions and indus-

150

tries in America. We used to wonder how in the world we could ever interest them in our kids. Then we just began going out and telling them our story, and very soon we discovered that they were not only willing to help, but that once they were given a chance many of these fine people proved that they loved our kids just as much as we did.

Recruiting kids from all over the city was part of it, too. We went everywhere to sell the school. One day Cole and I traveled to a Bronx school which was the only building standing for at least a four-block radius. We spoke to an audience of youngsters and afterward met with one of the assistant principals. She expressed fear and loathing at sending her students to school in East Harlem. "Listen," we said politely. "Look out the window. Come to East Harlem and look at what we're doing. You'll find a vibrant community." We picked up a number of applicants from that visit.

When the 1982–1983 school year began we had staged a formal opening for the new high school. Mayor Koch and other city officials attended, and I will never forget the sight of Chancellor Macchiarola getting out of his car and hearing the East Harlem Performing Arts School combo playing disco music. He began dancing on the street (very well, I might add) and kept it up for a full ten minutes. The Manhattan Center was off to a good start.

From the very first assembly we told our kids, "You're going to college." It was the power of positive thinking. For the first time in Colman Genn's life he wore a suit to work every day. And it made an impression—so much so that one day when we took a class on an outing to Great Adventure one student asked, "Mr. Genn, where did you get jeans?" So Cole answered, "At Hertz."

The school began to take off. Everyone got involved. Parents came in and gave lectures on their fields of knowledge. Teachers were encouraged to share their specialized interests that they normally couldn't get across in a classroom. And things began to come together, even exceeding our dreams.

The first graduation, in 1986, was incredible. It landed us on the front page of *The New York Times*. One hundred and fifty kids—all but four of the students who had entered the Center four years before—were graduating. And every one of those

150 was going on to college. Every kid! This on the campus of a school that had so recently been graduating only 7 percent!

As college admissions had come in that spring, and we realized the magnitude of what was happening, we held our collective breath. Every day that April, Ellen Sheinbach, the college adviser, would come running down the hall to Genn's office. "We got an acceptance to M.I.T.!" she'd shout one day. "We got an acceptance to Amherst," she'd cry out another. One student went to Harvard. Another to Williams. Others were accepted by equally fine schools, such as Cornell, Colby, Trinity, Wesleyan, among others. What a celebration we had when Genn realized that every youngster was a success and every one was going to college. It was a dream come true.

A lot of people had said that District Four was crazy to start a new high school, but we kept trying, and that graduation made everyone realize the power of being able to find and choose a good school. Although the Manhattan Center was offered the auditorium at Hunter College for the ceremony, Genn insisted on having the graduation on the Manhattan Center campus, in the presence of the entire community. It was inspirational. Genn said it was "like Camelot."

There were so many great kids at the Manhattan Center that by mentioning any in particular I leave out many others just as remarkable. Jeffrey and Gregory Anderson, for example, were persuaded to come to Manhattan Center by Gene Brown. They immersed themselves in the curricular and extracurricular life of the school, participating in many sports and student organizations. Jeffrey went on to M.I.T. and is now finishing two years of advanced study in Japan. Gregory graduated from Amherst and has begun his business career in New York City.

Luis D'Espagne was a bright boy who studied hard and played on the baseball team. He was courted by Yale and went for a weekend. When Genn asked him how it went, Luis became upset. Like all of the students at the Manhattan Center, he idolized Genn. He also knew how prestigious it was for the school that Yale was interested in him, and the last thing he ever wanted to do was to let his principal down. So when Genn asked Luis how his weekend in New Haven had gone, Luis began to cry. Genn comforted him and when Luis settled down, they began to talk. Luis explained that there was nothing wrong with Yale, but he had also gone to visit Wesleyan and had fallen in love with it. I wish we always had such problems! Genn assured Luis that it was up to him to choose the college that was best for him, and that the Manhattan Center would be as thrilled and supportive of him going to Wesleyan as they would be if he went to Yale. Then Genn helped Luis secure a scholarship to Wesleyan, where he did very well.

Not everyone who came to the Manhattan Center had so easy a time of it. Nathaniel M., for instance, was brought to see Genn by his grandmother. They lived on East 115th Street in the James Weldon Johnson projects, and he had gone to P.S. 57 around the corner. Fearful of the neighborhood, his grandmother walked him to school in the morning and back in the afternoon, and never let him go out alone. The boy's mother was an addict, his father had long since relieved himself of familial responsibilities, and his grandmother was desperately trying to raise him to be an upright man. Because of his isolation, when Nathaniel first came to Manhattan Center he had no socialization skills whatsoever. When you threw a ball at him he ducked! Genn and the staff of the Manhattan Center worked hard with him, and Nathaniel did a great job himself. He became a fine student and went on to attend the United States Maritime Academy.

And there was another, larger-scale turnaround in the Manhattan Center's success story. The astronomical dropout rate that had plagued its predecessor, Benjamin Franklin, completely disappeared. In fact, in 1986 *The New York Times* reported that the Manhattan Center had the best individual performance for a full four-year secondary school in the city. Only one of its 728 students had dropped out the previous year, whereas other city high schools experienced annual dropout rates as high as 25 percent.

One of our major objectives at the Manhattan Center for Science and Mathematics was to encourage young women to enter and do well in the science and technology fields of study. Our student population reflected that goal: 50 percent of our students were girls.

Debra Grady is representative of our female population. She was active in school activities, serving on the school newspaper and yearbook in addition to competing in the academic olympics. She went on to Skidmore College, where she graduated with a degree in biochemistry. She currently attends New York University, seeking a postgraduate degree in rehabilitative therapy.

Brontie Venn was one of the first members of the Mount Sinai Medical Scholars program. She attended the Rensselaer Polytechnic Institute, graduated with a degree in biomedical engineering, and today is employed in the dermatology department at the Mount Sinai Hospital.

Mara Frank was a talented musician and dancer at the Manhattan Center. She was a close friend of Debra Grady's and went with her to Skidmore College, where she majored in psychology. Today, Mara runs the computer systems for *Kirkus Reviews*.

Not all the young women at the Manhattan Center entered the technology fields; Cheryl Diggs graduated from Vassar College with a Bachelor of Arts in business and then spent a year at Emory College studying theology. She is currently working in New York City at a major insurance company as an executive trainee.

Tessie Scroggins, a very popular student at the Manhattan Center, excelled in academics, the arts, and sports. She also graduated from Vassar College and is working as a financial aid officer at Columbia University. The point worth making is that our female students did well in their math and science courses and then chose to enter a variety of fields of interest.

A key ingredient in the Manhattan Center was Isaac Newton Junior High School, a seventh- and eighth-grade math and computer school founded by Lenny Bernstein. A white-haired, pink-faced man, Bernstein grew up in the Bronx and early in his life was pointed toward a career in music. "But with my name," he says, "they were expecting a symphony or an oratorio every week and I couldn't take it." So after attending the High School of Music and Art he went to Brooklyn College, stayed on to receive his master's degree, and began a career as a high school biology teacher. Along the way he wrote several successful textbooks in the life sciences.

Bernstein came into District Four from District Five at the northern end of Manhattan. Having always concentrated his teaching activity on students at the low end of the spectrum, the Isaac Newton J.H.S. presented an opportunity for him to do something completely new and extremely challenging. He devised the program and curriculum, including the lab techniques.

He actually built the laboratories for his new school with his own hands. When Isaac Newton started at P.S. 109 in 1981, Bernstein and Manny Kostakis, then the assistant director and now Newton's director, moved soapstone laboratory tables weighing four hundred pounds apiece from a government surplus warehouse downtown and hoisted them up five flights of stairs. It took them all summer, and people said they were crazy. But they felt that had to do it. They needed a lab for their kids.

Only one year later, the school was moved to Franklin and became part of the Manhattan Center. Manhattan East lucked out; when they expanded and took over the top floor of P.S. 109, they got the laboratory tables, which are still in use today. Newton got eight new labs on wheels.

In each succeeding year, Bernstein refined, improved, and built his program further. We started the Mount Sinai Scholars Program in concert with Mount Sinai Medical Center, the goal of which was to produce minority students who would go to medical school and come back to East Harlem to deal with the terrible public-health problems there. Bernstein began by talking to the kids in ninth grade, asking them to consider becoming doctors. He assured them that he would help them to develop the skills that they would need in school and in life. And he followed through. In the first year of the program, four kids were awarded $17,000 Ralph Bunche scholarships upon their graduation. Recruiters seeking outstanding minority students began to contact the school. The Mount Sinai Medical School offered a slot to any student who maintained a 3.7 grade point average in college.

Sometimes it takes a while for the message to get through. One kid, Donneer Missouri, came from a broken home and was being raised by his grandmother. He was acting out, and in a regular school situation would quickly have been back on the street. Bernstein brought him into the office one day and Donneer said, "You're going to expel me, right?"

And Bernstein said, "Nope. You're stuck with me for two more years."

After that Donneer buckled down and did beautifully. Later

he said to Bernstein, "I did it because you were the only one who believed in me." That boy scored one hundred on his math Regents (New York's state-wide examinations) and went to Cornell.

Bernstein has had quite a few students move on to Cornell, and when he takes seniors around to visit schools he gets his former students to come out and have dinner with the group. Each of his kids know, no matter how many years ago he graduated, that he can still call Bernstein collect at home or at the office any time he needs to.

Maritza Ortiz, for example, still stays in close contact with Bernstein. She was a warm but very shy girl when she came to Newton, but she quickly developed close relationships with Bernstein and with Rush Putnam, her English teacher. Maritza was given love and encouragement and developed into a fine, self-confident young woman. In 1992 she graduated from the State University of New York, Stony Brook School of Nursing, where she won the Eleanor Roosevelt Award and three additional awards for community service and leadership. Today Maritza works at the New York University Medical Center and has begun graduate studies.

One of the most compelling success stories is that of Nancy Nava, a shy, soft-spoken young lady. Her loving (and very protective) parents escorted her to school and often waited for her at the end of the school day. The positive attitude, concern, and support of her parents paid off richly. Nancy became an honor student, excelling in science, math, and computer sciences.

When presented with the opportunity to send Nancy to a private school following her graduation from Isaac Newton, Nancy's parents were reluctant to allow her to leave New York City. After many meetings, interviews, and more than a share of persuasive arguments and assurances, however, it was agreed that Nancy would attend Brooks Academy in Massachusetts. She did very well there, graduated and was accepted at Yale University where she is studying languages. During her sophomore year, Nancy studied in Spain, returning to Yale where she continues to excel.

Incredibly enough, because of success stories like these, other principals around the city have called Bernstein an elitist, but he always replies, "Hey, you want to compete with me? Go ahead. I'll help you." They have never taken him up on his offer. In his words,

I love it here. Harlem has been very good to me. At one point, for personal reasons, I took a transfer to a white school in the Rockaways, where these kids would listen to me describe photosynthesis one day, and the next day turn in a six-page, impeccably typed paper on the subject which included much more information than I had given them.

They had encyclopedias at home and parents who helped them with their work at night. So I went to the principal and told him, "I hate it here. I want to go back to Harlem. I'm not doing anything for these kids. You could put a gorilla up in front of them and they'd learn. In Harlem I feel like I'm doing something."

In its first six years, students from the Manhattan Center consistently outperformed their peers in other New York City high schools. A full 87 percent of those who had entered had earned a diploma, versus the city-wide average of 51 percent. Almost half the students graduating from the Manhattan Center earned a Regents diploma, indicating that they had passed the state's most stringent set of course and examination requirements. The site of the city's worst school now housed a proud and effective institution of learning. School reform coupled with choice had worked better than anyone dared to hope.

The Manhattan Center was the first of several experiments in District Four with multilevel education in the same school building. We had noticed that when you combine a vigilant principal with parents escorting their children to elementary school, you make the school safer for the rougher junior high and high school kids who like to congregate in the area. So we set about improving another area, the neighborhood around J.H.S. 117 on East 109th Street, by building what we called the Alternative Education Complex, at that location.

"The regular junior high school at 117 was not a functioning school at the time," Carlos Medina recalls.

There was a lot of apathy around the place. The teachers were burned out. Attendance was dismal. There was no interaction with the parents. It wasn't fair to anyone to keep it open the way it was, so Sy and I decided to do what we did best—reorganize the school.

We converted it from a junior high school to a prekindergarten through ninth-grade school. We brought in several alternative programs under one roof because we thought it would make for an exciting environment for students to have so much going on around them, and because it worked so well at Manhattan Center. We had the talented and gifted program for the district moved there, and we brought in teachers and equipment that had been dispersed around the district to that location. In other words, we set it up so that kids of different ages were being educated together, which worked very well. We observed that given the chance and in the right environment, older students will do a lot to help younger ones out. We even started tutoring programs for kids to teach other kids.

The Harbor School and the Career Academy were already in the building; in fact, they had long made J.H.S. 117 their home. We moved Harbor to more hospitable surroundings on the third floor. (It had previously been located in the basement.) Then, figuring we had already included the brightest and most talented youngsters, we went out and brought in the Key School, which was a school for kids with real problems in learning. It was very small and relied on close supervision, a very low teacher-student ratio, and lots of support from the community and from outside agencies. We also moved in a special ed program.

To keep the various schools in harmony, we made sure we had a good principal, Bernie Diamond, who ran the Complex at J.H.S. 117 in an innovative fashion. He functioned as a kind of building manager, with the help of an assistant principal and a cabinet consisting of the directors from all the schools in the building. This worked very well. There were no disputes over the use of the gym, the library, or the lunchroom. The school was safe and secure. And since Diamond had formerly served as district business manager, he was able to help the individual schools' directors get funding and improve their finance procedures.

As we had intended, the Alternative Education Complex also worked very well for the neighborhood. East 109th Street, between Second and Third avenues, had previously been a block where parents feared for their children's safety when school ended at three o'clock. Drug dealing was prevalent, and elderly people had been beaten up and robbed on that block and on 108th and 110th streets. But the Complex, with its vigilant and cooperative principal, completely changed the character of the block, and after school, with parents of the schoolchildren in sight, the kids would talk and play. It became a safe block, and the community was very happy about that.

Later transformations in the district used the experience of the Alternative Education Complex as a model. In creating these new complexes and schools, our constant concern was that they not rest on their laurels but get better over time. We got heavily involved in teacher-training activities and sponsored a variety of after-school seminars, weekend retreats, and summer workshops. The teachers responded generously. There was no resentment or union interference. Working together, we had succeeded in creating a climate where neither teachers nor administrators objected to extra work. Everyone was willing to pay the price for educational success.

Early examples of this interplay of success and improvement were the Central Park East schools. In the wake of the success of the two CPE elementary schools and the 1982 creation of River East, Debbie Meier began to see the need for a secondary school to accommodate not only the graduates of her schools but other students who might respond to open classrooms. Though Meier had spent her entire career as an elementary school teacher, she was fascinated by the challenge of starting a secondary school that ran from grades seven through twelve.

About this time Professor Theodore Sizer of Brown University was organizing his National Coalition of Essential Schools. Sizer propounded nine principles. Briefly stated, these principles include the idea that less is more; that it is better to know some things well than to attempt to cover many things superficially; that high standards must be set for all students; that students demonstrate mastery of their subjects through exhibitions and portfolios; that teaching and learning be personalized; that students are perceived as workers and teachers as coaches; and, finally, that youngsters discover answers and solutions to problems by being active learners.

Meier approached Sizer and expressed hope that the new high school she was planning would become a member of the National Coalition of Essential Schools. This led to a series of meetings between Sizer and us in which we developed a working plan. We decided that J.H.S. 13, a failing school with few new applicants, would be an excellent home for Meier's new secondary school. Our plan was to phase out the old junior high and start CPE Secondary in that building.

The teachers of J.H.S. 13, however, took a different view. They mobilized a few of their remaining parents in an attempt to thwart the plan for the new school. In response, Superintendent Medina appointed a task force to study how the school might best be reorganized, with me, his deputy superintendent, as chairman of the panel. The plan this panel developed not only approved the establishment of CPE Secondary at J.H.S. 13, but also called for moving the original CPE elementary school into 13 as well, so that in one school building there would be a continuum of grades from pre-kindergarten to twelfth.

In order to accomplish this, a compromise was reached with the teachers of the old J.H.S. 13. The one outstanding feature of the school had been its band, and we hoped that that could become the nucleus of a new alternative school devoted to music, to be called Music 13. Music 13 had a brief life, but it was phased out in 1991 by Superintendent Marcelino Rodriguez when applications reached a low point. The school was failing and word got around. That happens in a choice system, and, although closing a school is always painful, it would be even more painful to force students to attend a school that wasn't doing its job.

Carlos Medina's faith in and support for Debbie Meier was borne out by CPE elementary school's test score results and by more subtle indicators. CPE school attendance, for example, was far above the city-wide average. In any given year only ten to fifteen CPE students changed schools. CPE students continued to perform very well as they moved into the upper grades. Data compiled in 1985 on CPE's first three graduating classes indicated that only one of the thirty-two elementary school graduates dropped out of school later. Twenty-nine had completed high school, and, of these, twelve had gone immediately to college. Out of the more than two hundred students who graduated from CPE in the years 1977 to 1984, only two are known to have dropped out of secondary school. In the city as a whole, more than 40 percent drop out; more than 60 percent of minority children drop out. Meier and her staff had imbued their students with positive attitudes about schooling in the early grades, and these attitudes enabled them to succeed at a disproportionate rate later on. CPE's success was not confined to the elementary school; the first two graduating classes of the CPE Secondary School in 1991 and 1992 had over 90 percent of those graduates go on to college.

Scores on city-wide standardized tests reinforce this picture of educational achievement. Since 1979, at least 90 percent of the school's sixth graders have scored at or above grade level— a startlingly high figure when one realizes that for most of the years under study, a large majority of CPE's second graders were reading below grade level. The data indicates that many CPE students caught up with and surpassed the national norm during their years in school.

Such statistics would be misleading if CPE had simply skimmed the cream of the community's students, selecting only the motivated and well-prepared children. But this was not the case. CPE generally followed a first-come, first-served policy, from which it deviated in only two ways: It strove to be racially integrated, and it gave preference to the younger siblings of current students. Indeed, in many instances the opposite of skimming took place. Many parents chose CPE because their children were not doing well in neighborhood schools and because CPE had a reputation for handling difficult children. Some 20 percent of the students at the CPE schools have learning disabilities, but they are "mainstreamed" into heterogeneous classes rather than isolated in special ed classes.

Just as impressive, in the school's first decade not a single student was suspended.

As we moved into the middle 1980s we could take some satisfaction that we had built a comprehensive alternative-schools network in District Four. We did it at the Manhattan Center; we did it at the first Alternative Education Complex; we did it at J.H.S./Music 13, where the original CPE elementary and secondaries are now located; and we did it in many other locations throughout the district as well. And around the city and the country people were beginning to take notice of what was happening in the schools of East Harlem.

But even as District Four was expanding the frontiers of education for its students, the walls were closing in on Tony Alvarado. Rumors about financial improprieties in the chancellor's personal life exploded into scandalous revelations in the late winter of 1984. The events began to unfold on February 27 of that year, when police discovered incriminating documents in a locked safe belonging to John Chin, a longtime Alvarado associate who was serving as assistant to the deputy executive director of pupil personnel services at the Board of Education. While investigating reports of gunfire from Chin's apartment, the police opened Chin's safe to find not only a cache of guns and illegal drugs, but also the title to Alvarado's car and two checks made out to Chin from the chancellor totaling $10,450.

The next day Alvarado admitted having borrowed at least $15,000, and perhaps as much as $20,000, from Chin in the late 1970s to ease a personal financial crisis. He wasn't sure of the exact amount, he said, and he had never repaid the money. But he assured reporters that he was otherwise clean: there were, he insisted, no other outstanding loans.

Even so, Chin was bad news. He was the unsavory figure whom East Harlem community activists had tried to force down our throat as the director of the Block School in 1978. In the intervening years Chin had ingratiated himself with district leaders, including Alvarado, who brought him downtown to 110 Livingston Street in 1983 and promoted him. Chin's new status gave him the right to earn overtime pay doing after-school and summer jobs, an abuse of the system that many others took advantage of as well.

The discovery of the loan to Alvarado from Chin set off alarms at the City's Department of Investigation and at the Manhattan and Brooklyn District Attorneys' offices. On Tuesday, March 6, the scope of the chancellor's financial misadventures widened as Alvarado admitted having borrowed roughly $80,000 from eleven other people, including eight subordinates. Alvarado claimed that these were business loans rather than personal obligations, citing his investment of some of the funds in residential real estate in Brooklyn. The next day he publicly repaid $19,750 in interest and principal and announced that he had no intention of resigning the chancellorship. Yet merely by alluding to the possibility he was revealing the weakness of his position.

Thursday, however, brought a potentially fatal blow: City Comptroller Harrison J. Goldin disclosed that over the previous four years at least six of the people who had lent Alvarado money had together received more than $100,000 in overtime pay. At this point in the emerging scandal the word "kickback" began to be heard for the first time. *The New York Times,* in a lead editorial, called for Alvarado's resignation.

After this week of stunning revelations, Alvarado seemed finished, but the pendulum slowly began to swing the other way. Jack Newfield and other longtime fans in the press rallied to the chancellor's side, and Alvarado himself began to realize that his position was stronger than he had first thought, given that there was no unambiguous proof of criminal conduct. Thus emboldened, he rejected out of hand a suggestion by James Regan, the president of the Board of Education, that he take a leave of absence until the situation was resolved.

But the respite was short-lived. Within a week Miguel Perez had written a column in the *Daily News* headlined, "Say Adios to Alvarado," and *The Amsterdam News,* an influential paper in the black community, had run an editorial calling on the chancellor to resign.

As each passing day brought new and more damaging revelations about Alvarado's mangled finances, the coup de grace was the revelation that he and his wife, Ellen Kirshbaum, owed $2,100 in unpaid parking tickets. "That hurt, that really hurt," a source close to Alvarado told Joe Klein of *New York* magazine. "The fact that he borrowed money from employees and got in over his head was bad, but people might have given him the benefit of the doubt. The parking tickets, though, made him look like a petty crook."

Though Alvarado paid off the tickets on March 13, it soon became clear that the city's top educator had not learned his lesson. On Sunday, March 18, he and Kirshbaum drove to a crucial meeting with his lawyer, Thomas Puccio (who would later become famous as Claus von Bülow's defense attorney), but parked illegally in a taxi zone near Puccio's office. It was not long before a forty-dollar ticket was fluttering under the car's windshield wiper.

Klein reported in *New York* magazine that when Alvarado's public-relations man, Mortimer Matz, came into the meeting to tell the chancellor of this latest parking ticket, Kirshbaum exclaimed, "Isn't that outrageous!" as if a grievous wrong had been inflicted on her family.

"At that moment," recalled one of the participants, "I realized that these people had lost touch with reality."

But reality was closing in. On March 21, Alvarado took a leave of absence to await the Department of Investigation's report. When it came within a few days, the result was devastating. The investigators charged that Alvarado had obtained the personal loans "in a manner that was inherently coercive and frequently deceptive"; that he had falsified his net worth on a mortgage application; that he had not disclosed the loans from his employees on his various loan applications; that on his income tax returns for the previous three years he had failed to report at least $128,000 of income; that the overtime payments to people who had had financial dealings with him represented an "overwhelming appearance of impropriety"; that Alvarado had himself "double-billed" on two occasions, fraudulently claiming overtime pay; that despite having been informed of John Chin's questionable activities, he nonetheless promoted him; and that he and his wife had bounced 124 checks (for more than $12,000) over the preceding two years.

Puccio disputed some of these findings when they were made public, but by then Alvarado's fate was sealed. He was suspended on March 25, and officially resigned on May 11, 1984.

The downfall of Anthony Alvarado was a personal tragedy, but it also cast a cloud over the very real accomplishments of District Four. People wondered if there might not be less to the District Four story than met the eye. Perhaps it had all been hype. Perhaps the alternative schools weren't really as great as they had been made to sound. Alvarado's vulnerability made for East Harlem's vulnerability. And the central board began to prod at the district to find a way to get even for what it perceived as past slights.

And here we see the fallacy in the search for, and dependence on, a Great Man to remedy the problems in the educational system. If ever there was a Great Man, it was Tony Alvarado, and if ever there was a situation where the demise of the Great Man failed to prevent his creation from moving forward, it was in District Four, where the energy Alvarado had unleashed flowed onward.

In the nine years since Alvarado's departure, there have been three permanent chancellors (Nathan Quiñones, Richard Green, and Joseph Fernandez) and two acting chancellors (Charles Schonaut and Bernard Mecklowitz). Such instability at the top tends to concentrate power in entrenched bureaucrats with seniority. Many of these people were delighted to have the opportunity to trim District Four's sails, and Nathan Quiñones, Alvarado's successor, did little to stop them.

Increasingly, battle lines began to be drawn, and friction between the district and the central board grew. Though East Harlem fought on, and indeed flourished for several years to come, a major collision was on the horizon.

11

"Not a District, but a Movement!"

There is a phenomenon identified by those who study animal behavior called "the hundredth monkey syndrome." Scientists observing a Pacific island with fifty thousand rhesus monkeys saw them pulling fruit off of trees and eating it. Then one mother washed a piece of fruit in the water before eating it. Slowly the other monkeys in her clan took up the practice, until there were nearly thirty monkeys washing before they ate. The practice spread, still at a slow rate, until the hundredth monkey began to wash his food before eating it. And at that point the entire population of fifty thousand monkeys rapidly adopted the technique.

A less illustrative phrase for what I am describing is "critical mass," the amount of material necessary to sustain a chain reaction.

Whichever image you prefer, it happened in the 1980s in District Four. We reached a certain point where things began to explode, as choice unleashed a creative energy that drove the entire district forward. Our activities increased, and so did our results.

At the district level we continued to support educational innovation and sought ways to expand our constituency. Carlos Medina initiated a series of breakfast meetings with local and state legislators to brief them on what we were doing and to win their support. We also established a council of ministers from the surrounding East Harlem churches who could advise us on their parishioners' needs and work together with us on projects of mutual interest, such as truancy reduction and "Just Say No" drug prevention campaigns. Finally, we upgraded our programs of outreach to families to assure that we were involving every parent, foster parent, and grandparent that we could.

Educators with the drive of Cole Genn, Debbie Meier, Beryl Epton, Bob Gyles, John Falco, Bill Colavito, Jeff Hansen, Mike Friedman, Etta Proshansky, Harvey Newman, and many, many others had transformed the district. As the 1980s progressed we concentrated on consolidating our gains and further improving our programs. We created fewer new schools, in part because once we had twenty-five alternative schools we had no more space in which to house new ones. But we constantly strove to upgrade what we had. And there were measurable results which demonstrated just how dramatically the schools of District Four had climbed.

In 1974, fewer than 16 percent of East Harlem's youngsters were reading at grade level. By 1988 this number had soared to 63 percent, and was within two points of the city-wide average. The number of students performing at or above grade level in math had risen from 33 percent (31st of the 32 districts in the city) in 1981 to 48 percent by 1988. Today it is 50.4 percent (22nd out of 32). In 1974, District Four had ranked last overall among the 32 school districts in the city. By 1983 it had risen to 23rd, and by 1988 we were between 15th and 17th, depending on how the statistics were interpreted. Some 23 percent of our students were attending superior high schools (the Manhattan Center, the elite city public high schools, or private schools), versus a city-wide average of only 8.9 percent. In 1987 alone, more than two hundred District Four youngsters attended Stuyvesant, Bronx Science, Brooklyn Tech, and LaGuardia, a performance nothing short of astounding. Another thirty-five students from District Four were placed into private schools that year on scholarships, including Andover, Westminster, Loomis Chaffee, Brooklyn Friends, Dublin, Hill, Spence, Dalton, Berkshire, Manhattan Country, and Columbia Grammar School. In other words, over a quarter of the district's middle-school graduating class had earned entrance to the kinds of schools that had been completely closed to East Harlem's youth a mere decade before.

Morale soared during those years. The sense of doing something revolutionary was in the air. The teachers, students, and administrators became celebrities around the country and overseas. Secretary of Education William Bennett often pointed to District Four as a poor district that nonetheless offered its students a superior education. President Ronald Reagan invited Carlos Medina and me to the White House for a celebration of outstanding model schools. British Prime Minister Margaret Thatcher sent her minister of education, Kenneth Baker, to visit East Harlem's schools, and followed up by sending Brian Griffiths, her chief domestic policy adviser, on two occasions. Many other educators came from overseas as well. The media were everywhere—all the networks, the *MacNeil/Lehrer News-Hour,* and many others. We were lionized at conferences and our techniques were studied at schools of education around the country.

Perhaps the greatest accolade of all was when word got back to us that the tour guides on the Circle Line cruise around Manhattan were pointing out the Manhattan Center to tourists and telling them it was "the miracle school in the the miracle district." To a bunch of hard-core New Yorkers, the White House and national TV were great, but the Circle Line! That was *really* something.

The ebullient mood of those years was summed up by Sid Schwager, who was the principal of a regular public school in District Four, and a valued comrade-in-arms to regular and alternative-school folk alike. In 1988 two hundred people from District Four had come out in the middle of a blizzard to a surprise party given in my honor, and, when he rose to make a toast, Schwager looked around the room and exclaimed, "This isn't a school district. This is a movement!" And despite hardships and reversals, time was to prove him right.

The New York Times headlined 1987 as a "Year of Honor in

East Harlem Schools," an assessment shared by the John D. and Catherine T. MacArthur Foundation, which awarded one of its vaunted "genius" fellowships to Deborah Meier that year. About the only body that didn't congratulate us was—naturally—the central Board of Education. What we had achieved in District Four not only annoyed them, it made them jealous, and very nervous, too. The only congratulations we received from 110 Livingston Street came for finishing the school year within our budget. But the board was not to remain even that passive for much longer.

Within two years, in fact, the alternative schools of East Harlem would be fighting for their lives as the bureaucracy rose up to reclaim its lapsed prerogatives.

For years the central board had been upset with District Four. It had never officially recognized our alternative schools. To this day, the Board directory does not include the names of the alternative schools in District Four, only of the larger school buildings in which they are housed. When reporting reading or math scores, the alternative schools were included as part of the school buildings in which they were considered registered, despite the fact that a good number were not even in the same building. After years of asking the central board to have the phone numbers of the alternative schools listed in the telephone directory—years during which it was not uncommon for parents to call directory assistance and ask for the name of their child's school only to be told such a school did not exist—I finally dealt directly with the telephone company myself and they agreed to list the alternative school numbers.

One year the principal of J.H.S. 99 received letters of commendation from the principals of two of New York City's most prestigious high schools congratulating him for having the highest percentage of youngsters accepted into their schools. In reality, not one of the J.H.S. 99 kids had been accepted. The acceptances were all for students in three of our alternative schools, who for administrative purposes were carried on the J.H.S. 99 register.

When the alternative schools first started this might have been defensible for a year or two, but after fifteen years of successful operation there was no reasonable excuse for continuing such an obsolete practice. Unless you looked at it from the central board's point of view: The teachers and administrators in District Four were "cowboys"; they ran roughshod over the rules; they were inconvenient; they were out of control; and they made the central board look bad because they were achieving great results.

The central board resented the fact that over the years District Four had competed for funds aggressively. Our response was that other districts could compete as aggressively for funds if they wanted to, so don't blame us for getting the most for our kids that we can. But the central board was determined to cut District Four down to size.

In 1988 something unexpected happened to me. Though I was very happy in District Four and had no plans to leave, I heard about another school district, District Twenty-eight in Queens, that was in the throes of a serious leadership crisis. I was asked if I would accept the superintendency there by a number of people on the board who had accepted the resignation of the previous superintendent, Joseph Petrella; at the same time, however, I was alerted that it would probably be a temporary position due to a pending court action by Petrella against the local school board. At first I was reluctant, but they made me an offer I couldn't refuse! For a fellow who's always advocating risk-taking, it seemed only natural that I take this shot. I left East Harlem to become superintendent of District Twenty-eight.

Within a year District Four suffered a severe blow, when Carlos Medina was suspended from the superintendency on charges of financial impropriety. The charges grew primarily out of political infighting for control of the District Four school board. Medina was suspended without pay while a district "special projects" fund was investigated. The fund had been established to enable the district to respond to needs in a timely fashion instead of being bogged down in the bureaucratic machine. The several thousand dollars in the fund had all been privately raised, and the district had reported on it monthly. No federal, state, or city funds were involved. At the request of Tony Rivera, a local school-board member, Medina had approved a hundred-dollar contribution from the account to buy Christmas presents for children at Metropolitan Hospital. Upon investigation, the central board found other irregular expenditures from the account, all of which showed the humanitarian nature of the funds: Coats had been bought for children who came to school in winter without them; donations had been made to organizations such as the United Negro College Fund; money had been given to parents so that they could bury children who had been killed in neighborhood violence. At the same time, however, accommodations at an education conference had been paid for from the fund which should have been charged differently, and loans had been made to Medina's colleagues. Unlike the loans Alvarado had requested from employees, however, Carlos Medina had not himself borrowed money, and the loans were all repaid. Although technically these were violations, it was not the stuff of scandal.

For a year the Board of Education did not pursue the investigation, and it was presumed dead. Then came the arrest of Matthew Barnwell, a principal in the Bronx who had been caught buying crack. The Inspector General's Office came under pressure to demonstrate that it could police Board of Education affairs, and so they chose a scapegoat. Carlos Medina became a victim of circumstance. He may not have been as vigilant an administrator as he could have been, but Medina's commitment to providing a superior education to the East Harlem community was total, and he never took so much as a cent for personal gain. Nonetheless, Medina paid an inordinately, perhaps uniquely, high price. His suspension was upheld because he did not follow standard operating procedures, and he was not allowed to return to his position—which was a great loss to the district—but no charges of wrongdoing were raised. Over the years Medina's concept of "institutional protection" of the educators in his schools had involved our practice of creative noncompliance with the rules in order to enable his people to realize their visions of what schools could be. Now the system had caught up with him and exacted its revenge.

The newly named acting superintendent, Shirley Walker, was a former deputy superintendent in charge of personnel. For the alternative schools, Walker's temporary promotion was the ultimate "bad news" transition, from a supportive leader to a manifestly hostile superintendent. It wasn't that she wanted to destroy the alternative schools per se; they simply did not figure in her scale of priorities, the alpha and omega of which was never to rock the boat at 110 Livingston Street.

The entire energy and spirit of the alternative-school movement, which so many dedicated teachers had labored to build over fifteen years, was put under severe stress by the new negativity that emanated from the district office. In case we had forgotten it before, the lesson learned once again was that schools are fragile enterprises, and insensitive leadership can be extremely damaging to them.

In this new atmosphere, John Falco, who had now become the Director of the Office of Alternative Schools, waged a valiant campaign to preserve and expand the alternative-school network. He had many valuable allies in the district office who fought alongside him, but the central board, sensing that its moment had come, went for the jugular. As part of the Medina investigation, John Falco was targeted for the flimsiest of reasons. Falco often volunteered to purchase liquor for district Christmas parties, taking advantage of the staff discount he received at a relative's store. Funds for these parties were contributed by district staff out of their own pockets. By securing the discount Falco was, in typical fashion, generously saving everyone money. But because the District accounted for the Christmas party fund in its financial reports, the auditors cited Falco for a "conflict of interest" and put a letter of reprimand in his file.

Then the central board decreed that Falco did not have the appropriate license for the position he filled so capably. He was fired and for the next six months continued to work as the unpaid director of the Office of Alternative Schools until he won reinstatement. Such is the extreme pettiness of the New York City Board of Education.

Colman Genn also came under pressure at the Manhattan Center. After the amazing success of the Manhattan Center's first graduating class, Genn was instructed to eliminate the extra classroom period he had included in the school's curriculum. The Board argued that it was "unfair" to students at other schools who did not have an extra period. We answered that if other schools wanted to add an extra period they should do so, but the central board continued to maintain that the Manhattan Center was "inequitable."

"Where were you when the graduation rate was only seven percent?" I demanded. "Was that equitable?"

We are all in favor of equity, but let's have an equity that

173

brings everybody up, not one that drags everyone down. However, we lost this particular battle, and the ninth period as well.

The central board also had the gall to complain to Genn that the attendance rate at Manhattan Center had declined one tenth of 1 percent, this after Genn had raised attendance levels from an abysmal 44 percent all the way up to 93 percent. As Mark Twain said over a century ago, "There is nothing more annoying than the setting of a good example."

Finally the board tried to remove Genn as the principal of the Manhattan Center because he had failed the necessary licensing exam. This was after he had engineered the greatest turnaround in one school in the history of New York City. Genn immediately appealed the licensing exam result, which was clearly an aberration. At the same time the East Harlem community rose up and threatened to close the school down and take the battle to the streets. In the end the central board backed down long enough for Cole Genn to get his principal's license after obtaining a court injunction preventing the board from filling the principal's vacancy.

In addition to the day-to-day harassment with which the alternative-school directors had become all too familiar, the central board assailed the district in every way it could through the budgetary process. Shirley Walker, true to form, supported the central board in every dispute, even siding with them on the district's deficit. Bryan Spears, director of New York Prep, was outspoken in defense of the alternative schools and thus drew the enmity of the acting superintendent, who blocked his promotion to assistant principal.

At one point the central board's Budget Office suggested that a good way to save money would be to eliminate the positions of the alternative-school directors. Although that idea was quickly squashed, it was no thanks to Walker. In the Office of Alternative Schools, John Falco found it increasingly difficult to operate his programs. Without moral support and with increasingly less financial aid, the situation of the alternative schools became progressively more difficult. The energy that had once flowed into innovative programs and educational vision was now no longer there.

The staff in District Four began to feel demoralized, and

students' achievement test scores began to decline for the entire district. Although it was still true that no New York school district had improved as much as District Four over the past twenty years, the vibrancy of an earlier time appeared to be spent. Many dedicated educators remained, but they found it difficult to maintain their enthusiasm in the face of the growing institutional inertia with which they were confronted.

The ultimate indignity was a 1990 audit of District Four operations, which the central board claimed showed that the district had overspent its 1989–90 budget by $2.5 million. If such a finding were upheld, the impact would have been nothing less than devastating.

Three District Four board members and the leaders of the Alternative Schools Parents Council invited me to assist them in the budget battle. My brief tenure as superintendent of District Twenty-eight was finished, and in 1989 I had retired from the New York City school system after thirty-two years of service. I started a new career as an educational consultant, and later that year I became the Gilder Senior Fellow at the Center for Educational Innovation, a branch of the Manhattan Institute, which seeks to study and promote innovative reforms that lead to excellence in America's public schools.

Using the center's resources, I wanted to sell the idea of public school choice to a wider audience. At the same time, I was determined to shore up choice in its original home. One of my first tasks, then, was to help buttress the alternative-school movement in District Four. No longer officially connected with the school system, I became instead a kind of Ambassador of Choice, continuing the rounds we had begun fifteen years before, listening, advising, exhorting, and helping out the alternative schools, now more than ever in need.

With the Manhattan Institute behind me, I was able to confront the central board's audit of District Four head-on. I suspected that a bogus charge was in the works, and, upon examining the audit findings more closely and conferring with my old associates in the district, we were convinced that the central board had indeed embarked upon a witch hunt. The Board of Education budget people seemed determined to settle old scores with District Four, even if that meant the destruction of schools of choice as a tool of educational reform.

The community school board arranged a meeting with Harvey Robins, the deputy schools chancellor for finance and budget, and asked me to attend. When I arrived at 110 Livingston Street I went up to Robins' office. When Shirley Walker came in and saw me she angrily demanded to know what I was doing at the meeting. Robins also asked me that question, and I replied that I had come at the request of the District Four board members.

At that point Robins left the room to seek guidance from the chancellor's office. When he returned he brusquely told me that I could not attend the meeting. The three members of the local board who were present apologized to me, and I left. The meeting was then held, and Robins, assisted by his staff, proceeded to lecture the community board members on their $2.5 million deficit. The acting superintendent acquiesced to the central board's presentation without making a single objection. The meeting so enraged the three community school board members that they, together with the Alternative Schools Parents Council, complained directly to Bernard Mecklowitz, then the acting chancellor, and he agreed to meet with Debbie Meier and me to discuss the issue.

After some confusion and another attempt to exclude me from the meeting, we aired our differences in a conference room at City College. The president of the Board of Education, Robert F. Wagner, Jr., also attended. At this point Wagner and Mecklowitz presumed that the Budget Office's allegation of a $2.5 million deficit was valid, and they were justifiably disturbed. Meier and I explained that we recognized that deficits were a serious business, but that the Budget Office's projections were nonetheless way off the mark; the true deficit, we said, would only be in the region of $600,000. If the district counted $300,000 in rollover funds from the previous year, the final deficit figure would only be $300,000, less than 1 percent of the total budget. Wagner and Mecklowitz assured us that, if our numbers were accurate, they would no longer have any problem with District Four. They agreed to bring in Jerry Posman, a former deputy chancellor for finance, and Charlotte Frank, former director of curriculum and instruction, two fine public servants, to act as intermediaries in the dispute. Posman, in fact, had told me before he had left his job at the central board a year or two earlier, "Sy, after I'm gone they will find a way to get you." Now I knew how right he was.

Mecklowitz and Wagner also promised us that if we were dissatisfied with the Budget Office's final figures they would agree to an outside auditor to settle the disagreement. The director of the Budget Office remained antagonistic, however, although he quickly revised his deficit estimate down to $2 million even.

The Budget Office assigned a special team to work in the district for six weeks, ostensibly to straighten out the district's finances. In fact, after repeated delays, what they ended up straightening out was their outrageously inflated estimate of our deficit. First they reduced their projection to $1.7 million and finally to $1.2 million.

Meanwhile Mecklowitz was being urged by his staff to "solve" the District Four budget "problem" by eliminating the alternative schools! But before making a decision, he decided to visit District Four's schools unannounced. He loved what he saw, and, to his everlasting credit, he assured us he would do everything he could to help us. Unfortunately, however, Mecklowitz did not have much time to be of help because a permanent chancellor, Joseph Fernandez, was soon named. The District Four board and parents group met with Fernandez, seeking his assistance on the ongoing dispute. Since there was still no resolution, they asked Fernandez to honor the commitment to bring in an outside auditor.

At the same time the Manhattan Institute invited the new chancellor to a "Welcome to New York" luncheon and offered its assistance. I had heard through the grapevine that the Budget Office was already lobbying Fernandez hard on the budget dispute with District Four. I wanted to raise the issue head-on at the luncheon, but Peter Flanigan, the chairman of the Center for Educational Innovation, asked me to be on my best behavior that day, and to be nice to the chancellor. Naturally, I agreed. Chancellor Fernandez arrived with Stanley Litow, the deputy chancellor for operations and Fernandez's chief lieutenant. Raymond Domanico, the director of the CEI, began the program by describing the Center's activities. But as soon as he mentioned District Four in a positive fashion, Litow attacked, belligerently asserting, after all that we had been through, that the district's deficit was over $2 million. I kept my word to Flanigan and was impeccably cordial to Chancellor Fernandez, but I engaged Litow in a heated dispute, during which I told him he had no idea what he was talking about.

The new chancellor was not terribly pleased. He informed Flanigan that he had agreed in his meeting with District Four's Parents' Council to an outside audit and asked if the Manhattan Institute might provide such a service pro bono. Flanigan agreed to the arrangement, and asked Stanley Goldstein, a trustee of the Manhattan Institute and a senior partner in a major accounting firm, to do so.

The audit found that District Four's deficit was approximately $600,000, just as we had said. This did not include the rollover of $300,000 from the previous year, making our total deficit a mere $300,000. Out of a $40 million budget, $300,000 is less than 1 percent. And in the context of a $6.7 billion budget for all of the New York City schools, much of it wasted on a self-serving central bureaucracy, it is a puny sum. If each of the City's thirty-two school districts were given a million dollars and could achieve just half of what we had with the extra $300,000, it would be the biggest bargain in educational history.

Instead, the district was subjected to relentless pressure and was forced to dismantle important elements of its operation. Programs that had been built up lovingly over the years were scrapped. Our chess team, which had traveled all the way to Moscow to play Soviet students, was eliminated. The Little League team was also abandoned. Initiatives in Math, a funded program aimed at developing mathematics skills in youngsters, ran out of money. Work with numerous outside agencies, which had provided professional support for many district programs, came to a halt. The face of the district began to change.

The alternative-schools staffs were no longer conceiving and implementing imaginative new programs. They were now put into a position of continuously having to defend existing schools against bureaucratic attack. In such a climate even the best schools atrophy, and within District Four a feeling of demoralization began to spread, which, if continued, would have been disastrous.

However, in June 1990, a new superintendent was selected

178

for District Four, and this time the appointment brought renewed hope. Marcelino Rodriguez was a successful elementary school principal in District Four who had himself created an alternative junior high school program. He believed strongly in the necessity to develop meaningful educational options for the children of his district. Amiable and highly regarded as a principal, Rodriguez understood that his first task was to re-unify the district. His deputy superintendent, Juana Dainis, had previously been the principal of a traditional elementary school in District Four, but she, too, was committed to the continuation of alternative programs. Her subsequent appointment to the President's Commission on Education was a welcome sign of the esteem in which District Four was held around the country, if not within the New York City educational establishment.

The district fought on. It launched what it called Phase Two District Four Choice Initiative. Acting on his belief that the East Harlem schools must become the center of their community, Rodriguez had brought a variety of resources—health clinics, after-school tutorials, and mentor programs staffed by Hunter College students—to P.S. 72, when he was its principal. As superintendent, Rodriguez now began to implement similar services at other District Four locations.

Rodriguez likes the concept of creating schools that run from kindergarten through the eighth grade. Some existing alternative junior high school directors voiced apprehension about this new emphasis, but Rodriguez has responded quite properly that such a system is merely an extension of choice. Rodriguez is also creating a new alternative-education complex at J.H.S. 45 by moving an elementary school in with the junior high.

One of the ongoing ways Rodriguez has promoted innovation is to encourage Steve Kahn in his effort to provide choices to students in special education. Kahn believes that choice is essential to successful education at all levels, and he has been battling to provide it, even for children with learning problems. In 1992 District Four inaugurated choice in special education. "People have to have choice," says Kahn, "but they have to be good choices. Then we have to help them become smart consumers."

Kahn estimates that the Central Board could save $27 million in its present cost-cutting drive by simply removing from special-education status all those students above the fifty-third percentile in math and reading tests. He argues that in practice this would merely mean removing students from programs they don't really need, allowing students in inner-city areas access to benefits that they are currently denied. Steve Kahn fights hard for his kids, and he has found that the addition of choice is often liberating for students with a history of learning difficulty. It lets them focus on what they really need and gives them a sense of self-confidence in their own abilities.

The students, parents, and teachers of District Four also continue to support choice. Attendance at the district's School Fairs has never been higher. Yet opposition and intransigence persists. When Chancellor Fernandez arrived in New York in 1990, he was skeptical of what we were doing in District Four. We invited him to come see the East Harlem alternative schools himself. He declined the offer with the *Alice in Wonderland* explanation that his Budget Office staff advised him not to go because, if he did, he might become prejudiced in District Four's favor!

Another stumbling block came in the person of Deputy Chancellor Stanley Litow, who had previously headed a coalition of educational associations called the Educational Priorities Panel and gained his current appointment after serving as the staff director of the selection committee that had proposed Fernandez for the chancellorship. Apparently, the central board considered John Falco's discount purchase of liquor for a Christmas party to be a conflict of interest, but Litow's appointment as deputy chancellor by the man he helped recruit to head the system was not.

Litow, who had never run a school in his life, became an outspoken critic of District Four. He even went so far as to deny that we had received assurances of fair treatment from Board President Wagner and Acting Chancellor Mecklowitz. Litow was also critical of choice, a problematic position for him when it came to light that Litow sent his own daughter to St. Ann's, a private, religiously affiliated school in Brooklyn. When confronted at a public meeting, Litow blanched, then admitted it, maintaining weakly, "It was her choice." At the same time, Litow's son was attending an outstanding public elementary school in District Three, which he must have chosen as well, since it was not his designated zoned school.

Yet Litow opposed choice for the one million other New York kids enrolled in schools across the city.

These stories would be merely pathetic if they did not involve the compromising of our children's education. Fernandez and Litow were not the villains of the piece by any means. They are only playing out the archetypal role of central bureaucrats. Indeed, in his third year on the job, Chancellor Fernandez became a vocal proponent of choice within the New York City public school system.

The answer to the woes of huge centralized school systems is not to install new leadership and hope for a powerful new personality to appear on the scene like a white knight to rescue a system in acute distress. There is no Great Man on the horizon, now or in the future. The answer, rather, is to restructure the system, decentralize it, provide a sense of ownership to those who use it, and make it fully accountable for its successes and its failures.

Around the country others saw the wisdom of this approach and were increasingly curious about choice. However, back in New York, choice still faced fierce resistance from within the educational establishment. It is a sad irony that the opponents of choice tend to be people whose concerns would be met most effectively by a choice system: those who fear resegregation, and those who fear that the most disadvantaged students will suffer. Unfortunately, they are joined by bureaucrats who fear the loss of their own power and by teachers who simply do not wish to be shown up by someone succeeding where they have failed. These people wield substantial power in schools, in legislatures, and even in the courts, making choice vulnerable on a number of fronts. What happened in District Four was in many ways so ephemeral that it can all be undone by a few small-minded people—if we let them.

Instead, we must continue, as we did all along in District Four, to create constituencies of students, parents, and teachers in the schools who will help us to initiate, fight for, and ultimately institutionalize meaningful educational reform.

In District Four the battle-scarred veterans of the choice wars continue to fight for and practice what they believe. In 1992

Debbie Meier's CPE secondary school graduated its second class, and for the second year in a row the graduating class had college placements that rivaled the Manhattan Center's—96 percent. One of the graduates, Lindsay Greene, had started at CPE in kindergarten and had stayed there through grade twelve. She is now attending Cornell University on a full scholarship.

Thus, District Four, which only a decade ago had little but frustration and probable failure to offer its students entering their high school years, has now developed two outstanding high schools, while continuing to send a good percentage of its younger students to the city's selective high schools.

And now the earlier group of educational innovators are being joined by a whole new generation of students, parents, and teachers who have embraced their ideals. Under Superintendent Rodriguez the district is moving again. In 1991 the district received New York State Magnet Funds for the first time, enabling it to strengthen further the quality of its alternative schools. The district opened Manhattan West in the fall of 1992, and three new alternative junior high schools are planned for 1993. One is the Peace Academy, whose curriculum will focus on conflict resolution, a topic very much on New Yorkers' minds as violence has escalated, not only on the city streets but in the schools themselves. The second school is a joint project with the Central Park Conservancy, the privately funded group which has so magnificently restored Central Park in the past decade. The third is the Hurston School Academy, which will open for at-risk youngsters, with small class sizes, individual instruction, and heterogeneous groupings. Further on the horizon is a program in conjunction with the Outward Bound organization. These new ventures are vivid reminders that original thinking and educational innovation are still very much alive in East Harlem, and that Phase Two of the District Four story is well under way.

Despite every effort to kill it, and in spite of occasional disappointments and defeats, in District Four both innovation and choice live on and grow stronger day by day. And the district continues to outperform many other districts with far higher per capita income levels.

In District Four the champions of schools of choice started as

182

outsiders but in due course became the district's backbone. The next step was to take choice to other districts, around the city and the country. So some of us have become "outsiders" again, working with schools and districts everywhere, hoping to make public school choice the backbone of our nation's public educational system.

12

Choice and Its Critics

Choice has become a word loaded with associations and connotations. It has no fixed definition, and its meaning often depends upon whether one favors or opposes it. In this chapter we will look at what objections have been raised against choice, how the real-life experience of a choice system stacks up against those criticisms, and the ways in which choice addresses the problems facing American education today.

Few would dispute that America's schools are in serious trouble. Since the publication of *A Nation at Risk* in 1983, educational reform has become one of the country's most widely discussed issues. But the numbers remain deeply disturbing. Grades, test scores, and drop-out rates all suggest that efforts at educational reform are failing. This result has come to pass not because reformers aren't trying hard and not because insufficient money has been spent. The problem, as I have tried to suggest in previous chapters, is that too many reformers are trying to change schools from above, instead of creating new incentives for change from within. Simply put, the things the educational bureaucracy can control generally make no difference in the quality of a school.

The kind of choice plan that evolved in District Four, in contrast, affords school professionals freedom—the freedom to design innovative and distinctive educational programs and to give parents and students the right to select their public schools. And, under these conditions, choice acts as a catalyst for change and makes for dramatic improvement in the quality of education provided by rich and poor school districts alike.

Some people oppose choice because they see it as an indirect way to foster or reintroduce de facto racial segregation in the schools. Others oppose choice because they fear it will lead to a more subtle but still insidious form of segregation. They fear that children of well-informed, activist parents will take up all the places in the best schools, leaving the children of less effective parents to make do with the rest. Choice, these opponents say, is not "equitable." Another point of contention is the conflict over whether parents or school directors should have the final word on school admission. Other critics cite problems of space or of transportation. Still others deplore the notion of schools competing, and say that choice will lead to "skimming" the best students and "dumping" the worst.

Our experience in East Harlem lays to rest all of these criticisms. In the first place, when we started out in East Harlem, the schools were about as segregated as they could get. There was only a tiny fraction of the once vibrant Italian community left in East Harlem, those who were too poor to leave. Otherwise the district was entirely black and Hispanic. By introducing choice schools we actually *integrated* District Four. Students began applying to our schools from all over the city. So from our perspective, the argument that choice will lead to segregated schooling is refuted by the actual experience of District Four.

Regarding the criticism that choice will favor those who are most competent to choose well and will leave others behind, one can readily acknowledge that this might turn out to be a problem, but, again, in District Four it didn't work out that way. The criticism presupposes that all the new alternative schools created in a given district will be targeted to serve the highest performing students, and that premise was simply not true in District Four, nor would it necessarily be true elsewhere. Educators come in many different varieties with many different motivations and interests. In District Four we were blessed to have people like John Falco and Mary Romer Coleman, who specifically devoted themselves to working with the most problematic sector of the student population. We had Beryl Epton, who decided that it was essential to start a new early elementary program to get kids with learning problems on the right track as early as possible. Mike Friedman and Sandy Rinaldo at the Bridge School also focused on students who were not, initially at least, likely Nobel Prize winners. And, as we have illustrated throughout this book, even in schools with outstanding success rates like CPE or the Manhattan Center, many kids with severe learning or emotional handicaps were accepted who flourished in the nurturing environments they found there.

Furthermore, the argument that a choice system will leave the poorest of the poor behind patronizes the poor and badly underestimates them. Our experience in East Harlem was that, when poor parents were provided with information, they fought as hard if not harder to educate themselves and their children as to their options and how to realize them within a choice system. I am all for sensitivity and concern for the poor, but only if it provides positive options, not if it is used, as some well-meaning people inadvertently do, to restrict poor people's limited range of choices even further.

A good choice system does not harm even the least skillful chooser, because in a properly functioning system of choice all of the schools are offering sound, viable programs. The idea is not that choice offers good schools if you are clever enough to discern which ones they are, but that choice offers a wide array of options, all of high quality. Under such a system inappropriate student to school match-ups can occasionally occur, but there is no reason to assume that a poorly chosen school should be any more injurious to a particular youngster than his assigned school would be. Remember, when we started in District Four, only 16 percent of the students were reading at grade level, and the further we got away from the assigned school system the higher the reading levels soared. And, unlike the student unhappily trapped in an assigned school, the student in a choice system caught in unhappy circumstances has the advantage of being able to transfer.

This raises the question of equity. Choice systems, some critics say, aren't equitable. I suppose what they mean by this is that since some schools offer one course of study and others another, some schools must be better than others. This is not necessarily so. As we have tried to make clear, the whole point of a choice system is to offer enough options for every student to learn in the way that is best for him or her as opposed to forcing every student to suffer through a stultifying, uniform curriculum decreed from above and taught without enthusiasm.

There is a further point to be made about equity. When District Four was the worst school district in the city *no one* raised the question of equity. They wanted to ignore the district entirely. But when we had tremendous success with the Manhattan Center, and every student graduated and went to college, the Board of Education became very concerned with the equity question. They examined the school closely and discovered that it had installed an additional class period each day to help get the students through its challenging curriculum. The board said that wasn't "equitable" and cut back its budget allocation for the following year.

"Where were you when this school was failing?" we asked. "Where were you when this place had a graduation rate of seven percent?" Not a soul had raised the equity issue then, but as soon as we had begun to achieve something worthwhile there were little minds who wanted to destroy it. It has been said that patriotism is the last refuge of a scoundrel. In education today, however, it is "equity." Equity is a great idea, and we are all in favor of it, but let's concentrate less on equities that level down and more on equities that level up.

A convincing rebuttal to the criticism that choice is too expensive is supplied by Debbie Meier. She points out that although her Central Park East Schools never received anything extra from the New York City school system, they did benefit from additional private and governmental resources which those in the district office secured. But Meier argues eloquently that the ultimate cost to society of operating effective centers of learning like hers is in the long run a net savings:

We have less teenage pregnancy, less truancy, less absenteeism; we maintain virtually all of our students regardless of handicapping conditions, and thus refer fewer students to expensive, self-contained special education classes. Thus, the costs that go with our smaller size can and should be balanced against the monies we save the city by solving real problems—not to mention the incalculable financial advantage of having better educated young people.

I keep thinking about a staggering figure. It costs $50,000 just to put one teenager on trial and another $50,000 if we put him or her away for a year. Programs like ours prevent results like that at a fraction of the cost.

Regarding the issue of whether the school or the student makes the final decision on admission, we came down on the side of the school making that decision. The critical point is to make sure a school admissions policy is fair to all concerned, unlike lotteries and other ersatz solutions. Although lotteries may be equitable (because the risks of not getting one's choice are the same for all), they are definitely not fair. Lotteries penalize students who are willing to work hard to get what they want and teach exactly the reverse—that luck is what matters most, and the system rewards truants and scholars equally.

In District Four, where we pioneered school-based management, it would have been hypocritical for us to force students onto schools. (Chapter 7 demonstrates how fairly our match-up system worked in practice.)

Choice does have real problems. Space can be a problem, especially when a school suddenly becomes popular. When that happens, however, it is always possible to expand the school the following year or, as we did with CPE, to start an entirely separate, new school operating on the same principles. Transportation can also become an expensive proposition in a choice system, especially in geographically dispersed districts. That, of course, was not a problem for us in the concentrated urban setting of East Harlem.

Some people consider it unseemly or unhealthy for schools to compete against each other for students. We found, however, that competition was good for our schools. That was one reason District Four put alternative and regular schools into the same building. If a school on the fourth floor is having interesting field trips, outside performers coming in, and other exciting things happening, it is unlikely that the students and teachers on the third floor will say, "That's fine for them, but not for us." Life doesn't work that way. At P.S. 50, where the East Harlem Performing Arts School was housed, the regular public school developed one of the strongest performing arts programs in the district. Competition helped to upgrade quality and to cross-germinate new ideas.

Perhaps the most famous outgrowth of this new entrepreneurial spirit came in the spring of 1981. Gus Torres, the principal of P.S. 121, read an article in *The New York Times* about a wealthy businessman named Eugene Lang, who had recently given Swarthmore College six million dollars. The article mentioned that Lang had attended P.S. 121, and so Torres invited the philanthropist to be the guest speaker at the upcoming sixth grade commencement. Lang accepted, returning to the school fifty years after his own graduation. He started his talk by recounting to the students how inspirational he had found Martin Luther King, Jr.'s "I Have a Dream" speech. Graduation should be a time of dreams for students as well, he said, at which point he departed from his prepared text and announced that he would personally pay the college tuition for each of the sixty-one students, if they successfully completed high school. This was the beginning of the "I Have a Dream" program. Lang later provided academic counseling for his adopted class through high school and met regularly with the students, providing enrichment experiences and support. Thirty-eight of the original sixty-one students have attended college. Other benefactors, following Lang's example, have sponsored thousands of students across the country. In District Four, five schools have participated in the program.

If a school is not providing its students with a superior education, no one should be forced to go to that school. Sure, some schools, teachers, administrators, and bureaucrats will be embarrassed if nobody chooses their school. But if the school is that bad it should be shut down, because no child should be forced to attend a failing school.

In District Four, when the Sports School failed to live up to our expectations, we reorganized it around a different theme and renamed it New York Prep. Thereafter, it thrived. When Music 13 did not meet the standards of other schools in the district, so many students opted out of it that it had to be closed down. On the other hand, when a school like Debbie Meier's CPE succeeded so impressively that it was swamped with applications, we did not just sit there and gloat. We started another school using the "open classrooms" methodology, CPE II, to accommodate the demand, and when that became oversubscribed we created a third, River East.

Many opponents of choice complain that not enough objective evidence is available to judge choice on its merits. But if one were to insist upon this experimental research standard to judge existing schools, it would also be impossible to say anything in education worked, from forty-five minute class periods, to division of functions for teachers, to the assignment of children to twelve grade levels. There is no research supporting these either. Even so, in Buffalo a study showed that schools of choice in a district improved general achievement, even in the traditional public schools. Studies of magnet schools in fourteen New York districts, in Montgomery County, Maryland, and in Montclair, New Jersey, have reached similar conclusions. And of course our experience in East Harlem amply documents and quantifies exactly how dramatically a choice system can transform student performance.

Moreover, there is plenty of data from District Four itself (see Appendix) as well as from educational researchers like Mary Ann Raywid of Hofstra University and others which back up our claims as to what has been accomplished when choice has been introduced. We also know they are true, not because we have analyzed the research material with the care of a social scientist, but because we have seen all of these things happen in practice in East Harlem.

Over the last twenty years the number of students in District Four reading at or above grade level increased 23 percent, twice as much as the New York City average. On a percentage basis, the district places almost three times as many of its middle school graduates into New York City's selective high schools as does the average New York City school district. Out of the June 1992 graduating classes over three hundred students were admitted to these elite institutions. The district's reputation is so widespread across the city that over a thousand students stream into East Harlem every morning to take advantage of its outstanding schools.

Finally, choice's opponents argue that choice alone will not make good schools. Indeed, a recent study by the Carnegie Foundation for the Advancement of Teaching, one of our country's most respected organizations, raised just this argument. Well, we agree. To build good schools you need committed, talented teachers, involved parents, and autonomy from the central school bureaucracy. As we indicated earlier, choice is merely a catalyst for change that can spur these schools to develop. Its importance lies in creating a break with a centrally controlled format where any form of innovation is discouraged.

It would be one thing to oppose choice if the present system were really doing its job. But the fact is, despite two successive waves of educational reform, our young people are falling farther behind their counterparts around the world with each passing year. Our schools are not performing as they should; a major part of the reason they aren't is that the students, parents, and teachers involved with them do not choose to be there.

Centralized educational bureaucracy reigns supreme, its own paramount concern being self-perpetuation while allowing little or no autonomy to its employees down the line. During the past twenty years the control of our country's schools has moved ever more in the direction of district offices, states, and the federal government. Schools have become not so much institutions of learning as agents of disaffection, and teachers and students alike have come to feel an increasing psychic estrangement from them. The principal does not choose his school. He is assigned. The principal does not choose his teachers. They, too, are assigned to him. Nor do the teachers choose their principal, or even their school. Neither the school nor the principal choose the organizing theme of the school, or the curriculum, or even the textbooks. Finally, neither the parents nor the children choose their own schools. They too are assigned, on the utterly arbitrary basis of where they happen to live. And no matter how unsuccessful such a school is, new students are assigned to it each fall.

Parents in general feel that they have little to say about the education of their children. Our social problems, particularly in the cities, are getting worse rather than better.

Is it any wonder, then, given this suffocating bureaucratic strangulation from above, that students grow disheartened, and fewer than 40 percent of inner-city high school students graduate on time? Furthermore, fewer than half of those who do graduate go on to college, leaving the rest at a severe disadvantage to compete in contemporary society.

Ironically, few of the criticisms of the potential problems in a choice system are ever directed toward the present public school system even though it could never refute them as convincingly as does our experience in District Four. The public school system has fallen prey to all the problems the critics ascribe to choice: It is often segregated, inequitable to those without political connections and a "dumping ground" for the most disadvantaged students. If we were starting out to build a public education system for this country from ground zero, would we give it the same structure we have now all over again? Of course not. So why not change what's wrong with it now?

The nationally perceived need for radical change in our system of education has given rise to a number of possible solutions. One that is frequently proposed is a voucher system, wherein public money is given not to a specific school, but to the individual student, who is then free to choose whatever school—public, private, or religious—he wishes to attend. In recent years, vouchers have attracted vocal support from private school and free market champions, and intense hostility from supporters of the existing public schools. Christopher Whittle's Edison Project proposes to build a thousand new model schools, run on a for-profit basis, although whether or not this is feasible without vouchers supplying some of the revenue is a subject of much debate among observers. Finally, a new kind of school, the charter school, is being attempted in a pilot program in Minnesota. Major charter school legislation has been passed in California, and the idea is catching on elsewhere. Charter schools are schools that meet minimum state requirements but are operated by colleges, foundations, community organizations, or even just by groups of like-minded teachers free of intereference from an intrusive and ineffective central bureaucracy. Although it is too early to tell, the charter school model could break the logjam between supporters and enemies of school vouchers, and may prove to be a potent new means of innovation and reform in the next generation of publicly funded American schools.

For the immediate future, however, there is already a tried-and-tested solution. After all, as I pointed out in chapter 1, 88 percent of our country's children attend public schools. Even if private schools were to double in size, 76 percent of America's students would still be attending public schools. It is there that improvement is needed most, and as quickly as possible. The best way to improve the nation's public schools is to set in motion the wheels of choice.

The results are difficult to dispute. Rather than repeat the statistics, I prefer to put it this way: Before we started the alternative-school movement in District Four, its schools were the worst in the city, and not likely to get better. That meant that the kids who were attending those schools were being consigned to a failing system which would leave them without the training or the confidence to escape what has been called the poorest neighborhood in the country. Within fifteen years, however, we were sending 25 percent of our middle school graduates to the most selective New York City high schools. Think of what that meant for those kids! And then we created two excellent high schools in District Four, which had previously had none. Thanks to choice, we were able to give thousands of kids a better future than they would otherwise have had.

But choice's benefits are not limited to students. Teachers also are liberated and inspired by choice. In District Four, a number of the alternative-school directors would have never become school leaders were it not for choice. Affirmative action programs, local politics, and the curious non-logic of the bureaucracy would have stymied many worthy educators. But the beautiful thing about choice was that it gave many great teachers the chance to do something special. Deborah Meier, Colman Genn, Beryl Epton, Bob Gyles, John Falco, and many other terrific people found in choice the means they had been looking for to express and develop their own individual educational vision.

Properly implemented, choice is the best hope America has for improving its public schools in general and its urban schools in particular. Although at the national level choice was originally embraced by the Republican Party, locally it has often been spearheaded by Democratic governors and state-level leaders. Regardless of ideology, people are attracted to something that works. And this is also true for the average American. A September 1992 Gallup poll found that 70 percent of those interviewed favored choice. Support among minority parents is higher, at 88 percent. And support for choice among parents with earnings under $15,000 is an astronomical 95 percent.

The transformation of East Harlem's schools can be a model for reversing problems in the schools and society on a national level. We believe that bureaucracy does not solve problems; it creates them. We understand better than ever today that there is no such thing as just one way to educate all children. These forces are leading us in the direction of de-bureaucratization, decentralization, school-site autonomy, and choice for parents, students, and teachers.

It worked in District Four, and, as I will discuss in the next chapter, despite every attempted attack on choice by its would-be critics, there is more than sufficient reason to believe that it will work in many other places as well.

13 Moving Beyond East Harlem

I n his weekly column, printed in *The New York Times* of August 9, 1992, Albert Shanker, president of the American Federation of Teachers, praised District Four as he had done several times in the past:

Everyone has heard about the great virtues of District Four in New York City. It's in East Harlem, a neighborhood where people expect to find lousy schools. Yet it has outstanding teachers and supervisors who have come up with exciting and original ways of teaching kids. Parents from all over the city try to get their children into District Four schools; people all over the country hold these schools up as examples.

Shanker went on to raise the crucial question of how well these results can be replicated in the rest of the city and in the country as a whole:

There are plenty of excellent alternative schools in the United States —and there have been for years. But they are a lot more like rare perennials than like the kind of flower that once planted spreads out until it takes over a garden. . . . Though District Four has been around for over a decade, it has hardly spread at all; there are no District Four spin-offs in Tulsa or Helena and only one or two others like it in New York City.

Well, we haven't quite reached Oklahoma and Montana yet, but that doesn't mean the East Harlem experience is not spreading. One of the most heartening aspects of the District Four story for me and for all of us who have been involved has been watching schools of innovation and excellence and the concept and practice of choice spread beyond East Harlem's borders to other parts of New York City and the country. So far District Three on Manhattan's Upper West Side has made the most progress in this direction, and, by 1992, had twenty-four alternative schools to offer its children, parents, and teachers. Later in this chapter I will explain more about this development.

But this is not the only good news to report. Things are beginning to change in New York City. We have finally made a major breakthrough at the central Board of Education. New York City Schools Chancellor Joseph A. Fernandez announced in August 1992 a plan to create thirty new theme high schools, of significantly smaller size, with the help of community and religious groups, cultural organizations, labor unions, and businesses. The New York City school system has now embraced the District Four model. Announcing the award of planning grants for fourteen of these new "theme" high schools, Chancellor Fernandez said, "Planned from the ground up by the community, parents, and teachers the schools will foster student choice and innovative instruction responsive to the diversity of our student population."

At the invitation of the Chancellor, District Four's own Debbie Meier will be creating seven to ten of these thirty new high schools on the model of her successful Central Park East schools. Working alongside Brown University professor Theodore Sizer, Meier will attempt to raise $3 million in three years from sources outside the tax rolls, in order to bring her innovative ideas into the mainstream.

The biggest boost of all came just one month later, on September 16, 1992, when Fernandez announced, according to *The New York Times,* that he "will let parents send their children to any school outside their district throughout New York City's five boroughs next year," giving the city one of the largest school choice arrangements in the nation. This plan was approved by the Board of Education in January 1993. (It would be the last time a majority of the central board and the chancellor would agree on any issue of importance. Before the month of February ended, the board decided not to renew Fernandez's contract.)

I am happy to say that my colleagues at the Center for Educational Innovation and I are already involved in helping to create important new schools all around the city. That shouldn't be surprising when one considers that two of my new associates are Carlos Medina and Colman Genn. Genn joined the Center as a senior fellow in 1991, after having served a tumultuous term as superintendent of District Twenty-seven in Queens, where he gained fame for going undercover to expose corruption by members of the local school board. Genn secretly taped board members offering bribes and kickbacks, and when the story hit the front pages of the New York papers in October 1989, he was celebrated as the "hero superintendent." In real terms, however, his whistle-blowing meant the end of a thirty-year career in the New York City public school system.

On the Center's initiative, a unique new high school for students suspended from regular high schools will be run by the Wildcat Services Corporation of downtown Manhattan, which has successfully rehabilitated former criminal offenders. We have several other irons in the fire: In District Fourteen in Williamsburg, Brooklyn, the Beginning with Children Foundation is creating a bilingual elementary school; the rigorously scholastic Frederick Douglass Academy in District Five in Harlem is being built from scratch by Principal Lorraine Monroe; and the innovative Flag and Mohegan schools and the accelerated P.S. 92 are a ray of hope in District Twelve in the South Bronx. Finally, after spending seven long years trying to change the failing Thomas Jefferson and Bushwick high schools, the East Brooklyn Congregations' two new six-hundred-student High Schools of Public Service in Bushwick and East New York will eventually replace them, and we are helping with this project. (These schools are explained in further detail later in the chapter.)

We have also been working with school officials in New Jersey, North Carolina, Maryland, Pennsylvania, and Puerto Rico to build systems of autonomous and academically diverse institutions. We are not, however, the only ones involved in spreading the gospel of choice and innovative schools—not by a long shot. Which is how it should be. A number of people haven't waited for us to show up. They've rolled up their sleeves and started building schools of choice for themselves. In cities such as Cambridge, Fall River, Milwaukee, Minneapolis, Rochester, San Francisco, and Detroit, choice programs of varying kinds are under way. And more are sure to follow.

Choice has already crossed national boundaries. After carefully examining District Four, the British government revamped its educational system and introduced a choice system in 1989. Local autonomy and the removal of bureaucratic interference have been vigorously pursued. In France, the Netherlands, Germany, and Canada choice systems have been installed to varying degrees.

In New York City, Manhattan's Upper West Side has led the way in following East Harlem's example, using choice to break the years-long pattern of uneven instruction. District Three, in fact, is more socially diverse than District Four; reaching from 57th Street to 125th Street, from the Hudson River to Central Park, it includes the neighborhoods around Columbia University, Lincoln Center, and Fordham University's midtown campus. There is middle-income co-op housing in the Lincoln Center area, and professors and their families in the Columbia area. The neighborhood became known in the 1980s for attracting young, upscale professionals, but there are also working-class housing projects in the center of the district, and tenements in central Harlem at the northern end. In the district's more than forty schools, with a student population of about fourteen thousand—similar to District Four's—white students account for only 11 percent of enrollment. The rest of the student population is mainly black and Hispanic.

Since 1974, however, a significant number of students from the Upper West Side have been transferring to the alternative schools in East Harlem as word of our success has spread. Other District Three students went to private schools, if they could afford the tuition. So, when Anton Klein became superintendent of District Three in 1986, he realized that the enrollment in the schools of his district had seriously declined and that it was up to him, as an entrepreneur of education, to attract his neighborhood's youngsters back to the neighborhood schools. To restore his district, Klein would have to compete with District Four.

The Wadleigh School was a natural place to start. Wadleigh stands at 215 West 114th Street, between Seventh and Eighth avenues. It is named for a nineteenth-century educator, Lydia Wadleigh, of Sutton, New Hampshire, who came to New York to run the Twelfth Street Advanced School for Girls and later helped to found the City Normal College, now Hunter College.

Many fine people came out of the old Wadleigh, but by the late 1980s it had become a nightmare. Scaffolding was permanently up around the building to protect students from falling masonry. The school, which had opened in 1903, had not received serious maintenance in many years. In some parts of the building, only the original coat of paint had ever been applied and had long since peeled away. Walls were falling down. There was water damage everywhere. Had the building been anything but a school it would have been condemned by the city long before.

Wadleigh's capacity was about fifteen hundred, but only enough space was minimally usable to house a five-hundred-student middle school. And even this was a disaster. Students were running wild in the halls. Closets were piled high with textbooks that had never been distributed. Classrooms were bare and bulletin boards were empty. Anything put up on them was ripped down or set on fire. On average, a third of Wadleigh's teachers called in sick every day.

The girl's gym was situated, believe it or not, directly above the library. But this didn't make any difference, because the last books had disappeared from the library years ago, and no one ever used it. Kids went into the lab rooms when teachers weren't there and threw glass jars filled with fetal pigs and gallon bottles of hydrochloric acid out the windows and five stories down onto 114th Street.

District Four's John Elwell had been named by Superintendent Klein as director of District Three's Office of Alternative Schools. Soon after Elwell began his new job in District Three, he asked me to visit Wadleigh with him and recommend what should be done with it.

I was shocked. It was the worst school I had ever seen in my life.

"John," I said, with an intensity that surprised even me, "You've got to close this place and figure out how to clean it up before you let them use it as a school."

It was an extreme remedy, but one that had to be taken. The school was a disgrace.

Elwell agreed with me, as did Superintendent Klein. And yet it was no easy task to close the school down. Parents were afraid that their school was being taken from them. They had been promised many things over the years by the central board and had been cruelly disappointed every time. The chairperson of the local UFT chapter particularly resisted the change. If the school were to close, she wanted to control the process, in order, in Elwell's sardonic phrase, "to be able to continue doing the same wonderful job they had always done."

And if the old Wadleigh were to close, what was the new Wadleigh to be? A thousand-student high school featuring a biomedical studies emphasis was suggested by one group, but they never presented a formal proposal for the idea. After canvassing the community and looking at how best to optimize the district's strengths, Elwell and Klein swung into action with a plan that soon won a broad local consensus.

They envisioned a successful complex of three alternative middle schools within the old Wadleigh. In addition to vastly improved facilities for children, there would be research libraries, conference rooms, and suitable offices for teachers. Knowing nothing would ever be achieved if they worked only within the system, Elwell approached me to ask about the possibility of outside support.

It so happened that, at the recommendation of Peter Flanigan, chairman of the CEI, I had recently met a most impressive individual, Reuben Mark, the chief executive officer of Colgate-Palmolive, a corporation whose annual revenues run into the billions of dollars. At the time he was also chairperson of the New York Partnership educational committee. Mark is passionately convinced that our nation needs to transform its education system, but when I was sent to see him, he was opposed to school choice, and we wanted the Partnership to endorse the idea of public school choice.

I showed Mark a tape of a *MacNeil/Lehrer NewsHour* segment on District Four's schools of choice and, in response, he asked me a series of thought-provoking questions about how such a system operates. Mark and I got along well, and he gave me some good suggestions on better ways to market the choice concept. It was clear to me that Mark is a man who likes action. So I said to him, "If you really want to get involved in a challenging situation, I want to get you involved in the Wadleigh School complex." I gave him a brief description of what Wadleigh looked like to me, and he was obviously interested.

I then set up a meeting with Klein, Elwell, and Mark at Colgate-Palmolive's offices. The meeting went well, and Mark agreed to visit the school the next day.

Thus began one of the most successful corporate-school relationships in effect today. Within a matter of days, Mark's enthusiasm and innovative dynamism had turned this modest plan into a major $48 million project in which the entire building would be rebuilt. Colgate-Palmolive would be heavily involved, not only financially but also in helping to plan the new complex and in working with students.

We met initial resistance to the plan from the District Three community school board, but after a stormy board meeting, the plan was approved.

The three schools to be housed at Wadleigh are the School of Writing and Publishing, the School of Science and Technology, and the Wadleigh Alternative Arts Middle School. Writing and Publishing concentrates on the use of language and "writing with a purpose." The school operates its own publishing company where students produce books, magazines, and a newspaper. Colgate contributes personnel to work in the school, and staff development and technical assistance are provided by the Bank Street College of Education and Columbia University Teachers College.

The Science and Technology School aims to provide each student with the cognitive and cultural skills necessary for success in an increasing technological society. It has separate labs for computer training, scientific reasoning, and technology workshops. When the Science and Technology School experienced a rocky beginning and failed to control its original students, the school was completely revamped, and a strong new director was brought in.

The Wadleigh Alternative Arts Middle School is committed to educating the whole child. It provides a small, supportive environment, and, although the curriculum is arts-driven, it is designed to teach critical thinking skills. The Alternative Arts School has programs with the Juilliard School, the Whitney Museum, the Studio Museum of Harlem, and corporate support from Colgate and Time Warner.

All of the Wadleigh alternative schools are up and running this year at other locations in the district. Thus, the new complex will not be starting from scratch when it opens in the fall of 1993. The new schools will be moved into the new Wadleigh over the summer in time to start the school year, and Wadleigh will be well on its way to becoming a true community of learning.

After redesigning Wadleigh, the leadership of District Three was more convinced than ever that a system of district-wide choice was the best possible answer for the district's long-term needs. Superintendent Klein established a Committee on School Choice to help design components of a choice policy. District leaders held weekly strategy sessions, and eventually a Blueprint for Choice emerged. As the plan was refined, Klein enlisted the support of the district's educators. Some were initially apprehensive about change, but their skepticism disappeared once they realized that choice would enable them to design and run the kind of schools they had always dreamed of —schools that put learning first. Parents were easier to convince. After all, for more than a decade a significant number of District Three parents had been sending their children to the schools of choice in District Four.

But before they could begin, the District Three community school board had to approve the new choice plan. The Upper West Side has always been a hotbed of political activism, and District Three has a notoriously combative board, with, as one wag described it, "twenty-one different caucuses for only nine members." Despite some fierce debate and backstage maneuvering, however, in early 1991 the motion to adopt a district-wide choice plan won unanimous approval from the District Three board.

Like East Harlem before it, the Upper West Side is proving to be fertile ground for educational innovation. The Crossroads School, housed on the fifth floor of P.S. 165 on West 109th Street, is the first middle school to be accepted by Theodore Sizer's Coalition of Essential Schools. Under the guidance of Director Ann Wiener, Crossroads is dedicated to a rigorous yet personalized education, and its special focus is writing. All children work on computers, there is a community service program, and the Chase Manhattan Bank has given the school an Active Learning Grant.

The Family School opened in the fall of 1991 with combined district and private support. Directed by David Liben, who worked with Elwell at the Sports School in District Four, the Family School seeks to address one of the most crucial of inner-city problems—familial disintegration—by creating a family atmosphere within its walls. School does not end after six hours. There are significant before-school and after-school support groups. Younger siblings and parents are instructed in addition to primary students. The school is open during the summer months to provide a sense of continuity in young lives that are all too fractured. A family assistance worker acts as a counselor to all fifty families involved in the school. Whatever crises arise, support systems are in place to help. The Family School follows the work of James Comer at Yale University and addresses head-on some of the problems described by Jonathan Kozol in his 1991 book, *Savage Inequalities*. It started with two kindergarten classes and will grow, a year at a time, to a full kindergarten through grade five school over the next five years.

An exciting partnership between the district and the American Museum of Natural History has resulted in the creation of the Museum School. Richard Gilder, chairman of the Manhattan Institute and a trustee of the museum, is the driving force behind this extraordinary development. His support of the project comes with significant financial assistance.

One of the most vibrant centers of alternative education in District Three is the O'Shea Complex at Intermediate School 44 on West 77th Street. The O'Shea Complex is composed of six mini-schools: Arts and Humanities, Bilingual, the Discovery Program, Environmental Studies, Science, and SEEK (Students Entitled to Enrichment and Knowledge). Discovery is a special education program for those students who have both a learning impairment and a gift or talent in an academic or arts area. SEEK is also a special education mini-school providing handicapped students a small, self-contained classroom experience. Both special ed programs mainstream students into as many school-wide activities as possible, including general education, sports, and choir.

The prime mover behind the O'Shea Complex is I.S. 44 Principal Bill Colavito, another alumnus of East Harlem. Inspired by Pop Cavello's book, *The Heart Is a Teacher*, Colavito entered the school system in 1963, a year after graduating from City College of New York. His first taste of working in an alternative school came at the Harbor School in District Four, where he taught English and reading. He recalls his time there:

We were buried in the basement of a building the way alternative schools usually are. The people in the traditional school upstairs complained that whenever they yelled at our kids, they simply answered, "Harbor!" The upstairs dean complained to me. "They act like they have diplomatic immunity. They act like they own the school." And I answered, "They do own the school! That's what we're all about."

Colavito had succeeded Colman Genn as the director of Harbor, and later served as the assistant director of the Office of Alternative Schools in District Four. He is, therefore, as experienced as anyone teaching today in implementing choice programs. Unlike many turf-conscious principals who fear the erosion of power that comes with sharing authority with alternative-school directors, Colavito has welcomed and even recruited schools of choice to I.S. 44. It has become District Three's first Alternative Education Complex. Still, even Colavito is surprised at the rapidity with which District Three has moved to embrace choice. "Two years ago I remember saying, 'I hope I live to see the day choice comes to District Three.' Suddenly, it's here."

It is indeed. Twenty-four schools of choice were established in District Three as of 1992, as many as in District Four. The School Fairs organized by the district every fall since 1991 produced an overwhelming turnout. More than twelve hundred students and their parents attended the fairs each year, held in school cafeterias, where alternative-school directors and teachers stood behind display tables "selling" their educational programs to prospective "buyers."

John Elwell and his assistant director, Liz Sostre, have brought parent participation to new heights in the district by forming a coalition of parents and teachers who meet regularly to discuss operational aspects of their schools. A key concern among some black parents in this 89-percent minority district was that after years of neglect of the Harlem schools of District Three, their revival would lead to an invasion of white students taking away the available places of local residents. A formula to prevent this, reserving a set percentage of places in Wadleigh and the other schools for those students who live in the immediate area, has been devised and endorsed by all sides. At the same time, as school districts across the country show a trend toward gradual resegregation, the effect of introducing choice in District Three has been to integrate schools there more than they have ever been before.

The early results of District Three's program are promising. By Christmas 1991, 98 percent of the two thousand fifth graders in District Three had already made their choices for the following September, a remarkable record for the first year of a radical new program. Sostre has been organizing staff development seminars to help teachers inform their students about their full range of options. Along the same lines, a Middle Schools Directory for District Three has been written and distributed to assist the parents in choosing middle schools for their children.

The cost of all this, moreover, is surprisingly low. The start-up costs for most alternative schools range between $7,500 and $10,000, primarily for books and materials. The key is to start small, with only one or two classes at first, allowing the new schools to solve their initial problems and refine their missions. Elwell ensures that the needs of the alternative-school directors are met, assisting in everything from the ordering of textbooks to the allocation of classrooms. "Once the parents grasp the potential of choice to do good for their children," he says, "no one can stand in their way. The parents won't let them."

At the same time, Elwell continues to encourage teachers and other school-level professionals to come forward with their own educational visions. The ideas are subjected to a rigorous review and the most promising proposals are submitted for approval to the community school board's Alternative Schools Committee, and, ultimately, to the Board of Education. If approved (and they are increasingly so), Superintendent Klein and Director Elwell allocate funds and fill the small number of staff positions necessary to start a new school.

Enthusiasm is running so high for the schools of choice in District Three that there will be three or four new middle schools opening in the next several years and five to ten alternative elementary schools, one of which will be housed in each traditional elementary school building. Then, as happened in District Four, the alternative schools will likely spur the traditional schools to do better. Excitement is growing in the district. Parents who had previously felt disenfranchised have begun to return to the community. They are creating a demand for good schools which the district leadership will have to fill.

District Three is alive with ideas, energy, and excitement. Middle school enrollment has grown by 43 percent, as many of those who fled the district in its weaker years are now coming back. In 1992 over 500 students returned to the public schools in District Three.

Even longtime opponents of choice seem to sense that something special is going on, and want to be involved. David Sherman, the vice president of the UFT, told Elwell, "This is the best thing happening for teachers and kids in all of New York City."

Most amazing of all, the central board itself, which had for so long made a practice of ignoring choice and denying alternative schools official recognition, has at last expressed interest in capitalizing on the choice program offered by District Three. Even Deputy Chancellor Stan Litow has jumped on the bandwagon. He is hoping to set up minibus tours of the district schools of choice for CEOs of companies that might support New York City schools in the same way that Colgate and Time Warner are supporting Wadleigh.

After touring District Three as its conversion to a choice system began, Professor Nathan Glazer of the Harvard University School of Education sounded a note of optimism: "District

Three is now expanding choice, with its accompanying requirements of encouraging enterprise among teachers, creating new
schools, and educating parents and students to a new approach
to public education. I believe it cannot but be for the best."

With parents choosing and children learning, District Three
is well on its way to justifying the faith that Sherman, Litow,
Glazer, and others—most important, its students and parents
—have invested in it.

And other districts around the city, the state, the country,
and the world are not far behind.

In Bushwick and East New York, a grass-roots coalition of
church groups called the East Brooklyn Congregations, who
have already enjoyed immense success in providing low-income
housing to poor neighborhoods through the Nehemiah Project, are now planning two new autonomous high schools that
will be truly responsive to their community's needs. The zoned
public high school for the area, Thomas Jefferson, is a failing,
violence-ridden institution, the site of three tragic student kill-
ings in the 1991–1992 school year. The new schools, the East
Brooklyn High Schools for Public Service, will integrate school-
based community service into the curriculum with the intention
of communicating to young people the nobility of public service
while at the same time teaching them techniques of community
empowerment. These two new alternative high schools say they
will offer "hope at home"; that is, for the first time there will
be meaningful education in the communities where their students live. Both institutions will, of course, be schools of choice.

Chancellor Joseph Fernandez has given his approval for
these new schools to go forward, embracing the concept of
smaller high schools organized around communities and
themes, and even expanding this plan to the building of thirty
new such public high schools. Without explicitly crediting District Four, the Board of Education has adopted its philosophy.
Colman Genn is working closely with the East Brooklyn High
Schools of Public Service to help ensure they achieve results
similar to those at District Four's innovative high school, the
Manhattan Center.

All of the veterans of District Four, including those of us
at the Center for Educational Innovation, are moving in the
direction recently outlined by the chancellor. We are pleased

to see the Board of Education come around to our way of thinking at last; we will do everything we can to help.

Carlos Medina, now a senior fellow and director of the Innovative Schools Project, is working closely with Principal Jeff Litt and his staff at another alternative school of choice, the Mohegan Elementary School, in District Twelve in the South Bronx. Situated in the burnt-out landscape of the Tremont neighborhood (infamous for the Happy Land Social Club, where eighty-seven people lost their lives in a tragic fire in 1990), the Mohegan School's curriculum is based upon E. D. Hirsch's concept of cultural literacy. The mission of the Mohegan School is to provide its youngsters with the cultural and educational information they need to compete when they enter middle school. Already there have been requests for additional alternative schools in the South Bronx, and we are working to help them get off the ground.

Two other innovative schools we are helping to launch are the Wildcat Academy and the Beginning with Children Foundation School. Wildcat is being sponsored by the Wildcat Services Corporation, a not-for-profit organization on Hudson Street in downtown Manhattan which since 1972 has had great success in training ex-convicts for jobs when they reenter society. The Board of Education has awarded Wildcat a contract to start and independently operate a high school for youngsters who have been suspended from other schools.

Beginning with Children, a bilingual elementary school started in 1992 in the Williamsburg section of Brooklyn, is a unique partnership between private philanthropists Joseph and Carol Reich and the Board of Education. After three years of struggling through the hierarchy of the central board, the Reichs and their partner, the Pfizer Corporation, have realized their dream of starting a new school. The school's unique governance structure consists of an advisory board with representatives from the Reichs' foundation, the Board of Education, the teachers' union, and community leaders.

The opening of Wildcat and Beginning with Children is historic because both schools will operate autonomously, with the blessings of the central board. They are, in effect, schools organized on the charter-school model which (as noted in chapter 12) is one of the most exciting and potentially important trends advancing schools of choice in public education today.

210

We see that there is hope on the horizon. The miracle in East Harlem has faced some hard times and some persistent opposition, but its example has, finally, made an impression on New York City and on the rest of the country. We started as hopeful young teachers ourselves, asking, "But is it good for kids?" and then asked other teachers, many of whom were frustrated by the weight of the system but still hopeful, to dream with us. We created a network of small schools, schools that were true communities of learners, from scratch, right in the middle of the older, regular schools, starting modestly in the beginning. Because we were doing what was best for kids, and it was obvious to all, the teachers in our new schools worked harder and longer than they had done in the schools without hope, and the results were enormously gratifying and rewarding to everyone concerned. Students began to read who could not read before. A whole generation of youngsters stayed in school instead of dropping out, and went on to high schools and colleges of top quality. We got their parents involved and active in choosing the schools they wanted for their children, the schools that were best for their children with all their varied needs, and in the process we helped teach them how to recognize a good school. We financed our reforms in three ways: with our share of the city's tax levies, by raising money from interested parties in the community, and by soliciting competitive grants from the federal and state grants. Of these three, reliance on competitive grants was most critical to our success. In fact, it became such an important factor that, at one point, we had three or four staff people whose primary jobs were to write proposals. And almost like a miracle, because we were doing the right thing, the money for our dreams was there, and more and more money began flowing in our direction.

Finally, we have even won over the principals who once stood on the sidelines watching us, as well as the doubtful administrators, the central Board of Education at 110 Livingston Street, who are, at last, following our lead. Public school choice is a catalyst to better education for all, but it needs other elements with which to do its work. Good schools need to be small, they need to be autonomous, they need a clearly defined and communicated vision, they need parent involvement, they need site-based management, they need to work like true communities. It's a new paradigm of public education we discovered, one that we worked out slowly over the course of two decades, and it is the right paradigm because it works for children, for teachers, for parents, and for the community. Thousands of youngsters, more than two generations of children, have been rescued from the desolate streets of East Harlem. And many millions more can be taught using our model by hopeful teachers, parents who demand a say in the matter, constructive politicians, and visionary educators, in New York City and throughout the United States.

14 The Route Home

E ast Harlem, autumn of 1992. On 110th Street the body
shops are still stripping cars by day and awaiting new ar-
rivals at night. The Thomas Jefferson Baths have been refur-
bished east of First Avenue. Looking west across the flats from
First Avenue, Morningside Heights rises in the distance,
topped by the still climbing spires of the Cathedral of St. John
the Divine. Not yet finished after a hundred years, and being
built anew after a period of inaction, it could be a metaphor for
Harlem's schools, or schools anywhere.

On the wide boulevard of 116th Street, department stores
and the Banco de Ponce vie with street merchants selling their
wares from the sidewalk. Construction workers sip coffee on a
morning break. Music store employees hustle boxes of cassette
tapes into the shop. The bodegas in this part of town display
posters showing black models happily smoking cigarettes. Cars
are double and triple parked on the street, and an idling UPS
truck blocks traffic completely while its driver ambles into a
store.

On 119th Street near Pleasant Avenue, outside a rubble-strewn tenement with a "Vote for Bush" sign—from 1988—pasted on the door, an elderly Hispanic couple embraces their daughter as the postwoman arrives with the morning mail. The Operation Greenthumb garden on First Avenue is empty save for the deep-green mural of campesinos busily digging. Farther west on 119th Street, amid burnt-out buildings with broken furniture and tons of trash dumped outside, another smaller vegetable garden, the "Garden of Love," has been harvested, and the ground is brown. Last summer's scarecrow still bears witness to a growing season long gone. A boy in a green hat wheels an old tire down the sidewalk. On 120th Street and Second Avenue, near the bust of Senator Robert F. Wagner, a sports team and its coach cross the street. Their t-shirts read P.S. 57 KICKBALL.

Housing projects stand on Lexington Avenue between 117th and 121st streets with no stores and little street life. On 120th and Fifth, the huge boulders and elevated look-out sights of Marcus Garvey Park are especially beautiful in the early-morning light. But at Fifth Avenue and 119th Street the reality of East Harlem reintrudes, as burnt-out buildings dominate both sides of the street. At 115th Street the big projects start: the Taft project on 113th Street, the James Weldon Johnson Houses at 112th Street and Park Avenue. At Lexington Avenue and 111th Street, a sign adjacent to a vacant lot reads, PLEASE DON'T DO DRUGS IN THIS YARD. CHURCH AND SCHOOL OPEN. The school is the Bridge School.

A lot of drugs are going down at Lexington Avenue and 110th Street. A condemned five-story building next to a barbershop has a padlock on the door which a young boy opens from inside to admit two teenagers. The crack houses are flourishing, the crime rate is high, the murder rate is rising, and the city in general is a tougher place to make a life than it has been for a century—particularly a young life.

For nearly two decades the alternative schools of East Harlem have helped kids make something good out of their lives even as the temptations of the street have loomed ever larger. In the final analysis, no matter how innovative we have been in the schools, our efforts would have counted for nothing had we not been able to offer our students the chance for a better life. In many cases we did, and it is worth recalling a few of those young people now.

In 1985 Pedro E. came to the Key School as a seventh grader with low test scores. He had already been held back once and was in danger of falling behind even further. Instead he found himself in the supportive educational atmosphere of the school. He flourished during his time there, went on to Park East High School and today is a proud member of the New York City Police Department.

Jimmy W. arrived at the Creative Learning Community in the late 1980s. His reputation had preceded him, and it was terrible. His grades were poor as well. Under the care of Mike Fisher, the current director, and his staff, Jimmy turned around. With their encouragement he found that he could learn, and that he wanted to. He became the most improved student in the school and was honored at graduation. Today he is studying at the Manhattan Center.

Michael Pagan, a genial, hardworking son of Ecuadorian immigrants, attended East Harlem Tech before entering one of the city's premier Catholic high schools, Cardinal Hayes, as a member of the Student-Sponsor Partnership, (a coalition of young students, their sponsoring mentors, and inner-city Catholic and Lutheran high schools). He recalls:

My interest was in science and Tech challenged me to take it as far as I could. It prepared me to be disciplined and creative in designing experiments. It would have been much harder to make the transition to Hayes from a regular public school.

Michael has consistently achieved honor-level grades at Cardinal Hayes and is now hoping to attend Columbia University's pre-law program.

Sam Johnson was a student at Isaac Newton Junior High who entered the Mount Sinai Scholars program. He remembers his experience:

In my school I was treated like an individual. Our program focused on critical thinking skills and helped me solve problems that at first I thought were too hard. So I now have some confidence that I can go on and do the things that I didn't think I could do before.

215

Today Sam is a successful undergraduate at Union College and hopes to become a doctor.

There are thousands of other District Four graduates with similar stories to tell. Schools of choice opened up new horizons for them, and they took advantage of them. They deserve all the credit in the world for doing so, but the schools of District Four can claim their share, too.

Like many teachers, I still get letters from my former students. One of them, Sara Chopkow, recently wrote to me from Oakland, California. She recalled the day, twenty-five years ago, when she failed to win admission to Hunter College High School, where many of her closest friends were going. "I wanted to die," she wrote, "but you lifted up my chin and looked me in the eye and said, 'Sara, you are going to be all right.'" Many years later and now a successful editor in a San Francisco publishing house, she took the time to write me how important that moment in her life had been. "Since then, whenever things have gotten hard, I've remembered your words, and they've always helped me to get through."

I had many great students in my teaching career, but I also had some failures. We had one student at P.S. 146 who began as an illiterate gangster. When he left I could only say that he was now a literate gangster. He blew up a telephone booth, got arrested often and became famous for the number of times he escaped from Rikers Island Prison. His brother killed a Burger King manager and was sent away for life. The only time I ever saw the two excited in school was the day their buddy brought in a hat from his home that had once belonged to Al Capone.

You can never win them all, and poverty takes its toll across racial lines. Thus, it heartens me when I get a call from former students, as I did recently from Lewis Jones, now a senior vice president of Chemical Bank and chairman of the East Harlem Tutorial and Counseling Service, who telephoned to invite his old teacher out to lunch—at the Harvard Club. The number of kids I taught who have overcome the odds to make something worthwhile out of their lives is deeply satisfying.

You can never underestimate the impact you have on a developing child or adolescent. We once had Sidney Poitier and Harry Belafonte visit P.S. 146. They performed and spoke to a school assembly. Afterward the principal and assistant principals discussed with them how important it was for our youngsters to come in contact with such successful role models. I told them that for many of the kids it would be the highlight of their school experiences. Then the principal asked Harry Belafonte, a product of the New York City public schools, what teacher or experience had had the biggest impact on his life. I have never forgotten the answer he gave: "The day Paul Robeson visited my school."

Of course, my years in District Four were not spent as a classroom teacher. By then I had moved up to the supervisory level. But I had the greatest pleasure in watching my colleagues form their own lasting bonds with the students who came into their schools, hungry for learning, for role models, and for answers to their questions about how to live their lives.

Many other teachers in District Four continue to have a deep and lasting rapport with their old students. Lenny Bernstein encourages his former pupils to call him from college twice a month, collect. Beryl Epton has gotten letters from her students over the thirty years she has taught in East Harlem. Not long ago she got one from a young lady who wanted her to know that she had passed the bar and was now practicing law in Houston, Texas.

Cole Genn often refers to his "son," Stephen Oates. Stephen could have become the biggest hoodlum ever to come to school in District Four. His street name was "Fish" because he worked mornings in the seafood section of La Marqueta, the market on 116th Street, and when he came into a room at J.H.S. 17 (now the Alternative Education Complex) after work, you knew it. Stephen was very violent and aggressive when he first came to Genn's attention. He got kicked out of the few classes he didn't cut, and was forever getting into fights. Genn took an interest in Stephen, got him into the shower at school, and took him home for family dinners. But it was when Genn arranged for Stephen to go to Camp Beaver Lake in the Catskills with him one summer that Stephen really responded. In the eighth grade he knuckled down to his studies and developed an insatiable appetite for reading. Other teachers saw what was happening and began to get involved with him. Stephen joined a weekly tutoring and sports program at St. Peter's Lutheran

Church on Lexington Avenue. He began to learn about jazz and the theater, and his horizons grew. He became a constructive force in his own gang as well, because he was still a leader in the streets, and while he was committing himself to going to school, his friends and followers did as well.

Genn paid for Stephen to go to Rice High School in Harlem, where the Christian Brothers have done such an excellent job with a structured curriculum and strict discipline over the years. At the end of his high school years, Stephen won a scholarship to Gustavus Adolphus College, a marvelous school in St. Peter, Minnesota. There he found a new world. From a violent, confrontational, nearly illiterate street kid, he had become a gregarious, sociable, and intellectually inquiring student. Stephen majored in classics at Gustavus Adolphus, learning Hebrew in the process, and today converses regularly with Genn by telephone in that language. He is happily married and the father of two children. He is the director of youth services for Pillsbury Neighborhood Services, a settlement house in St. Paul. And he has not stopped learning; he is continuing to pursue a graduate degree in comparative religion at St. John's College.

Mike Friedman got a letter recently from one of his former students. Christine Alvarado had graduated from the Bridge School with a scholarship to a private boarding school in New Hampshire. Here is an excerpt from an essay she wrote while there:

During my first few months at the Dublin School I detested the place. I called home every day and cried to my mother. When I went home for vacation I would cry so I did not have to return to school. My mother was about to file papers to have me removed. On my second vacation I returned to the Bridge School and spoke to Mr. Friedman. Before I could explain how awful I felt at Dublin, he told me how proud he was of me and how he knew I would succeed. I tried to explain my difficulties. He sympathized but urged me to make it through the first year. I started trying to think positively. By that spring no one could remember how unhappy I had been.

Now, as I look back at the three wonderful years I've spent at the Dublin School, I do not ever regret coming here. But most important I'll never forget my mother or the man who pushed and guided me through this period of my life, Mr. Michael Friedman, my principal and my friend."

When you come right down to it, letters like that are why one becomes a teacher. Love of learning is a great thing, and holding a position of responsibility in the community is okay, but what really matters, and what really motivates teachers is the opportunity to make a difference in a young person's life. What we are trying to do with choice, essentially, is to get the best out of every student, whatever that might be. We are trying to provide every kid with the means to learn and to believe in himself or herself, not only in school but throughout their lives. Yes, we believe in choice, but we believe in it because over many years we witnessed its transforming power on the lives of thousands of wonderful, though impoverished, youngsters in a tough neighborhood on whom the system had given up.

My wife likes to kid me by saying that whenever we head back from an evening in Manhattan to our home in Queens, no matter where we've been, the route always leads through East Harlem! It's true. The place is in our blood. Cole Genn and I drive by District Four almost every day, and we frequently recall the great moments we had there, like that first graduation day at the Manhattan Center, or the trip our Dance Repertory Company took to Paris to perform before European audiences, or the two separate occasions when our students traveled to Moscow to take part in intercultural programs.

We consider it our privilege and good fortune to have spent so much of our working lives among the inspirational young people we came to know in East Harlem. And we will continue to help the current teaching and supervisory staff of District Four to build their educational programs.

But we're not stopping at that. All students in this country should be able to choose the schools in which they learn, just as teachers should be able to choose the schools in which they teach. The miracle in East Harlem must now become a national movement. District Four demonstrated that public school choice is the surest way to revitalize American education, and now we must use what we learned there to help build good schools throughout the country.

We cannot do it alone—we need all the help we can get. Students, teachers, parents, community groups, charities, corporations, local government—all the entities that make up American society—have got to get involved. The fight for choice in public education will be a hard battle, but if we really care about our children's future, it is one we have got to wage.

It can be won, if we summon the will to make it happen. Millions of young people have put their faith in our educational system and we cannot afford to disappoint them. Their lives depend upon the quality of the education they receive, and the position of the United States in the world of the twenty-first century depends upon the education we provide them. The implementation of a broad-based program of public school choice on the East Harlem model will be the catalyst that energizes our educational system to provide the superior education our young people deserve.

It is up to all of us to join together to fight for the transformation of our country's schools. If we do, there is every reason to believe that by the year 2000 the miracle in East Harlem will be well on its way to becoming what we all dream of and hope for —a miracle across America.

Chronology

1973   Anthony Alvarado, thirty-one years old, is selected as superintendent of Community School District Four in the East Harlem section of Manhattan.

1974   The first alternative schools in District Four are established. They are: Central Park East, run by Debbie Meier; the East Harlem Performing Arts School, led by Ellen Kirshbaum; and the B.E.T.A. School, overseen by John Falco.

1975   Sy Fliegel is named acting principal of P.S. 108. The East Harlem Middle School, the Harbor School, and the Children's Learning Center are founded.

1976   Superintendent Alvarado names Fliegel the district's first director of the Office of Alternative Schools. The East Harlem Career Academy, the School of Communications and Health, and the Block School open their doors.

1977   Jeff Hansen is named assistant director of the Office of Alternative Schools.

1978   The Bridge School and the Sports School are founded.

1979   With the establishment of the Maritime School, a dozen new schools are now in operation, and the Office of Alternative Schools is expanded to include three curriculum specialists, Mary Anne Marripodi, Helene Steinbeck, and Etta Proshansky.

1980   Two of District Four's pioneers expand their horizons: Debbie Meier's success inspires the creation of Central Park East II, while Colman Genn leaves the directorship of the Harbor School to found the Academy of Environmental Sciences.

1981   The Children's Workshop joins Manhattan East and the Isaac Newton School for Science and Mathematics as the newest schools in District Four.

1982   A district-wide choice system is established for all junior high school students in East Harlem. Students are no longer assigned to a school according to their home address; rather, they and their parents must actively select the school they wish to attend. Their options continue to expand with the founding of the School for Science and Humanities, River East, and the Key School. District Four also establishes its first high school program at the Manhattan Center for Science and Math (under the leadership of Colman Genn) and reaches out to special education students through Project Mainstream. A *New York Times* editorial endorses the district's reforms.

1983   A year of heady personnel changes as Tony Alvarado succeeds Frank Macchiarola as New York's schools chancellor and is replaced by Carlos Medina in District Four. Sy Fliegel is promoted to deputy superintendent, while John Falco takes over at the Office of Alternative Schools. The College for Human Services Junior High School is founded.

1984   Alvarado's meteoric rise is followed by an even more rapid fall, as he resigns the chancellorship under a cloud of alleged financial improprieties.

1985   Debbie Meier expands her vision once again, creating the Central Park East Secondary School, the district's second high school program.

1986   The Manhattan Center triumphantly graduates its first class: All 154 seniors receive diplomas, and all go on to college in the fall. The East Harlem School of Bio-Medical Studies is founded.

1987 Debbie Meier is awarded a MacArthur "genius" grant for her work at the Central Park East schools.

1988 Sy Fliegel is named acting superintendent of District Twenty-eight in Queens. Within one year the former superintendent of that district is reinstated to his post and Fliegel retires from the New York City public school system.

1989 In the midst of attacks on District Four from the central Board of Education for allegedly overspending its budget, Carlos Medina is removed as superintendent and replaced on an interim basis by Shirley Walker. The B.E.T.A. School is closed as the district determines that its students can be better served through the now extensive network of alternative schools.

1990 Marcelino Rodriguez is selected as the new superintendent of District Four, and a renewed expansion of the alternative schools begins. The first to be founded during Rodriguez's tenure is the Art Institute–Manhattan West.

1991 District Three, on the Upper West Side of Manhattan, adopts district-wide choice on the East Harlem model and hires District Four veteran John Elwell as director of the Office of Alternative Schools.

1992 The Hurston Academy opens in East Harlem in September, and later that month Schools Chancellor Joseph A. Fernandez announces that a city-wide program of public school choice will take effect the following fall. Commentators cite District Four as the example the city should follow in instituting the Chancellor's plan.

1993 The miracle in East Harlem continues, with the founding of the Urban Peace Academy, the Central Park Conservancy School, and the Harbor Academy—with others on the way.

Appendix

Student Performance in East Harlem, 1974–1992

The student population of Community School District Four in the East Harlem section of New York City mirrors the community from which it is drawn. The district serves 14,353 students; 60 percent are Hispanic, 35 percent are black, 4 percent are white, and 1 percent Asian. Almost 80 percent of the students are eligible for free or reduced lunch programs due to their low-income status; this is a higher percentage than eighteen of the city's thirty-two school districts. Ten percent of the district's students are classified as Limited English Proficiency (LEP); these students come from homes where English is not the primary language, and they have scored below a cutoff (the 20th percentile) on a test of English language ability. This is a higher percentage of LEP students than thirteen of the city's thirty-two districts. (Many more students in the district come from homes where English is not the primary language, but these students score above the LEP cutoff.) Reflecting the difficulty of their surroundings the students' average daily attendance is 85 percent in elementary schools and 82 percent in middle school.

Reading Achievement

The most widely used indicator of success or failure in the New York City public school system is the reading achievement level of students. Although not without flaws, this statistic is often the sole measure by which the public judges particular schools or districts within the system. Prior to the establishment of the alternative schools and the parental choice system, District Four had the lowest reading achievement scores of any of the thirty-two community school districts in New York City. In 1974, only 15 percent of the students in District Four could read above grade level, less than half the city-wide average. By contrast, in 1988, 62.5 percent of District Four's youngsters were reading at or above grade level. This figure was only 2.5 percentage points below the city-wide average.

Because the absolute level of reading achievement can be affected by changes in the testing instrument used from year to year, it is often useful to examine achievement in relative terms by looking at a district's rank among all thirty-two districts in the city. In 1974, District Four ranked thirty-second among the city's thirty-two districts. By 1982, the district had moved to fifteenth, and it remains solidly in the middle level of districts today. In 1988, the district ranked nineteenth. This represents a slight decline over the last few years, but the community districts are very tightly clustered in the middle range, with the sixteenth-ranked district achieving reading scores only 1 percentage point higher than District Four.

Clearly, reading achievement has increased dramatically in District Four, a district that was the worst in New York in terms of reading achievement and one that continues to serve an entirely minority, low-income population, now performing at the city-wide average on reading tests. This is an example of real across-the-board improvement in District Four attributable to the implementation of school choice within the district.

Mathematics Achievement

District Four's mathematics scores have also improved since 1983, the first year that New York City administered a system-wide mathematics test. In 1983, 49 percent of the district's students scored above grade level in mathematics. In 1988, 47.8 percent of the district's students scored above grade level on a newer and tougher mathematics test. The improvement in mathematics achievement in District Four may be seen in its ranking relative to other districts in New York City. In 1983, the district ranked twenty-third out of thirty-two districts; by 1988, it ranked nineteenth in mathematics achievement. The district now performs in the mid-level of performance for New York City's school districts.

Admission to Selective Public High Schools

Although achievement test scores are important and receive much public attention, the placement of students in selective high schools is a powerful indicator of a school district's success. The New York City Board of Education operates many different types of high schools through its central Division of High Schools. The elite of these institutions—Stuyvesant, Bronx High School of Science, Brooklyn Tech, and the LaGuardia School of Music and the Performing Arts—are highly selective and are among the finest schools in the country. A second tier of New York City high schools, referred to as "education option," or "screened" schools, also selects their student bodies according to objective criteria and tend to perform at high levels of achievement compared to traditional, zoned high schools. The ability of a community school district's students to gain entrance to these selective high schools is a strong indicator of the ability of that district to prepare its students for the most demanding higher levels of schooling.

New York City has high schools that vary greatly in terms of the quality of their educational programs. The top four schools (listed above) are specialized high schools. Students must pass a stringent entrance exam, or audition for Performing Arts, to be admitted to these schools. The second tier of New York City's high schools is the "education option" or "screened," meaning that they are open to all but students must be selected according to certain criteria adopted by the central board. Each year these selective high schools accept only 8.9 percent of the entire city's graduates. In 1987, 22 percent of District Four's graduates went on to attend these schools, and in 1992, 20 percent did so. District Four officials report that in the mid-1970s only a handful of their graduates were admitted.

Admission to Private High Schools

Thirty-six students from District Four were accepted into selective private schools in 1987. Among the institutions accepting students from District Four were Andover, Westminster, Loomis Chaffee (2 students), Brooklyn Friends Dublin School, Dana Hall (3), Hill School (3), York School, The Rhodes School (6), Storm King School, George School (2), Trinity, Friends, Berkshire, Spence. The 355 students placed in private high schools or selective public schools represent the truest indicator of District Four as a conduit for expanded opportunities for the graduates of the East Harlem district. Over a quarter of the district's graduating class earns entrance to the kinds of schools that were closed to the community's youth scarcely a decade ago. The reforms instituted in District Four over the last fifteen years have paid substantial dividends to the community it serves.

The Manhattan Center for Science and Mathematics

The Manhattan Center for Science and Mathematics is a high school that is unique in New York City because it was the first secondary school designed and established by District Four. The school's curriculum requires math and science students to take four years of English, math, and science, and three years of a foreign language. All students take coursework in a sequence that includes classes in computer science, technical drafting, and either electronics or advanced computer science. The curriculum includes advanced placement courses for college credit in English, history, math, and chemistry.

The Manhattan Center's admissions policy is to accept students who are above or close to grade level in reading and mathematics and who express interest and commitment to math and science. The school gives some preference to students from District Four who meet these general criteria. Students in the Manhattan Center for Science and Mathematics outperform their peers in other New York City high schools. Data from the latest available study indicate that 82.1 percent of the students who had entered in September 1983 had earned a diploma by June 1990. In comparison, the city-wide average was 54.1 percent. At least half the students graduating from the Manhattan Center earn a Regents-endorsed diploma, indicating that they have satisfied the state's most stringent set of course requirements. The graduating class of 1988 consisted of 245 students; of these, 210 enrolled in four-year colleges and 31 enrolled in two-year colleges. Although the Manhattan Center is now independent of District Four, and its future success or failure cannot be attributed to the district, it does provide an example of the improvement that can come from a redesign effort accompanied by the imposition of a choice policy. The former site of one of the worst schools in the city now houses a proud and effective institution of learning. School choice is a powerful tool in an effort to improve educational performance.

PERCENTAGE OF STUDENTS READING AT OR ABOVE GRADE LEVEL

Year	District Four	NYC
1974	15.3	33.8
1975	28.3	45.2
1976	27.9	42.6
1977	20.8	40.1
1978	25.9	43.0
1979	25.7	40.3
1980	35.6	46.7
1981	44.3	50.8
1982	48.5	51.0
1983	52.3	55.5
1984	48.1	52.8
1985	53.1	56.8
1986	62.6	65.0
1987	62.2	63.5
1988	62.5	65.0
1989	41.5	47.8
1990	40.2	47.3
1991	42.0	49.2
1992	38.3	46.4
Change '74–'92	+23.0	+12.6

Note: From 1974 to 1977, New York City administered the 1970 version of the *Comprehensive Test of Basic Skills;* from 1978 to 1985, the 1977 version of the *California Achievement Test;* from 1986 to 1988, the 1982 version of the *Degrees of Reading Power Test;* and, from 1989 to 1992, the 1988 version of the *Degrees of Reading Power Test.*

Only one district, Fifteen, in Park Slope, Brooklyn, made greater improvement over these years than did District Four.

RANKING OF DISTRICT FOUR IN READING
ACHIEVEMENT AMONG NEW YORK CITY'S
32 SCHOOL DISTRICTS

Year	District Four's Rank
1974	32
1978	28
1982	15
1986	18
1988	19
1990	21
1992	22

PLACEMENT OF DISTRICT FOUR'S STUDENTS
IN NEW YORK CITY'S SELECTIVE HIGH
SCHOOLS FOR ENTERING HIGH SCHOOL
CLASSES OF 1987 AND 1992

Percent of Junior High Graduates
Entering These High Schools

High School	From New York City	From District Four: 1987	1992
Brooklyn Technical	2.2%	2.5%	1.0%
Stuyvesant	1.1%	1.1%	0.5%
Bronx Science	1.2%	1.6%	1.6%
LaGuardia	1.2%	4.8%	2.2%
Murry Bergtraum	1.1%	1.9%	4.8%
A. Phillip Randolph	0.5%	1.3%	5.1%
Norman Thomas	1.3%	5.0%	4.8%
Total for These 7 Schools	8.6%	18.2%	20.0%

Bibliography

Alvarado, Anthony. Farewell speech upon leaving chancellorship. *New York Times,* March 22, 1984.

Bensman, David. *Quality Education in the Inner City: The Story of the Central Park East Schools.* New York: Kramer Communications, 1987.

Brandt, Ronald, ed. "Schools of Choice." *Educational Leadership* (December 1990).

Carnegie Council on Adolescent Development. *Turning Points: Preparing American Youth for the 21st Century.* Washington, D.C.: Carnegie Council on Adolescent Development, 1990.

Carnegie Foundation for the Advancement of Teaching. *School Choice, A Special Report.* Princeton, N.J.: Carnegie Foundation for the Advancement of Teaching, 1992.

Center for Educational Innovation. *To Design a New Generation of American Schools.* New York: Center for Educational Innovation, 1992.

Chubb, John, and Terry Moe. *Politics, Markets and America's Schools.* Washington, D.C.: The Brookings Institution, 1990.

Community School District 3, *Middle School Directory, 1991–92.* New York: Community School District 3, 1991.

Coons, John E., and Stephen D. Sugarman. *Education by Choice: The Case for Family Control.* Berkeley: University of California Press, 1978.

Clune, William H., and John F. Witte, eds. *Choice and Control in American Education.* London: Falmer Press, 1990.

Domanico, Raymond. *Model for Choice: A Report on Manhattan's District 4.* New York: Center for Educational Innovation, 1989.

———. *Recommendations for a County-wide Schools of Choice Policy for Guilford County, North Carolina.* New York: Center for Educational Innovation, 1990.

———. *Restructuring New York City's Schools: The Case for Public School Choice.* New York: Center for Educational Innovation, 1990.

——— and Colman Genn. "Putting Schools First." *City Journal,* Spring 1992.

D'Souza, Dinesh. *The Politics of Race and Sex on Campus.* New York: The Free Press, 1991.

Durant, W. Clark III. "Freedom of Choice, Local Control Are Ways to Run School System." *Detroit Free Press,* November 25, 1988.

Fantini, Mario. *Regaining Excellence in Education.* Columbus, Ohio: Merrill Publishing Co., 1986.

Feller, Michael Alan. "The Performing Arts Alternative School: Case Studies." Ph.D. diss., Columbia University Teachers College, 1982.

Finn, Chester E., Jr. "The Choice Backlash." *National Review,* November 10, 1989.

Fishman, Katherine Davis. "The Middle Class Parents Guide to Public Schools." *New York,* January 13, 1986.

Freedman, Samuel G. *Small Victories.* New York: Harper & Row, 1990.

Genn, Colman. "Director's Message to Graduates." Harbor School for Performing Arts 1977 Yearbook. New York, 1977.

Glazer, Nathan, John Chubb, and Seymour Fliegel. *Making Schools Better.* New York: Manhattan Institute for Policy Research, 1988.

Glenn, Charles. *Choice of Schools in Six Nations.* Washington, D.C.: U.S. Department of Education, 1989.

Grant, Gerald. *The World We Created at Hamilton High.* Cambridge: Harvard University Press, 1988.

Gutmann, Stephanie. "Is School-Based Management Working?" *City Journal* (Autumn 1991).

Kidder, Tracy. *Among Schoolchildren.* Boston: Houghton Mifflin, 1990.

Klein, Joe. "Tony Alvarado Flunks Math." *New York*, April 2, 1984.

Kozol, Jonathan. *Savage Inequalities*. New York: Crown, 1991.

Lieberman, Myron. *Privatization and Educational Choice*. New York: St. Martin's Press, 1989.

Maynard, Robert C. "If a School Can Prosper in Harlem." *Oakland Tribune*, April 2, 1987.

Meier, Deborah. "Choice Can Save Public Education." *The Nation*, March 4, 1991.

————. Unpublished memo to Chancellor Bernard Mecklowitz, et al., November 27, 1989.

Murray, Charles. *Losing Ground: American Social Policy 1950–1980*. New York: Basic Books, 1984.

Natale, Jo Anna. "Friedman Does the Right Thing." *The Executive Educator*, August 1990.

Nathan, Joe, ed. *Public Schools By Choice*. St. Paul: Institute for Learning and Teaching, 1988.

National Commission on Excellence in Education. *A Nation at Risk*. Washington, D.C.: National Commission on Excellence in Education, 1983.

New York City Board of Education. "Cash Funds." *Standard Operating Procedures Manual*, February 1991.

New York City Department of Investigation. Investigation into the Matter of Anthony Alvarado. March 1984.

————. Carlos Medina Hearing Transcript. June 6, 1987.

Osander, John. *Making Their Own World in East Harlem*. New York: Fund for the City of New York, 1981.

Postman, Neil, and Charles Weingartner. *The School Book*. New York: Delacorte, 1973.

Price, Janet R., and Jane Stern. "Magnet Schools as a Strategy for Integration and School Reform." *Yale Law and Policy Review*, Spring 1987.

Ravitch, Diane. *The Great School Wars*. New York: Basic Books, 1974.

Raywid, Mary Anne. *Research Evidence of School Choice*. New York: Center for Educational Innovation, 1992.

Rogers, David. *110 Livingston Street Revisited*. New York: New York University Press, 1983.

Silberman, Charles E. *Crisis in the Classroom*. New York: Random House, 1970.

Stewart, Donald. *A Short History of East Harlem.* New York: Museum of the City of New York, 1972.

Tan, Norma. *The Cambridge Controlled Choice Program: Improving Equity and Integration.* New York: Center for Educational Innovation, 1990.

Tashman, Billy. "Hobson's Choice: Free Market Education Plan Vouches for Bush's Favorite Class." *The Village Voice,* January 21, 1992.

Thernstrom, Abigail. *School Choice in Massachusetts.* Boston: Pioneer Institute for Public Policy Research, 1991.

U.S. Department of Education. *Schools That Work.* Washington, D.C.: U.S. Department of Education, 1987.

Van Dyk, Jere. "Growing Up in East Harlem." *National Geographic,* May 1990.

Viteritti, Joseph P. *Across the River: Politics and Education in New York City.* New York: Holmes and Meier, 1983.

Young, Timothy, and Evans Clinchy. *Choice in Public Education.* New York: Columbia University Teachers College, 1992.

Index

About the Authors

SEYMOUR FLIEGEL is the Richard Gilder Senior Fellow at the Manhattan Institute's Center for Educational Innovation, where he has been involved in the advocacy and implementation of "choice" programs for school districts in New York City and elsewhere.

Mr. Fliegel has been a teacher, assistant principal, and principal at P.S. 129 and P.S. 146 in New York City's East Harlem—two schools cited for excellence in Charles Silberman's *Crisis in the Classroom.* In 1976 Mr. Fliegel became the director of the Office of Alternative Schools for Community School District Four, where he developed a system of choice among alternative schools that has brought accomplishment to the children of East Harlem. He has been a deputy superintendent and a superintendent in New York City and an adjunct professor of education at Hunter College.

A native and lifelong New Yorker, Mr. Fliegel received his bachelor and master of science degrees from the City College of New York. He is married to his childhood sweetheart, Sonia, and is the father of three fine adults.

JAMES MACGUIRE is a fellow at the Center for Social Thought and a founding board member of the Student-Sponsor Partnership. His articles have appeared in *The New York Times, The Wall Street Journal,* the *San Francisco Chronicle, Esquire, National Review,* and *The City Journal,* and he is the author of *London and the English Countryside* and *Campion* (a play co-written with Christopher Buckley). He lives in New York City.